Ensuring Risk Reduction in Communities with Multiple Stressors: Environmental Justice and Cumulative Risks/Impacts

National Environmental Justice Advisory Council

December 2004

Prepared by the
National Environmental Justice Advisory Council
Cumulative Risks/Impacts Work Group

NATIONAL ENVIRONMENTAL JUSTICE ADVISORY COUNCIL
CUMULATIVE RISKS AND IMPACTS WORK GROUP

† Judith Espinosa, Surface Transportation Policy Project, Albuquerque, New Mexico **(Co-Chair)**
Sue Briggum, Waste Management, Inc., Washington, DC **(Co-Chair)**
Neil Carman, Long Star Sierra Club, Austin, Texas
David Clarke, American Chemistry Council, Arlington, Virginia *
Calvert Curley, Navajo Nation Environment Department, Window Rock, Arizona
Bahram Fazeli, Communities for a Better Environment, Huntington Park, California
Timothy Fields, Jr., TetraTech EMI, Inc., Reston, Virginia
Kenneth Geiser, University of Massachusetts/Lowell, Lowell, Massachusetts
Hector Gonzalez, Laredo Health Department, Laredo, Texas
† Walter S. Handy, Cincinnati Health Department, Cincinnati, Ohio
† Jodena "Jody" Henneke, Texas Commission on Environmental Quality, Austin, Texas
Darryl Hood, Meharry Medical College, Nashville, Tennessee
H. Patricia Hynes, Boston University School of Public Health, Boston, Massachusetts
Karen Medville, Arizona State University, Phoenix, Arizona
Shankar Prasad, California Air Resources Board, Sacramento, California
Kenneth Sexton, University of Texas/Brownsville, Brownsville, Texas
Peggy Shepard, West Harlem Environmental Action, New York, New York
† Wilma Subra, Louisiana Environmental Action Network, New Iberia, Louisiana
† Connie Tucker, Southern Organizing Committee for Economic and Social Justice, Atlanta, Georgia
Holly Welles, Pacific Gas and Electric Company, San Francisco, California
Janet Phoenix, National Safety Council, Washington, DC *(Liaison to EPA Children's Health Protection Advisory Committee)* **
Charles Lee, EPA Office of Environmental Justice *(NEJAC Designated Federal Officer [DFO])*
Dennis Utterback, EPA Office of Research and Development *(Work Group Co-DFO)*
Susan Conrath, EPA Office of Air and Radiation *(Work Group Co-DFO)*
Paul Locke, Consultant

* Served until December 2003
** Served until August 2003
† Member of the NEJAC

Other Members of the NEJAC:
Veronica Eady, Tufts University Department of Urban and Environmental Policy, Medford, Massachusetts (NEJAC **Chair**)
Mary Nelson, Bethel New Life, Incorporated, Chicago, Illinois (NEJAC **Vice-Chair**)
Charon Asetoyer, Honor the Earth, Lake Andes, South Dakota
Charles Collette, Florida Department of Environmental Protection, Tallahassee, Florida
Richard Gragg, Florida A&M University, Tallahassee, Florida
Jason S. Grumet, National Commission on Energy Policy, Washington, D.C.
Robert L. Harris, Pacific Gas and Electric, San Francisco, California
Phillip Hillman, Polaroid Corporation, Waltham, Massachusetts
James Huffman, Lewis and Clark Law School, Portland, Oregon
Lori F. Kaplan, Indiana Department of Environmental Management, Indianapolis, Indiana
Pamela Kingfisher, Austin, Texas
Richard Mason, Shintech Corporation, Houston, Texas
Juan H. Parras, De Madres a Madres, Houston, Texas
Chris Peters, Seventh Generation Fund, Arcata, California
Graciela Ramirez-Torro, Inter-American University of Puerto Rico, San Germán, Puerto Rico
Andrew Sawyers, Maryland Department of the Environment, Baltimore, Maryland
Kenneth J. Warren, Wolf, Block, Schorr and Solis-Cohen, Philadelphia, Pennsylvania
Tena Willemsma, Coalition on Religion in Appalachia, Charleston, West Virginia
Terry Williams, The Tulalip Tribes, Tulalip, Washington
Benjamin Wilson, Beveridge and Diamond, P.C., Washington, D.C.
Lily Yeh, Artists Without Borders, Philadelphia, Pennsyslvania

 **NATIONAL
ENVIRONMENTAL JUSTICE
ADVISORY COUNCIL**

December 17, 2004

Administrator Michael Leavitt
U.S. Environmental Protection Agency
1200 Pennsylvania Avenue, NW
Washington, DC 20460

Dear Administrator Leavitt:

Please find attached a copy of the report entitled **"Ensuring Risk Reduction in Communities with Multiple Stressors: Environmental Justice and Cumulative Risks/Impacts,"** December 2004.

The U.S. Environmental Protection Agency (EPA), through its Office of Environmental Justice, requested the National Environmental Justice Advisory Council (NEJAC), to provide advice and recommendations on the following question:

> *In order to ensure environmental justice for all communities and tribes, what short-term and long-term actions should the Agency take in proactively implementing the concepts contained in its Framework for Cumulative Risk Assessment?*

The EPA Charge to the NEJAC was developed in conjunction with the Office of Air and Radiation and the Office of Research and Development. OAR and ORD also provided financial and staff support to this effort. This report reflects the advice and recommendations that resulted from pre-meeting preparation, public comments, and subsequent analysis. The preparation included a public meeting devoted to the issue, on April 13 through 16, 2004 in New Orleans, Louisiana. Individuals and organizations with varied backgrounds and interests offered comments, suggestions and recommendations on how EPA should address this important issue.

In response to this charge, the NEJAC developed eight overarching themes. As a whole, they provide a long-term vision for addressing issues of environmental justice and cumulative risks/impacts.

- To institutionalize a bias for action within EPA through the widespread utilization of an Environmental Justice Collaborative Problem-Solving Model;
- To fully utilize existing statutory authorities;
- To address and overcome programmatic and regulatory fragmentation within the nation's environmental protection regime;

- To fully incorporate the concept of vulnerability, especially its social and cultural aspects, into EPA's strategic plans and research agendas;
- To promote a paradigm shift to community-based approaches, particularly community-based participatory research and intervention;
- To incorporate social, economic, cultural, and community health factors, particularly those involving vulnerability, in EPA decision-making;
- To develop and implement efficient screening, targeting, and prioritization methods/tools to identify communities needing immediate intervention; and
- To address capacity and resource issues (human, organizational, technical, and financial) within EPA and the states, within impacted communities and tribes, and among all relevant stakeholders.

In addition, the NEJAC recommends 12 specific actions that EPA can take immediately to lay the groundwork for the larger changes called for by the 8 overarching themes. Successful implementation of these recommended actions will place the Agency in a stronger position to make the transition to being more capable of effectively responding to cumulative risks and impacts in people of color, low-income, and tribal communities. These actions should be part of the Agency's efforts to engage a coherent collaborative problem-solving methodology to ensure risk reduction in disadvantaged, underserved and environmentally overburdened communities and reflect the Agency's bias for action in addressing cumulative risk and impacts.

- Initiate community-based, collaborative, multi-media, risk reduction pilot projects;
- Develop a toolkit of implementable risk reduction actions;
- Provide resources for community-based organizations;
- Develop and utilize tools for targeting and prioritization of communities needing urgent intervention;
- Promote incentives for business and industry;
- Conduct scientific and stakeholder dialogues in ways that enhance scientific understanding and collaborative problem-solving ability;
- Lay the scientific basis for incorporating vulnerability into epa assessment tools, strategic plans, and research agendas;
- Produce guidance on greater use of statutory authorities;
- Elevate the importance of community-based approaches;
- Establish an agency wide framework for holistic risk-based environmental decision making and incorporation of Tribal Traditional Lifeways in Indian Country;
- Strengthen EPA's social science capacity and community expertise; and
- Integrate the concepts of the NEJAC's Cumulative Risks/Impacts Report into EPA's strategic and budget planning processes.

The NEJAC is pleased to present this report to you for your review, consideration, response and action. In addition, the NEJAC appreciates any assistance you can provide in processing the advice and recommendations in this report through the various EPA program offices, in particular, the Office of Research and Development and the Office of Air and Radiation.

There is perhaps no more fitting way to summarize this report than the words of its final paragraph, which read:

> *"The issue of cumulative risks/impacts is a unifying one, because it is a vehicle through which the impressive array of tools now available to ensure pollution prevention and risk reduction can be brought together and applied in new, innovative, and more effective ways. Exciting new approaches, partnerships, and models will surely emerge. Ensuring that these new possibilities will blossom will require a critical appraisal of past Agency policies and practices. Ensuring that this new day in environmental protection will come to pass will require committed individuals willing and able to provide foresight, analysis, and leadership."*

We want to thank you and others at EPA for the resources and support that the Agency has provided to our efforts to produce this important document.

Sincerely,

Veronica Eady /S/   **Judith Espinosa** /S/   **Sue Briggum** /S/

Veronica Eady	Judith Espinosa	Sue Briggum
Chair of the NEJAC	Co-Chair, Cumulative Risks/	Co-Chair, Cumulative Risks/
	Impacts Work Group	Impacts Work Group

A Federal Advisory Committee to the U.S. Environmental Protection Agency

TABLE OF CONTENTS

APPENDICES

ENSURING RISK REDUCTION IN COMMUNITIES WITH MULTIPLE STRESSORS: ENVIRONMENTAL JUSTICE AND CUMULATIVE RISKS/IMPACTS

National Environmental Justice Advisory Council
December 2004

EXECUTIVE SUMMARY

"I am sick and tired of being sick and tired." This poignant plea for assistance has been voiced at every single meeting of the National Environmental Justice Advisory Council (NEJAC) and echoed by numerous environmentally overburdened people of color, low-income, and tribal communities throughout the nation. This plea reflects profound disappointment in such communities with the status of their health, frustration with the public health community's failure to assist in improving health, anger over the unresponsiveness of many businesses complacent with the adequacy of their regulatory obligations and unresponsive to the health problems their neighbors face, and bewilderment at the government's failure to understand and correct these shortcomings. Communities richly understand the degree to which they are burdened, yet find the government unwilling to seek their counsel and to provide the resources needed for communities to exercise their full voice in regulatory decisions that impact their lives. For many communities facing stresses from factors beyond their control, living with a myriad of polluting facilities, this affront is compounded by the impacts of racial and economic discrimination.

The sense of anguish expressed above and uniformly experienced by disadvantaged, underserved, and environmentally overburdened communities reflects a complex web of combined exposures. In recent years, this combination has come to be described as "cumulative risks and impacts." Manifested in the above plea is the concept of vulnerability, a matrix of physical, chemical, biological, social, and cultural factors which result in certain communities and sub-populations being more susceptible to environmental toxins, being more exposed to toxins, or having compromised ability to cope with and/or recover from such exposure.

It is in the context of this kind of community experience that the U.S. Environmental Protection Agency (EPA), through its Office of Environmental Justice (OEJ), has requested that the National Environmental Justice Advisory Council (NEJAC) address the following question:

> *In order to ensure environmental justice for all communities and tribes, what short-term and long-term actions should the Agency take in proactively implementing the concepts contained in its Framework for Cumulative Risk Assessment?*

This report is the product of eighteen months of work by members of the NEJAC's Cumulative Risks/Impacts Work Group (hereinafter referred to as "NEJAC Work Group" or the "Work Group"). This Work Group consisted of representatives from communities, academia, business and industry, non-governmental organizations, and state, local, and tribal governments. The report also is the product of public input from a NEJAC's Public Meeting in New Orleans, Louisiana (April 13 through 16, 2004).

DEFINING THE ISSUE: MULTIPLE STRESSORS AND MULTI-MEDIA APPROACHES

The issues of cumulative risks and cumulative impacts are inherently multi-faceted, interconnected, and complex. The NEJAC began its work with an understanding its focus must be the real life context of communities confronting environmental justice issues. The NEJAC chose to begin with a discussion of two key definitional topics: (1) the idea of using multiple stressors as a common starting point of discussion, and (2) the need for multi-media approaches to address cumulative impacts in a holistic way and to overcome programmatic and regulatory fragmentation. With respect to the identification of multiple stressors, the NEJAC quickly recognized a need to ascertain and mitigate these stressors in a time frame shorter than traditionally envisioned by cumulative risk assessment. This early identification and response has come to be termed the NEJAC Work Group's "bias for action." With respect to the latter, the report suggests that a comprehensive, integrated, and unified approach toward communities burdened by environmental hazards that cross multiple environmental media over time. The Work Group stresses that adequately addressing these cumulative, multi-media impacts will require a unified, place-based approach that transcends the single-media, single program focus of current environmental regulation.

CORE MESSAGE: ADOPTING A COMMUNITY-BASED COLLABORATIVE PROBLEM-SOLVING MODEL FOR ADDRESSING CUMULATIVE RISKS AND IMPACTS

EPA's *Framework for Cumulative Risk Assessment* (hereinafter also referred to as the Agency's "Cumulative Risk Framework") provides important tools and mechanisms to begin to address the multi-faceted impacts felt by overburdened communities and to determine the depth of vulnerability to harm these communities experience. The NEJAC Work Group argues that combining the Agency's new Cumulative Risk Framework with a collaborative problem-solving approach is the **fastest and surest way** to bring about tangible and sustainable benefits for disproportionately impacted communities and tribes. Significant experience and lessons are now emerging in the use of an Environmental Justice Collaborative Problem-Solving Model. Such lessons can be of great value to operationalizing the concepts of the Agency's Cumulative Risk Framework. Together, they provide a critical set of strategies and tools for achieving the ultimate goal of both environmental justice and the Cumulative Risk Framework, i.e., healthy and sustainable communities.

This report acknowledges that the Agency's *Framework for Cumulative Risk Assessment* represents a profound advancement in the kind of thinking that will help communities and tribes address their concerns. The Cumulative Risk Framework is important because, for the first time, it opens the scope of risk assessment to include the environmental, health, social, and cultural factors that are key to understanding community risk. It allows for a focused discussion of multiple sources of physical impact, as well as the social and cultural factors included in the concept of vulnerability. Within this framework, the community can enter into a dialogue about risk that realistically incorporates the factors experienced by disadvantaged, underserved, and environmentally-overburdened communities and tribes.

The NEJAC recognizes, however, that cumulative risk reduction will not occur simply because the cumulative burden is identified. For tangible results, there must be a conscious effort to develop a collaborative process bringing governments and all sectors of the community together in a problem-solving mode. This means that all relevant stakeholders will need to engage in an open and deliberative discussion of causes of risk and be willing to contribute to a community-wide effort to reduce it. Moreover, there must be a commitment to address capacity and power imbalances inherent in all collaborative processes. Collaborative problem-solving must strive to ensure equity, empowerment, and authentic processes. This collaborative problem-solving approach is a paradigm shift of equal importance to the paradigm shift embodied in the cumulative perspective on risk laid out in the *Framework for Cumulative Risk Assessment*.

DISCUSSION OF KEY CONCEPTS

Stressors: The report notes that EPA's *Framework for Cumulative Risk Assessment* places no limitation on the definition of stressors, explicitly stating that they include not only chemicals but also socioeconomic stressors such as lack of health care. This is one reason why the Framework is such an important milestone, laying the basis for a realistic and meaningful dialogue about comprehensive risk in disadvantaged, underserved, and environmentally-overburdened communities and tribes.

Vulnerability: The concept of vulnerability goes to the heart of the meaning of environmental justice. Vulnerability recognizes that disadvantaged, underserved, and overburdened communities come to the table with pre-existing deficits of both a physical and social nature that make the effects of environmental pollution more, and in some cases unacceptably, burdensome. As such, the concept of vulnerability fundamentally differentiates disadvantaged, underserved, and overburdened communities from healthy and sustainable communities. Moreover, it provides the added dimension of considering the nature of the receptor population when defining disproportionate risks or impacts.

The EPA's formal definition of vulnerability, i.e., susceptibility/sensitivity, differential exposure, differential preparedness, and differential ability to recover, allows an analytical framework to understand how a disadvantaged community may face greater impacts from pollution than the general population. Moreover, it takes on new meaning when linked to concepts like health disparities. Vulnerability and health disparities are integrally related concepts, and in some ways, *health disparities are both an outcome of and a contributor to vulnerability*.

Community-Based Participatory Research: The National Institute for Environmental Health Sciences defines community-based participatory research as "a methodology that promotes active community involvement in the processes that shape research and intervention strategies, as well as the conduct of research studies." Community-based participatory research can be an extremely useful tool not only to obtain valuable information for cumulative risk/impact assessments, but also to empower the affected community and to engender more effective prevention/intervention efforts.

Proportional Response: The concept of proportional response is a direct outgrowth of the NEJAC Work Group's thinking on conducting cumulative risk analysis in the context of a bias for action and its promotion of a collaborative problem-solving model for addressing cumulative risks and impacts. First, the idea of proportional response seeks to match the needs of communities and tribes with an appropriate level or type of analysis and action at any given point. In other words, analysis should be commensurate with community needs and the nature of the intervention to be taken. Secondly, response must be proportional to the harm caused.

Qualitative Analysis: An integrated analysis of cumulative risk and impacts will require making both quantitative and qualitative judgements. The report notes that there exists a body of literature in the area of environmental impacts analysis and cumulative impacts analysis that may prove to be useful to such an integrated analysis. For example, the White House Council on Environmental Quality (CEQ) published a report entitled "Considering Cumulative Effects Under the National Environmental Policy Act" in which CEQ provided eight principles and eleven methods for conducting cumulative effects analysis.

Other Key Concepts:

- Efficient Screening, Targeting, and Prioritization Methods/Tools;
- Unifying the Fields of Public Health and Environmental Protection; and
- Social Capital.

Special Concerns of Tribes: For tribes, issues of multiple and cumulative risks and impacts cannot be separated from the historical legacy of habitat loss. A proactive approach towards cumulative risks and impacts in a tribal context must include assessments of the ecosystem and pursue the goal of ecological restoration. EPA has begun to explore issues of cumulative risks and impacts in the Native American context through what are sometimes referred to as" tribal traditional lifeways." Tribes have consistently raised concerns that EPA's programs, risk methodologies and regulatory approaches are generally not sensitive to tribal traditional lifeways, neither do they give a whole or comprehensive view of the health of the people or their environment. Tribes have also called upon EPA to address the environmental impacts which threaten tribal treaty rights, including traditional and customary hunting and fishing areas. The health of the environment is of critical importance to the Native Americans because of their spiritual and cultural connection to the Earth. Tribes traditionally fish, hunt and gather native foods to sustain their way of life and their culture. Without the ability to hunt, trap, fish and gather, opportunities for story telling and sharing experiences that instruct the young are lost–their language, knowledge and skills are lost. Their spirit and culture are irreversibly altered. In addition to adverse long-term changes to the environment, the presence of toxins and pollutants in natural resources has had a severe impact on the ability of tribal people to continue their traditional and cultural practices, including spiritual ceremonies. Tribes point out that pollution impacts "the web" or "circle of life" which is critical to maintaining Native American health and culture.

OVERARCHING THEMES

The NEJAC has decided to frame its proposed advice and recommendations under the eight major interrelated themes. These themes are intended to promote long-term change in Agency *action*, a change in Agency *thinking*, and a change in Agency *capacity*. **As a start, EPA should incorporate all relevant concepts and recommendations of this report in any and all work growing out of the Agency's *Framework for Cumulative Risk Assessment* and the development of Agency cumulative risk guidance.**

- To institutionalize a bias for action within EPA through the widespread utilization of an Environmental Justice Collaborative Problem-Solving Model.

- To fully utilize existing statutory authorities.

- To address and overcome programmatic and regulatory fragmentation within the nation's environmental protection regime.

- To fully incorporate the concept of vulnerability, especially its social and cultural aspects, into EPA's strategic plans and research agendas.

- To promote a paradigm shift to community-based approaches, particularly community-based participatory research and intervention

- To incorporate social, economic, cultural, and community health factors, particularly those involving vulnerability, in EPA decision-making.

- To develop and implement efficient screening, targeting, and prioritization methods/tools to identify communities needing immediate intervention.

- To address capacity and resource issues (human, organizational, technical, and financial) within EPA and the states, within impacted communities and tribes, and among all relevant stakeholders.

RECOMMENDED ACTIONS

Recognizing that the 8 overarching themes of this report envision significant paradigm changes in the way that the Agency does business and are long-term in nature, the NEJAC is providing the following 12 recommendations on actions which the Agency can take immediately. It is the NEJAC's view that successful implementation of these 12 recommendations will lay the groundwork for the larger changes called for by the 8 overarching themes. Successful implementation of these recommended actions will place the Agency in a stronger position to make the transition to being more capable of effectively responding to cumulative risks and impacts in people of color, low-income, and tribal communities. These actions should be part of the Agency's efforts to engage a coherent collaborative problem-solving methodology to ensure risk reduction in disadvantaged, underserved and environmentally overburdened communities and reflect the Agency's bias for action in addressing cumulative risk and impacts.

1. Initiate Community-Based, Collaborative, Multi-Media, Risk Reduction Pilot Projects: EPA should initiate a set of community-based, multi-media, risk reduction pilot projects in low-income, people of color, and/or tribal communities as part of a broad national community-based effort to address risks in such communities. These should be the focus of EPA's bias for action in addressing cumulative risks and impacts. There should be at least one per each EPA Region, as well as attention to tribal populations. Activities should include but not be limited to community-based assessment, partnership building, provision of resources, prevention/ intervention risk reduction efforts and application of the Agency's Environmental Justice Collaborative Problem-Solving Model. In addition, EPA should systematically take the lessons gained from the pilot projects and integrate them into EPA programs as part of the Agency's day-to-day activities. These pilot projects should be part of a short-term and long-term research agenda on community-based, multi-media, collaborative problem-solving approaches to achieve environmental justice and healthy communities. The projects, and its associated research agenda, should:

- include community-based participatory research elements in the selection criteria;
- consider racial, ethnic, economic, and tribal status in pilot selection;
- provide lessons on ways to overcome programmatic and regulatory fragmentation;
- involve other federal agencies, where appropriate;
- document and disseminate information from projects; and
- be incorporated into Headquarters and Regional Environmental Justice Action Plans.

2. Develop Toolkit of Implementable Risk Reduction Actions: EPA should develop a toolkit of early implementable actions to reduce risk and pollution in people of color, low-income, and tribal communities. The purpose of such a toolkit is to "jump start" and support results-oriented processes in impacted communities with proven strategies and methods. The actions should include tools designed for use in large businesses and public facilities, small businesses, schools, mobile sources, surface waters, and homes. Examples of such actions are provided in Appendix C of this report. These actions should include regulatory actions (such as enforcement), incentives for voluntary action, community-based participatory research and collaborative problem-solving. The Agency should ensure that appropriate means exist to disseminate information about and train the public in the use of such tools.

3. Provide Resources for Community-Based Organizations: EPA should ensure that adequate resources are being made available to community-based organizations. EPA should institute new and/or increase the amount of funding available to community based organizations, following examples of past and present grant programs. Additionally, direct support of community-based organizations should be incorporated into other areas where this goal is not a priority. These funds should be complemented by more innovative ways of ensuring that information on such programs are disseminated to community based organizations. Recognizing that community-based organizations require assistance in areas of grant management, the Agency should provide training on grant management. Last, EPA should proactively work with other groups, such as philanthropies, to ensure that resources and technical assistance are provided to community based organizations.

4. Develop and Utilize Tools for Targeting and Prioritization of Communities Needing Urgent Intervention: In the short run, EPA should recommend some methods or tools for screening and prioritization of communities with high cumulative pollution burdens to prioritize Agency activities in those communities. In order to accomplish this task over the next two years. EPA should inventory and review existing screening methods and tools to ascertain: (1) strengths and weaknesses of existing cumulative impact evaluation tools; (2) ways in which these tools can be improved; and (3) recommend specific tool(s) that can be applied to a particular scenario, including guidance regarding minimum criteria for selection and use of a particular tool. In addition to methods and tools available at EPA, this inventory also should include methods used by other federal agencies, states, public health agencies, universities, etc. In the long run, EPA should identify and incorporate appropriate indicators of vulnerability into these screening tools. These development efforts should be done in conjunction with pilot projects and other community based activities (See Recommended Action No. 1), to "truth-test" the accuracy and comprehensiveness of such methods and tools. By "truth testing,"the NEJAC means that such methods and tools should be grounded in community realities. Scientific peer review, which is essential to ensuring sound methodology, must have robust community involvement. Scientific peer review, which is essential to ensuring sound methodology, should be informed by a robust understanding of community realities. Moreover, the Agency should engage in stakeholder dialogues to ensure that all stakeholders develop a common understanding of the purpose, parameters, and limitations of such tools, as well as ways to use them.

5. Promote Incentives for Business and Industry: EPA should develop an affirmative strategy to incentivize members of business and industry to go beyond compliance to reduce cumulative impacts in overburdened communities. Businesses and industry that reduce their proportional share of the cumulative impacts in such communities should receive appropriate rewards in the form of public recognition for their voluntary efforts and efficient permit processing that facilitates implementation of these pollution reductions. In developing this strategy, EPA should first consider the recommendations made regarding such rewards in the NEJAC's June 2003 report,"Advancing Environmental Justice Through Pollution Prevention." EPA should also evaluate the examples of "regulatory reinvention" projects that have been considered successful by both the impacted community and the business and industry project participants. Three criteria are fundamental to appropriate business and industry incentives: (1) the reductions in impact must go beyond regulatory compliance to tangibly improve community health and quality of life; (2) the level of incentive must be proportional to the degree of improvement and the expectation that the largest contributors to the community burden will make the greatest efforts to reduce negative impacts; and (3) the rewards are developed in the course of collaborative dialogue among impacted community members, business and industry and the regulators. In short, the business and industry incentives must be for voluntary action beyond compliance and reflect a fair acknowledgment of business or industry's actions to reduce environmental exposure and risk, improve community health and the environment.

6. Conduct Scientific and Stakeholder Dialogues in Ways that Enhance Scientific Understanding and Collaborative Problem-Solving Ability: EPA should convene, support, and promote a series of workshops, focus groups, stakeholder meetings, scientific symposia, conferences, and other dialogues to promote greater understanding and consensus around the concepts in this report. Such dialogues are critical to ensuring a sound scientific foundations as well as multi-stakeholder understanding. They are critical to building strategic partnerships–in the private and public sectors and in communities–for the collaborative undertakings called for by this report. In particular, they are critical to bringing diverse perspectives together, and holding them together through periods of experimentation and learning. Such dialogues can be useful catalysts for the long-term building of collaborative problem-solving capacity in the form of strong institutions, shared understandings and perspectives, and leadership and vision.

7. Lay the Scientific Basis for Incorporating Vulnerability into EPA Assessment Tools, Strategic Plans, and Research Agendas: EPA should develop a plan to ensure incorporation of the concept of vulnerability, particularly its social and cultural aspects, into the Agency's strategic plans, research agendas, and decision-making processes. This should begin with an Agency effort to lay the scientific foundations or understanding vulnerability, especially its social and cultural aspects. Issues papers, workshops, case studies and other approaches should be employed in such a foundation laying effort. Additionally, the Agency should initiate and promote dialogue with key partners and stakeholders on the subject. The Agency also should include the concept in its development of screening, targeting, and prioritization methods and tools. The Agency should also direct all offices whose missions relate to policy making, program implementation, regulatory enforcement, and professional and community training, to develop strategic plans for incorporating the concept of vulnerability into their operational paradigm. One vehicle for accomplishing this is each office's Environmental Justice Action Plans. Last, EPA should make it clear that although quantitative evaluation of vulnerability is precluded in almost all cases by a scarcity of scientific knowledge and understanding, this is not an excuse to ignore it. Vulnerability should be an integral part of cumulative risk assessment even it must be analyzed using qualitative measures.

8. Produce Guidance on Greater Use of Statutory Authorities: EPA should inventory, review, and promote the utilization of existing statutory authorities that can increase the capacity of EPA and its state, local and tribal government partners, impacted communities, business and industry, and other stakeholders to address cumulative risk in disadvantaged, underserved, and environmentally overburdened communities. EPA should work on identifying and clarifying existing legal authorities that could be useful in addressing cumulative risks and impacts, especially in disadvantaged, underserved, and disproportionately affected communities. This should build upon the Office of General Counsel's December 1, 2000 memorandum on environmental justice authorities. EPA program offices should translate the authorities into guidance for permitting procedures. In addition, EPA should make cumulative risk reduction as a goal in assessing penalties and authorizing Supplemental Environmental Projects. EPA should explore innovative ways to make use of these authorities to address cumulative risks and impacts, such the combined use of statutory authorities and alternative dispute resolution. In addition, integrated problem-solving approaches that combine multiple regulatory, enforcement, and voluntary emission reduction processes should be explored.

Last, EPA should explore a programmatic approach to integrating cumulative risk considerations into permits, rather than one permit at a time.

9. Elevate the Importance of Community-Based Approaches: EPA should develop and implement a systematic plan to elevate the importance of community-based approaches. Such a plan begins with the recognition that the effectiveness of Agency managers and staff, particularly those with a regulatory background, would be enhanced by an understanding of the positive role that community initiative can play in reaching the Agency's environmental and public health goals. This plan should be developed, therefore, around activities in communities that both result in tangible community benefits and demonstrate the success of this approach. All EPA Regional and Headquarter Offices should develop and implement activities to achieve this goal. The second part of this plan should include a systematic process of research, education, training, and dialogue among Agency staff on community-based approaches to environmental protection. These activities should be intended to promote awareness and understanding of the premises, methods, and experience related community based approaches. Areas of examination should include environmental justice, community-based participatory research, collaborative problem-solving, dispute resolution, and others. In addition, special meetings should be convened by offices and groups such as the Innovation Action Council, Office of Environmental Justice, Conflict Prevention and Resolution Center, Public Involvement Improvement Council, and their regional counterparts. As part of this plan, EPA also should facilitate dialogue among its federal, state, tribal, and local governmental partners, business and industry, universities, professional organizations, non-profit organizations, and philanthropies about working togther to promote community-based approaches. Last, the Administrator should provide vision and direction on the importance of community-based solutions in the next generation of environmental protection. Likewise, such direction should be provided by all EPA Assistant Administrators and Regional Administrators.

10. Establish an Agency Wide Framework for Holistic Risk-Based Environmental Decision Making and Incorporation of Tribal Traditional Lifeways in Indian Country: EPA should support the work of the EPA Indian Program Policy Council to establish a collective, multi-media Agency approach and determine what additional efforts are needed that will allow EPA to adequately consider tribal traditional lifeways when conducting scientific analyses, including assessing risks; developing and implementing environmental programs and regulations; and making decisions that protect human health and the environment in Indian country. In addition, EPA should identify examples of successful holistic risk assessment and collaborative problem-solving efforts that abide by the Native American World View of Health and promote ecological restoration in Indian County, and integrate the lessons from such successes into all of the Agency's policies, programs, and activities.

11. Strengthen EPA's Social Science Capacity and Community Expertise: EPA should develop an implement a plan for short- and long-term development of intramural and extramural expertise in the social sciences, community-based work, and collaborative problem-solving. expertise, and collaborative problem-solving skills. As part of this effort, the Agency should conduct a study to identify ways that such expertise can best be utilized and integrated into the Agency's programs. Part of this study should identify larger trends in environmental protection challenges that elevate in the importance of sociology in environmental decision-making and problem-solving. In addition, the study should identify ways to systematically develop the skills of in-house scientists and program personnel in social science areas and community assessment, not the least of which is requiring that program personnel and scientists spend time in communities to understand the real life context of the communities' environmental challenges. EPA also should encourage and support the development of community expertise and social science capacity within its governmental partners, business and industry, universities and the environmental protection field in general. Last, to focus broad based attention on the imperative to overcome the present structural limitations of the environmental protection field and its makeup, the Administrator should issue a policy statement to elevate the importance of the sociology and the social sciences in environmental protection and collaborative problem-solving. One goal of such a policy is to ensure an environmental protection work force that has a built-in bias for action.

12. Integrate the Concepts of NEJAC's Cumulative Risks/Impacts Report into EPA's Strategic and Budget Planning Processes: EPA should ensure that the concepts of this report are integrated into its strategic and budget planning processes. To that end, the Agency can focus on a number of actions. Each EPA (HQ) National Program Manager and Regional Office should update its Environmental Justice Action Plan to address the major actions associated with these recommendations. Using the principles in the Office of Enforcement and Compliance Assurance's (OECA) environmental justice targeting strategy as a model, each EPA (HQ) National Program Manager should identify the priority areas for application of this report's major concepts and action items into its operating plans. Each Regional Office should incorporate the major action concepts and action items of this Report into its Regional Strategic Plans. Last, the Assistant Administrator, OECA, Director, OEJ, and the Office of the Chief Financial Officer should work together to incorporate these concepts and action items into the next update of EPA's Strategic Plan.

CONCLUSION

In a very real sense, the fact that the NEJAC is addressing the issue of cumulative risks and impacts represents the maturation of environmental justice issues. The NEJAC's involvement with the issue of cumulative risk and impact did not start 18 months ago when this Work Group was formed.. It has been an issue that has been an explicit and implicit part of the environmental justice dialogue ever since it rose to national prominence in the 1980s.

For these reasons, the concepts and recommendations of this report are testaments to the greater ability of all sectors of American society to understand and address the issues of environmental justice. The NEJAC believes that the concepts and recommendations of this report provide a solid foundation for the Agency to be able to better address the issues of cumulative risks and impacts. The report places the Agency in a better position to make the transition to a new era of environmental protection, one that is characterized by place-based, collaborative and integrated problem solving. Finally, the Agency will be able to address systematically the "toxic hotspots" where disadvantaged, underserved, and environmentally overburdened communities and tribes have yet to reap the full benefits of our Nation's environmental progress.

The issue of cumulative risks/impacts is a unifying one, because it is a vehicle through which the impressive array of tools now available to ensure pollution prevention and risk reduction can be brought together and applied in new, innovative, and more effective ways. Exciting new approaches, partnerships, and models will surely emerge. Ensuring that these new possibilities will blossom will require a critical appraisal of past Agency policies and practices. Ensuring that this new day in environmental protection will come to pass will require committed individuals willing and able to provide foresight, analysis, and leadership.

Ensuring Risk Reduction in Communities With Multiple Stressors: Environmental Justice And Cumulative Risks/impacts

National Environmental Justice Advisory Council
December 2004

Introduction

> *"I am sick and tired of being sick and tired." This poignant plea for assistance has been voiced at every single meeting of the National Environmental Justice Advisory Council (NEJAC) and echoed by numerous environmentally overburdened people of color, low-income, and tribal communities throughout the nation. This plea reflects profound disappointment in such communities with the status of their health, frustration with the public health community's failure to assist in improving health, anger over the unresponsiveness of many businesses complacent with the adequacy of their regulatory obligations and unresponsive to the health problems their neighbors face, and bewilderment at the government's failure to understand and correct these shortcomings. Communities richly understand the degree to which they are burdened, yet find the government unwilling to seek their counsel and to provide the resources needed for communities to exercise their full voice in regulatory decisions that impact their lives. For many communities facing stresses from factors beyond their control, living with a myriad of polluting facilities, this affront is compounded by the impacts of racial and economic discrimination.*[1]

In a recent report, the Centers for Disease Control and Prevention (CDC) pointed out that: "Despite great improvements in the overall health of the nation, Americans who are members of racial and ethnic minority groups, including African Americans, Alaska Natives, American Indians, Asian Americans, Hispanic Americans, and Pacific Islanders, are more likely than whites to have poor health and to die prematurely..."[2] The CDC findings, together with the experiences of communities populated by people of color, Native American tribes, and the poor, have led to a deep frustration over the cumulative adverse conditions impacting their lives and a rising demand for the government, business and industry, and the public health community to take effective action to improve conditions.

The sense of anguish expressed above and uniformly experienced by disadvantaged, underserved, and environmentally overburdened communities reflects a complex web of combined exposures. In recent years, this combination has come to be described as "cumulative risks and impacts." Manifested in this plea is the concept of vulnerability, a matrix of physical, chemical, biological, social, and cultural factors which result in certain communities and sub-populations being more

---

[1] The phrase "I am sick and tired of being sick and tired" comes from renowned civil rights advocate Fannie Lou Hamer during the 1960s. It has come to embody the feelings of overburdened communities in the emerging environmental justice movement during the 1990s.

[2] *Racial and Ethnic Approaches to Community Health (REACH) 2010: Addressing Disparities in Health 2003,* Centers for Disease Control and Prevention.

susceptible to environmental toxins, being more exposed, or having compromised ability to cope with and/or recover from such exposure.

It is in the context of this kind of community experience that the U.S. Environmental Protection Agency (EPA), through its Office of Environmental Justice (OEJ), has requested that the National Environmental Justice Advisory Council (NEJAC) address the following question:

> *In order to ensure environmental justice for all communities and tribes, what short-term and long-term actions should the Agency take in proactively implementing the concepts contained in its Framework for Cumulative Risk Assessment?*[3]

The NEJAC is the formal advisory committee chartered, pursuant to the Federal Advisory Committee Act, to provide advice and recommendations to the EPA Administrator on matters related to environmental justice. Through its charter, the NEJAC has been charged with providing advice and recommendations on matters including, but not limited to, the "direction, criteria, scope, and adequacy of the EPA's scientific research and demonstration projects relating to environmental justice."

To address this question, the NEJAC constituted a Work Group consisting of representatives of communities; academia; business and industry; non-governmental organizations; and state, local, and tribal governments; which has worked diligently over the past 18 months. In addition, the NEJAC devoted its 19th public meeting, in New Orleans, Louisiana (April 13 through 16, 2004), to this issue.

SUMMARY OF REPORT

With the multiple challenges and frustrations confronting disadvantaged, underserved, and environmentally-overburdened communities and tribes in mind, the NEJAC has developed the following report containing advice and recommendations for both short-term and long-term actions. The NEJAC's proposed recommendations are structured around eight overarching themes. These proposed recommendations are preceded by a discussion of the need to adopt a community-based collaborative problem-solving model to operationalize the important concepts of the Agency's *Framework for Cumulative Risk Assessment* in the real life context of communities and tribes suffering environmental injustice. In addition, the report discusses some concepts critical to understanding and addressing cumulative risks and impacts within an environmental justice context, i.e., stressors; vulnerability; community-based participatory research; proportional response; qualitative analysis; efficient screening, targeting, and prioritization methods/tools; unifying public health and environmental protection; and social capital. As always, the NEJAC stresses the importance of ensuring that the special concerns of tribes are understood and addressed.

In the view of the NEJAC, the approaches recommended here will help EPA and other involved parties to systematically focus on the multiplicity of exposures, risks, impacts, and stressors facing communities—including a complex web of environmental, health, social, economic, and cultural factors—and to set priorities for action. But we recognize that before solutions can be implemented effectively, problems must first be defined clearly.

---

[3] The full text of the EPA Charge to NEJAC on cumulative risks and impacts is provided in Appendix A.

Thus, to institutionalize a bias for action within EPA, this report underscores the need to fully utilize existing statutory authorities to address environmental justice and cumulative risks and impacts. Recognizing that such authorities are fragmentary, we urge EPA to address and overcome programmatic and regulatory fragmentation within the nation's environmental protection regime. Recognizing the pivotal importance of the relationship between cumulative risks and impacts and vulnerability to environmental justice, we urge EPA to fully incorporate the concept of vulnerability, especially its social and cultural aspects, into the Agency's strategic planning and research agenda. To enhance the Agency's capacity to work with communities, we urge EPA to take steps to promote a paradigm shift to community-based approaches. As part of that shift, EPA must act to incorporate social, economic, cultural, and community health factors, including those related to vulnerability, in EPA decision-making. A vital need in addressing community needs is the development of cogent methodologies for timely, accurate, and comprehensive community assessment and characterization. Last, EPA must address the capacity and resource issues (human, organizational, technical, and financial) within EPA and the states, within impacted communities and tribes, and among all relevant stakeholders to ensure that community-based approaches have the wherewithal to succeed.

Section II of the report contains a set of appendices that provide illustrations of and background information to the key points made in this report. The appendices include:

Appendix A: Full Text, EPA's Charge to NEJAC on Cumulative Risks and Impacts.
Appendix B: Matrices Illustrating Multiple Stressors (Laredo, Texas).
Appendix C: Excerpts, Chelsea Creek Community-Based Comparative Risk Assessment Report.
Appendix D: Tables, Council on Environmental Quality Report, "Considering Cumulative Effects Under the National Environmental Policy Act."
Appendix E: EPA Risk-Reduction/Healthy Community Initiatives and Programs.
Appendix F: EPA Community Assessment Methods/Tools.
Appendix G: Implementable EPA Risk Reduction Actions and Tools.
Appendix H: Impacts of Economic, Racial, and Social Inequality on Health.
Appendix I: Community-Based Study of Vulnerability (WEACT-Columbia University Partnership).
Appendix J: Summary, EPA Human Health Research Strategy.
Appendix K: Background, Statutory Authorities Related to Cumulative Risks/impacts and Environmental Justice.
Appendix L: Pollution Burden Matrix.
Appendix M: Texas Commission on Environmental Quality Draft Cumulative Risk Activities.
Appendix N: Local Government Cumulative Risk Prevention/Intervention Effort (Portland, Oregon).

[Page Intentionally Blank]

DEFINING THE ISSUE: MULTIPLE, AGGREGATE, AND CUMULATIVE RISKS AND IMPACTS IN THE CONTEXT OF ENVIRONMENTAL JUSTICE

The authors of this report recognize that the issues of cumulative risks and cumulative impacts are inherently multi-faceted, interconnected, and complex. It is important, therefore, to clarify the nature of the problem that the EPA charge is requesting the NEJAC to address. One way of doing so is to provide the reader with a graphic illustration of the multiple and interconnected factors which are at play in communities confronting environmental justice issues. The table below provides a graphic illustration of such factors in the Mississippi River Industrial Corridor, a 2,000 square-mile area between Baton Rouge and New Orleans, in the State of Louisiana.[4]

Table 1
Multiple, Aggregate, and Cumulative Risks and Impacts in the Mississippi River Industrial Corridor

Demographics	Pollution Sources	Existing Health Problems & Conditions	Unique Exposure Pathways	Social/Cultural Conditions	Community Capacity & Infrastructure/ Social Capital
• African American: 63% • Caucasian: 35% • Asian: 3%	• Petrochemical facilities • Refineries • Wastewater treatment facilities not meeting permit limits and bypassing raw sewage due to under capacity • Drinking water taken from Mississippi River • Toxic organics, pesticides, and heavy metals in drinking water • Atrazine from Midwest agricultural fields present year round in raw and finished water • Pesticides, herbicides, and fertilizers applied to sugar cane crops • Aerial and tractor application drifts on to adjacent residential areas and school yards • Burning sugar cane during fall harvest season results in particulate matter and pesticides being dispersed into the air for 1/3 of the year	• Asthma • Respiratory distress • Skin rashes • High rate of a large variety of cancers • Lack of access to health care • Lack of trained environmental health physicians	<u>Air:</u> • Industrial facilities: semi-volatile and volatile organics, dioxins, pesticides and herbicides, toxic heavy metals, and smoke from sugar cane burning <u>Water:</u> • Drinking water contaminated • Surface water contaminated with industrial and agricultural chemicals and partially-treated waste water • Contaminated crops • Contaminated terrestrial game species • Seafood contaminated with pesticides, industrial chemicals, mercury from chlor-alkali facilities by way of air deposition.	• Very poor/ minority communities • Live off land and gardens contaminated with air deposited chemicals • Hunting and fishing of contaminated organisms • Generations have lived off the land and not profited by industrial development in the area.	• Good infrastructure in areas of low-income communities of color with respect to roads and rail; the industry needs these items. • Poor infrastructure within the communities: poor road conditions, improper drainage, waste water collection and treatment system inadequate. • Very little to no social capital: education system very minimal; the area was impacted by white flight; primarily African Americans attend the public schools.

---

[4] The table was developed by Ms. Wilma Subra, Louisiana Environmental Action Network. It is noteworthy that the above is an example of one of the methodologies for conducting cumulative effects analysis, i.e., matrices, which were described in the Council on Environmental Quality report, *Conducting Cumulative Effects Analysis under the National Environmental Policy Act.* A fuller discussion of such methodologies is found the Qualitative Analysis section of this report.

Communities and tribes confronting environmental justice issues typically are historically disadvantaged and underserved, environmentally-overburdened, and suffer adverse health conditions. The table above illustrates the range of cumulative risks and impacts as well as the factors which serve to decrease the ability of residents to cope with or recover from environmental exposures.

It would be instructive, at the outset, to thoroughly discuss two key definitional questions that are critical to ensuring sensitivity to community concerns and the bias for action so important to the NEJAC's views on the cumulative risks and impacts issue. They are the following: (1) the idea of using multiple stressors as a common starting point of discussion, and (2) the need for multi-media approaches to address cumulative impacts in a holistic way and to overcome programmatic and regulatory fragmentation.

Multiple Stressors

To be sensitive to community concerns, there must be a common conceptual framework and common definitions for understanding the issue at hand when one speaks of "cumulative risks and impacts." The lack of such is a major contributor to the lack of a coherent, consistent, and transparent framework for assessing and responding to situations involving cumulative risks and impacts. This, in turn, leads to the inability to create the confidence, trust, and capacity in the process that is fundamental to building the community capacity, institutional support, and social capital necessary to address over time the complex issues of community-wide risks and burdens. Hence, it is important to tease out what actually is meant when the terms "cumulative risks" and "cumulative impacts" are used.

Typically, regulators and risk assessors tend to see cumulative risks and impacts as a set of stressors (risks, impacts, burdens) for which there is a combined valuation. In the environmental risk assessment field, these combined valuations are usually expressed quantitatively. In the environmental impact assessment field, these combined valuations are usually qualitative in nature.[5] However, most members of impacted communities, as well as the larger public, use the term cumulative risks or impacts to mean a collection of individual stressors that occur simultaneously and multiply. This is precisely what is illustrated by the table on risks and impacts in the Mississippi River Industrial Corridor.

In most instances, a cumulative analysis, in the sense that most risk assessors or regulators understand the term, has yet to be conducted. If there is to be a bias for action that is sensitive to the needs of overburdened communities and tribes, then the starting point for examination of the problem at hand should not be "cumulative risks or impacts" but "multiple stressors." In other words, the contradictory understandings of what is meant by cumulative risks and impacts may be a "train wreck" in the making. Not having multiple stressors as the common starting point of reference will likely lead to more inaction and frustration. Hence, a common understanding by all parties of multiple stressors as the starting point for a dialogue is key to beginning the iterative process of building the confidence, trust, and capacity within the impacted community and among all stakeholders that is the foundation for a coherent, consistent, and transparent framework for assessing and responding to cumulative risks and impacts.

---

[5] The development of the environmental impact assessment field is closely related to conducting analyses under the National Environmental Policy Act. In the main, qualitative methods of analysis are used. See section on Qualitative Analysis in this report.

Multi-Media Approaches to Overcome Programmatic and Regulatory Fragmentation

Environmental protection in this country has grown by individual pieces of legislation, developed to address a particular environmental media or a pressing problem like abandoned toxic sites. Environmental law has not evolved from a master game plan or unifying vision. As a result, the statutes have gaps in coverage and do not assure compatible controls of environmental releases to all media from all sources.

While virtually all communities suffer from the statutory, regulatory, and programmatic fragmentation inherent within the Nation's environmental protection regime, its ill effects for people of color, low-income, and tribal communities are especially egregious. Recognizing the ways in which such fragmentation undermines a unified approach towards addressing cumulative risks and impacts and presents major obstacles to positive action is a critical starting point for understanding the issues confronting highly impacted communities. The following paragraphs, provided by Ms. Wilma Subra, describe how the Mississippi River Industrial Corridor is affected by such fragmentation.

> *The environment in communities along the Mississippi River corridor in Louisiana bear the environmental and health burden of programmatic and regulatory fragmentation. The regulation of the industrial facilities falls primarily under the regulation of the state environmental agency (Louisiana Department of Environmental Quality). Oversight is provided by the U.S. Environmental Protection Agency. Both the state program and EPA oversight have been extensively criticized in recent audits. Criticism has covered all program areas with particular emphasis on enforcement and compliance, expired permits, and lack of oversight.*
>
> *In addition to the pollution sources under the jurisdiction of environmental agencies, there are a number of other major pollution sources that impact the public health of the community members and the quality of the environment. The Louisiana Department of Agriculture and Forestry regulates agricultural crop programs and pesticide and fertilizer applications. The pesticide applications, surface water runoff, and burning of the agricultural crops result in a heavy pollution burden. These sources of pollution are never considered when evaluating environmental regulatory programs. The drilling and production of oil and gas is regulated by the Louisiana Office of Conservation. The air emissions, waste streams, glycol dehydration facilities, and compressor stations have produced a large environmental burden. Hundreds of oil and gas exploration and production sites are present in each community of the Mississippi River corridor and yet their pollution burden is never considered when evaluating environmental situations under current permitting and reporting processes. The Mississippi River water is a source of transportation as well as drinking water. The air emissions from ships, boats, and barges contribute to the air pollution in the communities but are not regulated or considered by the environmental regulatory programs. The contaminants in the Mississippi River water that are distributed to people in the communities are never considered as pollution burdens.*

Based upon the above, a comprehensive, integrated, and unified approach towards multiple environmental hazards in overburdened communities is critical to properly addressing cumulative risks and impacts. In the context of an environmental protection regime that suffers programmatic

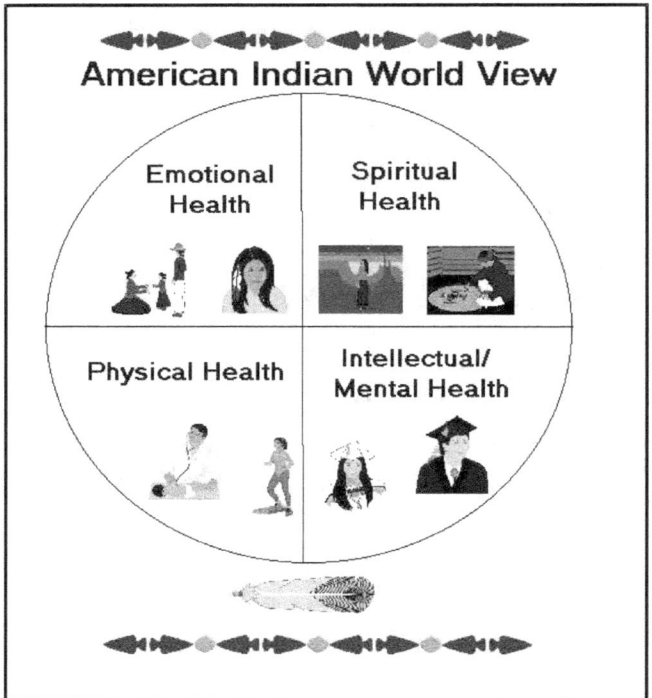

Figure 3: The four aspects of a healthy being must be considered in a cumulative risk/impact assessment. They are integral to the nature of American Indians and are reflected in the four cardinal points of the medicine wheel or sacred circle. When in balance, this will promote community health. Graphic developed by Karen Medville.

and regulatory fragmentation, a logical corollary to using multiple stressors as a common starting point for dialogue on cumulative risks and impacts is that of using multi-media approaches to overcome such fragmentation.

It should be noted that the above example is hardly unique. While there are many other similar situations throughout the Nation, space prevents us from providing a detailed description of them. All have different fact patterns and exhibit different types of environmental impacts and social dynamics. All evidence the adverse impact of multiple stressors and burdens. Therefore, it is important to highlight some implications of these kinds of communities for public health strategy and action that grow from an understanding of cumulative risks and impacts.

A NATIVE AMERICAN HEALTH PARADIGM

Many Native Americans are concerned about pesticide use, particularly in forested lands that are owned or managed by the federal government. The EPA Tribal Science Council has worked with the Agency to develop an alternative to traditional risk assessment that better incorporates Native American perspectives on wellness and health. Tribal relationship with the land is inseparable from Native American culture. If the land and water are not healthy, then people cannot be healthy. As Figure 1 illustrates, health is a strong aspect of traditional Indian culture, and has spiritual as well as mental and emotional components. Practitioners of traditional medicine and other members of the Native American community are called upon to enrich these components. For example, in the Mohawk culture, the canoe is used as a key symbol and represents the "holder of the culture."

SOUTHEAST LOS ANGELES: AN URBAN AIR HOT SPOT

Southeast Los Angeles, in California, is an air toxics "hot spot." It is the home of a cluster of polluting facilities as well as the stationary and mobile pollution sources that result from being a major goods-movement corridor. Some of these polluters are regulated by local ordinances; many are not regulated at all. According to a report by Communities for a Better Environment (CBE), the health effects caused by these multiple sources of pollution provide compelling reasons for timely action. The pollution sources create environmental injustice because they are overly burdensome to the Southeast Los Angeles community, harmful to its health, and lead to a lower quality of life. CBE's report concludes that current environmental policy ignores cumulative impacts, and that toxins are not regulated adequately to protect human health.[6]   A cumulative approach could help document the issues that the community faces.

WEST HARLEM: STUDYING CHILDREN'S HEALTH

In the Harlem neighborhoods of New York City that were studied by West Harlem Environmental Action (WEACT) and Columbia University's School of Public Health, children are impacted by a cascade of environmental and other stressors that negatively affect their health, welfare and quality of life. Living in deteriorating housing with substantial pest infestation results in a double whammy for developing fetuses and infants: high levels of pesticides results in widespread exposure to pesticides during pregnancy as well as *in utero* sensitization to multiple indoor pest allergens. Many of the children who live in these conditions start their lives as highly exposed individuals, and with developmental disorders, frequent respiratory symptoms, and other health deficits. Because of these cumulative impacts, even a small exposure to environmental toxins can be significant in this community.[7]

---

[6] Communities for a Better Environment, *Holding Our Breath: The Struggle for Environmental Justice in Southeast Los Angeles,* Los Angeles: Communities for a Better Environment, 1998.

[7] See Appendix I for detailed description of these studies.

[Page Intentionally Blank]

EPA's Framework for Cumulative Risk Assessment

In May 2003, EPA published its *Framework for Cumulative Risk Assessment*[8] (hereinafter also referred to as the "Framework" or EPA's "Cumulative Risk Framework"), which is a first step in the Agency's long-term effort to develop guidelines for assessing and responding to cumulative risks and impacts. While the Framework represents a profound milestone for the Agency's efforts to address the cumulative risk issue, it is especially significant for addressing the relationship between cumulative risks and environmental justice. In fact, many of the tenets of the Framework were informed by the attempt to develop a coherent approach to situations involving environmental justice issues.

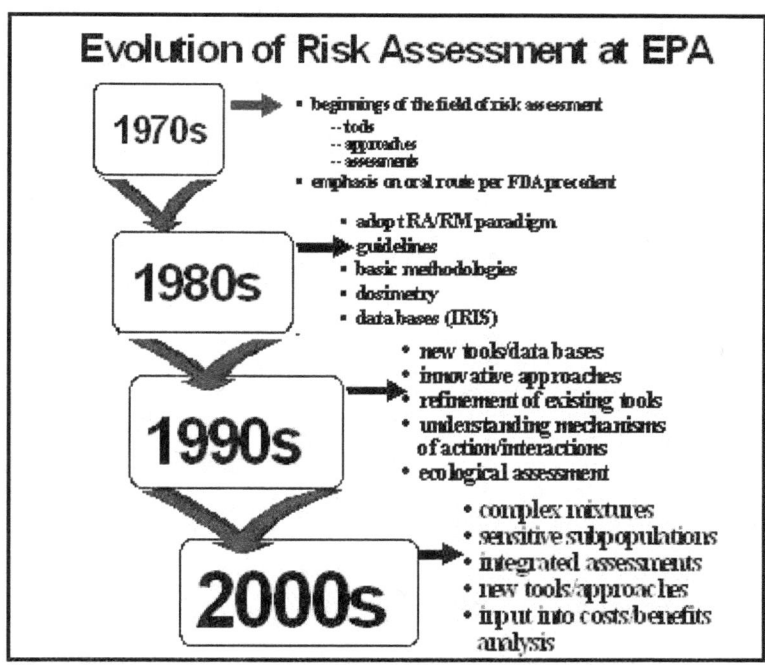

Figure 4: Thomas A. Burke, Johns Hopkins University, Bloomberg School of Public Health, Presentation to EPA Region 3 Cumulative Risk Workshop. May 28-29, 2003

Taken in historical context, past risk assessment approaches, and environmental protection principles generally, were geared to controlling sources of pollution through technology-based regulation or an individual chemical-by-chemical approach. It became evident that the broad national regulations produced uneven results and left significant pockets of higher exposure and adverse impacts. These pockets, in large part, were the many communities and tribes where issues of environmental justice are manifested. More often than not, these remaining pockets of higher exposure and adverse impacts are the "toxic hotspots" in which historically disadvantaged and underserved communities and tribes live, work, worship, and play. Some of the major tenets of the Framework (community-based approach; place-based and population-based analysis; multiple stressors; involvement of impacted community members and other stakeholders; and the concept of vulnerability) also are basic tenets of a strategy to remedy environmental injustice. The EPA *Framework for Cumulative Risk Assessment* represents a major advance in the Agency's quest to resolve these remaining challenges.

The Framework is key to ensuring the goal of environmental justice for all communities because of the following features:

---

[8] See U.S. Environmental Protection Agency, *Framework for Cumulative Risk Assessment*, EPA/630/P-02/001F, Washington, DC, USEPA, May 2003. The EPA *Framework for Cumulative Risk Assessment* is the first major document in EPA's efforts to develop approaches and methodologies for assessing and responding to cumulative risks. It provides the basis for eventual EPA guidance on conducting such assessments. The report is available on http://cfpub.epa.gov/ncea/raf/recordisplay.cfm?deid_54944.

■ **It takes a broad view of risk.** The Framework explicitly states that the formulation of risk can include areas outside EPA's regulatory authority, and poses questions for which a quantitative method or answer does not yet exist.

■ **It utilizes a population-based and place-based analysis.** Conventional human health risk assessments usually focus on the source or stressor ("a risk assessment for benzene, an industrial plant, etc.") and follow the stressor to various populations affected. Cumulative risk assessment, like many ecological assessments, will be done with the focus on a population or place, and consideration of various stressors affecting them ("a cumulative risk assessment for a community, etc.").

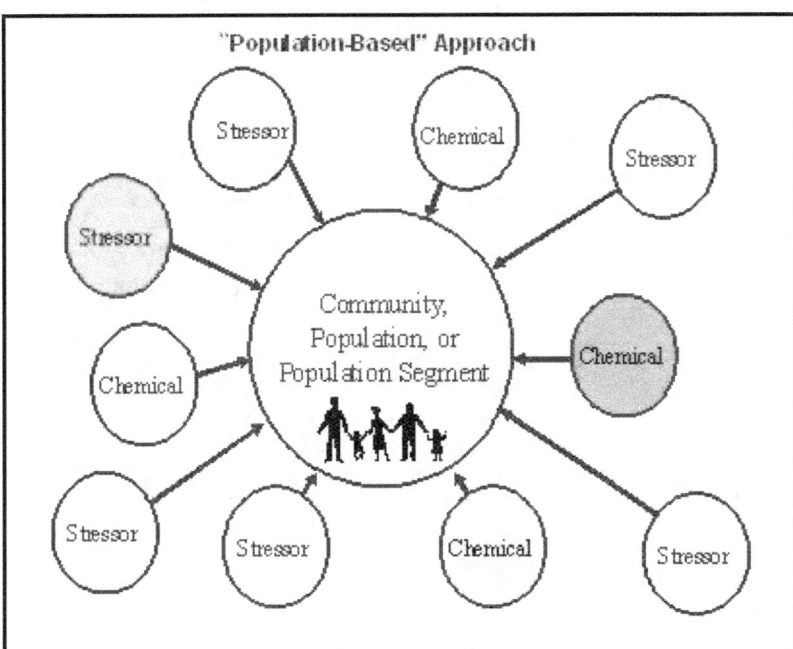

Figure 5: *Framework for Cumulative Risk Assessment, USEPA.*

■ **It promotes a comprehensive and integrated assessment of risk.** Although combining human health and ecological concerns has been a challenge for risk assessors for decades, the possible interaction between ecological and health risks makes this even more important in cumulative assessments than it has been in conventional risk assessment.

■ **It involves multiple stressors (chemical and non-chemical).** While past risk assessments have often addressed a number of chemical stressors individually, the Framework for Cumulative Risk Assessment requires the consideration of how these multiple stressors act together. It also discusses broadly considering not only chemical stressors, but also other stressors such as biological, physical, or even cultural, and how they affect the cumulative risk.

■ **It posits an expanded definition of vulnerability to include biological and social factors.** Using the definition of vulnerability from the Framework, "vulnerability" is broader than just another word for biological susceptibility or sensitivity. The Framework adopts a social science view of vulnerability which allows consideration of any number of types of stressors that result in a widely different effect for two populations who suffer the same intensity of insult.

■ **It places a premium on community involvements and partnerships.** Cumulative risk assessment will largely play out in geographically or population-based settings. Because of this, the Framework puts heavy emphasis on making use of local expertise of various sorts available within the areas studied.

- **It emphasizes the importance of planning, scoping, and problem-formulation.**
  Cumulative risk assessment has the potential to be much more complex than conventional
  risk assessment. It is essential that the questions to be answered be clearly identified and
  articulated, and that the participants have clear agreement on what is to be done and the
  limitations of the potential results of the assessments.

- **It links risk assessment to risk management within the context of community health
  goals.** Because of its potentially broad scope, including many different types of stressors,
  cumulative risk assessment has a high potential for bringing attention to a variety of sources
  of risk. Managing these risks may require a wide variety of approaches (not all regulatory)
  discussed jointly among the participants.

NEJAC'S CORE RESPONSE TO THE EPA CHARGE: ADOPTING A COMMUNITY-BASED COLLABORATIVE PROBLEM-SOLVING MODEL FOR ADDRESSING CUMULATIVE RISKS AND IMPACTS

The EPA Charge requests that the NEJAC provide advice and recommendations on what short-term and long-term actions EPA should take on the issue of cumulative risks and impacts to ensure environmental justice for all communities. After much deliberation, the NEJAC decided that it can add the most value by offering another perspective to the ones already articulated by the Framework. This added perspective is meant to address the question: ***How does one operationalize the important concepts in the Agency's Cumulative Risk Framework in a manner that is sensitive to the "real life" context of communities and tribes suffering environmental injustice?***

To answer this question, the NEJAC takes the position that, in situations where it is possible, combining the new Cumulative Risk Framework with a collaborative problem-solving approach is arguably the **fastest and surest way** to bring about tangible and sustainable benefits for disproportionately impacted communities and tribes. Some significant experience and lessons are now emerging in the use of an Environmental Justice Collaborative Problem-Solving Model, developed by the EPA Office of Environmental Justice through the Federal Interagency Working Group on Environmental Justice. Such lessons can be of great value to operationalizing the concepts of the Agency's Cumulative Risk Framework. Together, they provide a critical set of strategies and tools for achieving what is presumably the ultimate goal of both environmental justice and the Cumulative Risk Framework, i.e., healthy and sustainable communities.[9]

The Environmental Justice Collaborative Problem-Solving Model is an emerging community-based, interagency, multi-stakeholder model to address environmental justice issues and achieve healthy and sustainable communities. It is premised on the following:

- Seeks proactive, strategic, community-based solutions to environmental justice issues, building on community visioning and planning processes;

---

[9] See U.S. Environmental Protection Agency. *Environmental Justice Collaborative Model: A Framework to Ensure Local Problem-Solving* (EPA 300-R-02-001), Washington, DC: U.S. Environmental Protection Agency. Copies are available from: <*www.epa.gov/compliance/environmentaljustice*>. The environmental justice collaborative model is the basis of a new grant program administered by OEJ called the Environmental Justice Collaborative Problem-Solving Grant Program. Fifteen grants will be awarded to community-based organizations in FY2003 and another fifteen in FY2004. See U.S. Environmental Protection Agency, "Office of Environmental Justice, Environmental Justice Collaborative Problem-Solving Grant Program Request for Applications," *Federal Register*, June 6, 2003. Also see U.S. Environmental Protection Agency, *Towards an Environmental Justice Collaborative Model: An Evaluation of the Use of Partnerships to Address Environmental Justice Issues in Communities* (EPA/100-R-03-001) and U.S. Environmental Protection Agency, *Towards an Environmental Justice Collaborative Model: Case Studies of Six Partnerships Used to Address Environmental Justice Issues in Communities* (EPA/100-R-03-002). These reports were based on studies conducted by the EPA Office of Policy, Economics, and Innovation <*www.epa.gov/evaluate*>. The International City/County Management Association (ICMA) is nearing completion of a study on the IWG demonstration project collaborative partnerships, particularly looking at the community-local government interface. It is to be entitled *Not Business at Usual: Using Collaborative Partnerships to Address Environmental Justice Issues.* Last, see Lee, Charles, "Collaborative Models to Achieve Environmental Justice and Healthy Communities, " in Pellow, David and Robert Brulle, *People, Power and Pollution: A Critical Appraisal of the Environmental Justice Movement*, Cambridge, MA: MIT Press, forthcoming.

- Promotes an asset-building approach [10] to building community capacity and social capital, particularly for disadvantaged and underserved communities;
- Incorporates consensus building and dispute resolution principles and methods, including the "Mutual Gains Approach to Negotiations";[11]
- Utilizes community-based participatory research methodologies;
- Establishes multi-stakeholder partnerships to leverage human, organization, technical, and financial resources;
- Fosters an integrated approach to addressing environmental, health, social, and economic needs;
- Promotes multi-agency coordination to effectively utilize resources of all relevant federal, state, tribal, and local government agencies; and
- Integrates an evaluation framework and promotes replication of lessons learned and best practices.

To be sure, the Agency's *Framework for Cumulative Risk Assessment* represents a profound advancement in the kind of thinking that will help communities and tribes address their concerns. The Cumulative Risk Framework is important because, for the first time, it dramatically opens the scope of risk assessment to include the factors that are key to understanding community risk. It allows for a discussion of multiple sources, as well as social and cultural factors and issues of vulnerability. Finally, the community can enter into a dialogue about risk that realistically incorporates the factors experienced by disadvantaged, underserved, and environmentally overburdened communities and tribes. Past risk conversations have always had limitations that caused risk assessments to miss the target and sometimes even bias decisions against communities with multiple stressors.

As important an advance as the Agency's Cumulative Risk Framework is, the NEJAC fears that, by itself, the Framework will not lead to dramatic progress. Rather, the NEJAC fears that it can be used to slow down progress if it causes analysis of risk to be more complicated and time consuming in order to reach the answers needed for action to take place. In fact, the increased complexity can easily become an excuse for never taking action.

For this reason, the NEJAC sees the need to place this important advance in the context of a bias for action. Such a bias for action means that a Cumulative Risk Framework must be combined with other key strategies if it is going to make a meaningful difference in the health of impacted communities and tribes. To get to actions that will reduce risk means that the new expanded view of risk has to form the starting point for a process in the community that builds the community's capacity to actually do something about risk.

While the Cumulative Risk Framework opens up the possibility for a new and more realistic dialogue on risk, it will not, by itself, cause that dialogue to take place. To get results, a conscious

---

[10] Asset building is an approach towards community development and problem-solving that seeks to identify (asset-mapping) and build upon community-based assets such as the skills of local residents, power of local associations, resources of public, private and non-profit institutions, and the physical and economic resources of local places. See Kretzmann, John P. and John L. McKnight, *Building Communities From the Inside Out: A Path Toward Finding and Mobilizing A Community's Assets*, Chicago, IL: ACTA Publications, 1993.

[11] The "Mutual Gains Approach to Negotiations" was developed by Lawrence Susskind, Massachusetts Institute of Technology planning professor and president of the Consensus Building Institute. It calls for a process by which parties with different interests can create value by exploring mutually beneficially options. See: *<http://www.cbuilding.org>*.

effort to develop a collaborative process that brings governments and all sectors of the community together in a problem-solving mode must be combined with the expanded cumulative perspective. This means that all relevant stakeholders will need to engage in an open and deliberative discussion of causes of risk and be willing to contribute to a community-wide effort to reduce risk. This collaborative problem-solving approach is a paradigm shift of equal importance to the paradigm shift embodied in the cumulative perspective on risk laid out in the Framework.

Joining in a real, community-based collaborative process also will require difficult adjustments on all sides: Governments and risk experts must recognize that residents have an essential and vital role to play in the discussion of risk and risk management. Residents must be willing to look at risk broadly and use science to understand risk and to target risk reductions efforts. Industry must be willing to go beyond its narrow facility perspective, look at risk from the community perspective, and become willing partners in efforts that go beyond mere regulatory compliance to improve community health.

This collaborative process will create the capacity that is needed to get something done. Solutions to health problems in impacted communities will not come from government or from industry or from residents alone. It will take a collaborative partnership that brings everyone to work together to find solutions. A cumulative perspective on risk and a collaborative community process will bring the changes needed to finally address the longstanding needs of communities and tribes suffering environmental injustice.

The NEJAC cautions that using cumulative risk analysis alone to select a few targets for action under applicable regulatory authority will raise the bar for the level of analysis for those few and result in long delays and legal challenges. If only a few contributors to wide-spread community burdens are selected to respond to concerns about community health and welfare, those few contributors will spend their resources explaining why such selective enforcement is unfair rather than channel new resources to reduce the portion of community burden for which they are accountable.

We need to use the critical breakthrough that comes with the cumulative risk perspective to dramatize the accountability of all contributors for unacceptable cumulative community burdens. We need to use this perspective to help create a new conversation that brings all sectors together in a collaborative approach to reach some workable agreement resulting in action. This conversation will have to be an iterative one that gradually builds both trust and a better understanding of risk and ways to reduce it. It will start with a fairly quick screening of multiple stressors and deliberative conversation that will identify the risks that everyone can agree to address immediately. Actions will be taken on these immediate risks and vulnerabilities while the partnership works simultaneously to refine its understanding of the full scope and extent of a community's burden. The trust built through common action and the common knowledge built through further cumulative risk analysis will result in new, refined targets and more extensive and productive actions. This is a process that should continue indefinitely as a regular function of a healthy community.

In presenting the above perspective, the NEJAC recognizes that its enthusiasm for these eminently sensible concepts must be tempered with a realistic appreciation of the challenges which often confront disadvantaged and underserved communities and tribes. We realize that, despite the good efforts of many well-intentioned parties, some contributors to environmental burdens–be they business or government–still refuse to come to the table to acknowledge the environmental burdens for which they are accountable. In those instances, the NEJAC calls upon EPA, as well as delegated state programs, to exercise their regulatory and enforcement authorities to the fullest extent possible.

Taken together, the concepts articulated in both the Agency's Cumulative Risk Framework and in this report must be integrated in a manner that leads to a coherent, consistent, and transparent framework for conducting assessments and taking meaningful action to reduce risk on the part of all parties involved. Much of what will make the concepts articulated in both the Agency's Cumulative Risk Framework and in this report come to life is a unifying process that overcomes fragmentation, builds confidence, trust, and capacity on the part of the communities and all relevant stakeholders. The degree to which such confidence in the process, trust among all stakeholders, and capacity on the part of all parties involved, is achieved will determine, in large measure, the quality of the analysis and the meaningfulness of the actions taken to reduce risk.

Building on the NEJAC Pollution Prevention Report

In a very real sense, the recommendations of this report build on the recommendations of the NEJAC's report on "Advancing Environmental Justice through Pollution Prevention." In that report, the NEJAC confronted the issue of determining which of the myriad of currently available pollution prevention tools would be most effective in any given community or tribal situation, most of which suffer from cumulative risks and impacts. As a result, the NEJAC proposed a "multi-stakeholder collaborative model" to focus, in the first instance, on the assessment process but also to fashion a pathway to implementation of pollution prevention and risk reduction solutions.[12] The issue of cumulative risks and impacts that the EPA now requests the NEJAC to examine presents, in large part, a mirror image of the earlier question.

The NEJAC recognizes that equitable collaboration and community based approaches can be jeopardized when they do not build upon a strong foundation of community engagement. Community-based participatory research (CBPR) provides a process to develop an action strategy that evolves from a strong community foundation to involve many parties and stakeholders. It provides an avenue to ensure an understanding on the part of all parties of community concerns and ensures the involvement of impacted community groups in decision-making in an equitable, multi-disciplinary, and collaborative framework. Thus, CBPR can provide the foundation for successful utilization of the Environmental Justice Collaborative-Problem Solving Model. It is a systematic way of involving the community in finding the answers to questions or the solutions to problems. The particular strength of CBPR is that community members groups along with researchers, specialists, and other stakeholders, such as government and businesses, carry out projects in equitable partnerships. Moreover, CBPR partnerships begin with structures that maintain equitable power sharing.

The CBPR process begins with identifying community concerns and ideas through *Community Dialogue Sessions*. In these sessions, basic training is conducted on community-based participatory research. Methods utilized at Community Dialogue Sessions are designed to ensure that there is an organic involvement of the community. This is a critical first step for genuine community identification of problems, and to ensure long-term involvement of the community in equitable partnerships seeking to uncover solutions and promote action. The Dialogue Sessions allow participants to identify community (and other) information and data, and begin initial identification and assessment of community expertise, resource needs, and initial identification of partners.

---

[12] National Environmental Justice Advisory Council, *Advancing Environmental Justice Through Pollution Prevention*, June 2003. See *<http://www.epa.gov/compliance/environmentaljustice/nejac>*. A major recommendation of this report calls upon EPA to develop and implement a multi-stakeholder collaborative model to advance environmental justice through pollution prevention that ensures a meaningful role in design and implementation for impacted communities.

Analysis of the advantages of partnerships and the barriers to achieving effective partnerships also are explored, culminating in the development of principles which form a framework for equitable partnerships under the following premise:

> *Equitable partnerships require sharing power and resources, and a reciprocal appreciation of the knowledge of the other partner at each stage of a project–from defining the problem, to conducting the investigation, to evaluation, to determining actions and interventions.*

In conclusion, the NEJAC believes that adopting a community-based collaborative problem-solving model to address issues of cumulative risks and impacts is intended to accomplish the following:

- Address multiple stressors;
- Create a transparent process that instills confidence, trust, and other positive features of social capital;
- Institutionalize a bias for action;
- Develop a coherent and consistent framework for doing cumulative risk assessment;
- Incorporate community-based participatory research methods;
- Address issues of vulnerability in communities, when assessing cumulative risks/impacts as well as when undertaking prevention/intervention efforts;
- Utilize efficient screening, targeting, and prioritization methods/tools;
- Bring about significant risk reduction; and
- Employ regulatory authorities to bring recalcitrant parties to the table.

DISCUSSION OF KEY CONCEPTS

In the opinion of the NEJAC, the implications of adopting a community-based collaborative problem-solving model to address issues of environmental justice and cumulative risks and impacts can be profound. This section of the report discusses certain key interrelated and interdependent concepts critical to understanding these implications. Two were discussed earlier, i.e., (1) the idea of using multiple stressors as a common starting point of discussion; and (2) the need for multi-media approaches to overcome programmatic and regulatory fragmentation. Other concepts are: the EPA Cumulative Risk Framework's definition of stressors; vulnerability; community-based participatory research; proportional response; qualitative analysis; efficient screening, targeting, and prioritization methods/tools; unifying public health and environmental protection; and social capital. We have chosen to discuss these concepts because they are directly related to the NEJAC's thinking on promoting a collaborative problem-solving model to address and eliminate cumulative risks and impacts in disadvantaged, underserved, and environmentally overburdened communities and tribes and ensure environmental justice for all people.

Stressors:

The concept of stressors is used from the very beginning of this report. Hence, it is important to examine it more extensively. The EPA *Framework for Cumulative Risk Assessment* defines "stressor" in the following manner:

> *A stressor is a physical, chemical, biological, or other entity that can cause an adverse response in a human or other organism or ecosystem. Exposure to a chemical, biological, or physical agent (e.g., radon) can be a stressor, as can the lack of, or destruction of, some necessity, such as a habitat. The stressor may not cause harm directly, but it may make the target more vulnerable to harm by other stressors. A socioeconomic stressor, for example, might be the lack of needed health care, which could lead to adverse effects. Harmful events, such as automobile crashes, could also be termed stressors. Obviously, calculating risks from different types of stressors can use widely differing methods, including probabilistic estimates of disease via dose-response relationships or looking up rates in statistical tables of historical events, among others.*[13]

Notably, the Framework says that "...There is no limitation that the 'agents or stressors' be only chemicals."[14] For example, the above definition specifically mentions socioeconomic stressors, such as lack of health care. This is one reason why the Framework is such an important milestone; it lays the basis to begin a conversation about comprehensive risk in an impacted community or tribe.

From the perspective of the Framework, stressors are those things that cause or promote both risks and impacts. However, the meaning of the term "risk" has been shaped by a historical association with quantitative risk assessment. Risks has been defined as the probability of harm and heretofore has been expressed quantitatively as a metric. As a result, impacted communities have had a strong aversion to the concept of risks and risk assessment. They see the historic concept of risk as being as overly narrow, overly technical, and highly removed from the reality of their situations. Residents of impacted communities see themselves as living with the impacts, or "harm or adverse effects found

---

[13] U.S. Environmental Protection Agency, *Framework for Cumulative Risk Assessment*, pg. 2

[14] Ibid, pg. 7

in populations or individuals as a result of a stressor or stressors," and believe that their knowledge of community conditions, community needs, and community assets are important to any effort to assess and address risk in their community. A good description of this tension is described in the report of the Chelsea Creek Community-Based Comparative Risk Assessment.

> *Risk assessment is a tool created to compare and rank environmental problems based on the potential for environmental and public health impacts. Traditionally, risk assessments draw together a number of experts in fields such as toxicology, economics, and natural resources. These experts are expected to use "pure science" to assess the risk to public health from contaminants, and identify appropriate resource investment or mitigation measures. This approach does not generally allow for public participation or input into the process.*[15]

A major concern of environmental justice is the timely, accurate, and comprehensive characterization of communities inundated with multiple sources of pollution. These sources may include, but certainly are not limited to: industrial facilities; noxious land uses; deteriorated housing; contamination in air, soil or water; transportation related emissions; and/or food consumed as a result of subsistence diets.

As previously stated, and as the above definition of stressors shows, the EPA *Framework for Cumulative Risk Assessment* seeks to think about risk in a broad and unified manner. Some implications of this integrated approach are:

- It provides flexibility in terms of the assessment scope and the type and nature of the input data, i.e., to able to take communities as you find them;
- It promotes the development of ways to characterize and use information differently, including thinking and making judgments in both a quantitative and qualitative manner;
- It requires the assessment to be more data intensive, and include collection and analysis of data pertinent to all the factors relevant to multiple risks and impacts;
- It involves additional areas of expertise to do the assessments;
- It places a greater premium on involving and getting input from impacted communities and tribes; and
- It fosters the development of partnerships among multiple disciplines and multiple stakeholders.

The concept of stressors is important because, as discussed earlier, it represents the logical common starting point for the discussion of how to characterize disadvantaged and overburdened communities and tribes and how to describe vulnerability. The concept also provides a way to dramatically open the scope of risk assessment to include the factors which are key to understanding community risk and community health.

The NEJAC cannot overemphasize the reality that in impacted communities and tribes, both residents and risk assessors initially confront a situation with a set of multiple stressors, the combined risks and impacts of which have yet to be ascertained. While one goal is ultimately a comprehensive characterization of such combined risks and impacts, the impacted community

---

[15] *Chelsea Creek Community-Based Risk Assessment Report*, Chelsea Creek Action Group and U.S. Environmental Protection Agency, Spring 2003. Excerpts from the report are provide in Appendix C. The full report can be obtained at http://www.epa.gov/region01/eco/uep/boston/bprogress.html.

should not have to wait until such a full characterization of combined risks and impacts is completed before action can be taken.

Vulnerability:

The concept of vulnerability goes to the heart of the meaning of environmental justice. Vulnerability recognizes that disadvantaged, underserved, and overburdened communities come to the table with pre-existing deficits of both a physical and social nature that make the effects of environmental pollution more, and in some cases unacceptably, burdensome. As such, the concept of vulnerability fundamentally differentiates disadvantaged, underserved, and overburdened communities from healthy and sustainable communities. Moreover, it provides the added dimension of considering the nature of the receptor population when defining disproportionate risks or impacts.

The Framework includes a definition of vulnerability that can serve as a starting point for discussing this concept.[16] According to the Framework, a subpopulation is vulnerable if it is more likely to be adversely affected by a stressor than the general population. There are four basic ways in which a population can be vulnerable: susceptibility/sensitivity, differential exposure, differential preparedness, and differential ability to recover. Each of these types of vulnerabilities is discussed below.

> **Susceptibility/Sensitivity**: A subpopulation may be susceptible or sensitive to a stressor if it faces an increased likelihood of sustaining an adverse effect due to a life state (e.g., pregnant, young, old), an impaired immune system, or a pre-existing condition, such as asthma. A subpopulation could have been previously sensitized to a compound, or have prior disease or damage. In some cases, susceptibility also could arise because of genetic polymorphisms, which are genetic differences in a portion of a population. For example, a community with a large subpopulation of young children could be more susceptible to the effects of lead poisoning. A community with many elderly residents could be more vulnerable to a stressor such as a heat wave. And a community with a high number of asthmatics will be more susceptible to air pollution. The environmental justice implications of this phenomenon are significant. For example, given the fact that children are considered to be a highly susceptible subpopulation, then children in low-income and people of color communities must be considered an even more susceptible group within that subpopulation.[17]

> **Differential Exposure**: A subpopulation can be more vulnerable because it is living or working near a source of pollution and is therefore exposed to a higher level of the pollutant than the general population. Children living in older, deteriorated housing are more likely to receive greater exposure to lead paint dust, and their breathing zone is closer to the ground where such dust is more likely to be found. Communities situated close to the fence line of a facility that is emitting air pollutants, or living near a major roadway, will most likely experience higher levels

---

[16] The following definition was provided by Roger Kasperson, noted environmental risk expert and executive director of the Stockholm Environmental Institute. Among other things, Dr. Kasperson was the first social scientist appointed to the EPA Science Advisory Board.

[17] See EPA, *America's Children and the Environment: Measures of Contaminants, Body Burdens, and Illnesses*, EPA 240-R-03-001, February 2003.

of air pollution. Due to contaminated fish or wildlife, subpopulations, such as Native Americans, that are dependent on subsistence consumption represent another example of differential exposure.

In reviewing differential exposure, it is important to take into consideration what is sometimes referred to as background exposure or historical exposure. It is particularly important to recognize historical exposures in communities and tribes suffering environmental injustice. In some cases, community members were exposed to pollutants for many years in the past from facilities that are no longer functioning or in business. These past exposures could act to increase the body burden of a subpopulation so that vulnerable individuals start off at a higher dose. Even if the dose-response curves among the subpopulation are the same as the general population, starting off at a higher point on this curve puts the members of the vulnerable subpopulation at greater risk for exposure to the same amount of a compound than the general population. This fact is highly pertinent to the historical legacy of racial and economic discrimination, and the relationship of vulnerability to health disparities. In this sense, it may be productive to explore the relationship between health disparities and susceptibility.

Social, economic, and cultural factors can play a role with respect to differential exposure. An intriguing example of a lessened ability to prevent environmental insult and resulting exposure is found in the research of Professor Manuel Pastor, Jr. and his colleagues. They found a strong correlation between periods of greatest community demographic change and the introduction of noxious land uses. It is surmised that this is a period when the community's social capital, in terms of stable leaders, networks, and institutions, is perhaps lowest. Pastor's colleagues coined a term to describe this phenomenon, i.e., "ethnic churning."[18]

While it is clear that social, economic, and cultural factors can play a salient role in the area of differential exposure, they are perhaps more prominent with respect to the next two categories of vulnerability, i.e., differential preparedness and differential ability to recover. Moreover, as previously noted, these factors cut across the different categories of vulnerability.

Differential Preparedness: Differential preparedness refers to subpopulations which are less able withstand an environmental insult. This is linked to what kind of coping systems an individual, population, or community has: the more prepared, the less vulnerable. Examples of lessened ability to withstand insult include lack of actions to prepare for a stressor (vaccination, for example, to ward off disease) or poor access to preventive health care (which has the potential to improve community response to stressors). Poverty, poor nutrition, or psycho-social stress may affect the strength of one's coping system. Preparedness against many stressors also can depend on the general state of social and cultural health of a subpopulation. As the American Indian World View of Health in Figure 1 shows, preparedness in these

---

[18] Manuel Pastor, Jr. is a professor of Latin American and Latino Studies at University of California at Santa Cruz and director of its Center for Justice, Tolerance and Community. He has authored numerous publication on the subject of environmental justice. Dr. Pastor presented on his research on issues of "ethnic churning" and facility siting to the NEJAC Enforcement Subcommittee in December 1999. His presentation was based on the following article: Pastor, Manuel, Jr., Jim Sadd, and John Hipp, "Which Came First? Toxic Facilities, Minority Move-In, and Environmental Justice," *Journal of Urban Affairs* 23(1)1-21, 2001.

communities often will be linked directly to the balance between emotional, physical, spiritual, and mental health.

Differential Ability to Recover: Differential preparedness and differential ability to recover are closely related categories of vulnerability. Some subpopulations are more able to recover from an insult or stressor because they have more information about environmental risks, health, and disease; ready access to better medical and health care; early diagnosis of disease; or better nutrition.

Clearly, social factors, including but not limited to income, employment status, access to insurance, discrimination in the health care system, language ability, and the existence of social capital, can play an important role in determining the ability to prevent, withstand, or recover from environmental insults. Last, isolation, whether economic, racial, linguistic, or otherwise, leads to less connections, less access to information or influence, and, thus, less ability to prevent, withstand, or recover from environmental stressors. Indices which measure such isolation, such as dissimilarity indexes, may be useful in this area.[19] Once again, this may point to the relationship of health disparities to all four categories of vulnerability.

This formal definition of vulnerability takes on new meaning when looked at within the context of a community and provides a framework for understanding how a disadvantaged community faces greater impacts from pollution than the general population. As already illustrated, linking vulnerability with the concept of health disparities can produce a very powerful analytical tool. Vulnerability and health disparities are integrally related concepts, and in some ways, **health disparities are both an outcome of and a contributor to vulnerability**. Greater vulnerability of individuals to a stressor can result in health disparities to an entire community. For example, if an entire community receives higher exposure to a single or multiple pollutants, this may result in the community having a higher incidence of disease, such as asthma or cardiovascular disease, resulting in a health disparity. If these same individuals are also more susceptible to a stressor, are in poor health to begin with and do not receive proper medical attention, the potential for health disparities and the magnitude of the disparities from the higher exposure increases. Once a community shows disparities in various diseases, the community members have a compromised state of health, the community is more vulnerable. This cycle of multiple exposures coupled with vulnerability can lead to a downward health spiral to greater disparities.

EPA's Cumulative Risk Framework is a good place to begin to understand the concept of vulnerability because it lays the groundwork, perhaps for the first time in an EPA document, to incorporate those social (as well as physical) factors which are numerous in historically disadvantaged and underserved communities but heretofore have not been considered part of the scope of an environmental risk assessment. While vulnerability has yet to be clearly or fully articulated as a salient factor, it has been an implicit part of the debate over risk within communities and tribes suffering environmental injustice. One example is the proposal that a protocol for characterizing communities with environmental justice issues must take into account preexisting risk conditions. This was proposed by Jerome Balter, of the Public Interest Law Center of Philadelphia.

---

[19] See discussion in Appendix H by H. Patricia Hynes and Russ Lopez (Boston University School of Public Health) about different indices available for examining vulnerability factors such as the impacts of economic, racial, and social inequality on health.

In essence, Mr. Balter was suggesting that vulnerability factors, as described in this report, be taken into account.[20]

As previously stated, the concept of vulnerability goes to the heart of the meaning of environmental justice, that is, the idea that disadvantaged, underserved, and overburdened communities come to the table with pre-existing deficits, of both a physical and social nature, that will make the effects of environmental pollution more and, sometimes, unacceptably burdensome. Some will make the case that the concept of vulnerability is bigger than the risk assessment process or that it deals with things which fall outside of EPA's jurisdiction. They would argue that it speaks to larger questions like poverty, education, or employment opportunity. Or the concept of vulnerability speaks to a community's cultural or linguistic practices, access to information, capacity to engage in the decision-making process, social networks and assets, and other aspects of the community's social infrastructure. The NEJAC would argue that these are the very things which must be considered in order to obtain an accurate characterization of community risk. Moreover, they are critical to meaningfully involving impacted communities in the risk assessment process and to developing and implementing risk reduction and community health solutions.

There is, in fact, a rich literature on the social determinants of health that makes a compelling case for the role of social factors in significantly affecting the health of a community. These social factors include poverty; unemployment, poor nutrition; housing and transportation, deprivation in early childhood; exposure to drugs; lack of control over one's life; poor social relations, discrimination and segregation, and others.[21] Researchers in the field have concluded that health disparities within populations are most commonly caused by environmental factors, where environment includes social, built, and physical environments, and not by individual genetic susceptibilities to disease alone.

There needs to be more examination of concepts like racial and economic discrimination as a social stressor with health outcomes, as well stress which grows out of such discrimination. Clearly, many of the issues raised require long-term research. However, this should not be an excuse for lack of action in the short term. To the extent possible, the social, cultural, and community health factors which can be incorporated into EPA's decision-making process should be identified. On the other hand, there will be factors which fall outside of EPA's jurisdiction. This requires leadership on the part of EPA, as well as all interested parties, in identifying the appropriate agencies, be they health, transportation, housing or others, which need to be brought to the table early on as part of initial scoping, planning, and problem-formulation.

Last, the NEJAC believes that the area of vulnerability should be pursued systematically as part of the EPA's basic and applied research agenda. Such a systematic effort should address the questions, array of concepts, body of theory, and assemblage of tools and methods that can characterize the condition of social, political, economic, and environmental vulnerability; its variable distribution within a population; and its social and psychological meaning. Investigations need to consider the various factors that lead to the generation of differentiated vulnerability and to the social and economic disparities that result from those differences. Such a science is by nature multi- and inter-disciplinary, drawing from many of the social sciences for its concepts, theories, and methods but

---

[20] Jerome Balter, Testimony at the National Environmental Justice Advisory Council Meeting, May 24, 2000, Atlanta, Georgia. Mr. Balter was the attorney for the plaintiff in *Chester Residents Concerned for Quality Living v. Seif*, 132 F.3d 925 (3d Cir. 1997), the famous case involving use of Title VI of the Civil Rights Act of 1964.

[21] See discussion in Appendix H by H. Patricia Hynes and Russ Lopez, referenced previously.

focused upon questions directly drawn from the experience of people living in vulnerable communities. It should be reiterated that understanding vulnerability and the economic, social, and cultural aspects of community risk are key to identifying and implementing effective community-based prevention and intervention strategies. This is especially true when one links the concept of vulnerability to that of social capital. Hence, this research will be most effective if it were done in such a way that employs community-based participatory research and is geared towards studying prevention and intervention strategies and the achievement of healthy and sustainable communities.

From O'Neill M, et.al., "Health, Wealth, and Air Pollution: Advancing Theory and Methods," *Environmental Health Perspectives*, December 2003

We structure the discussion with an interpretative framework based on three related propositions. First, groups with lower SEP (socioeconomic position) may receive higher exposure to air pollution. Second, because lower-SEP groups already experience compromised health status due to material deprivation and psychosocial stress, they may be more susceptible to the health effects of air pollution. Third, because of the combination of greater exposure and susceptibility, these groups are likely to suffer greater health effects.

Conclusions:

Research may show that groups most likely to be made ill from air pollution also receive the highest exposure, and this exposure then exerts larger effects on their health than it does on the average or reference population. The public health and regulatory implications of such a finding could be significant because most air pollution standards aim to reduce average exposure over large regions, rather than targeting exposure reduction and mitigation programs to those areas receiving the highest exposure. Thus, targeting exposure reduction would be justified on the grounds of maximizing public health benefits. Differential distribution of adverse health effects (as addressed in this article) also need to be considered alongside differential distribution of the benefits (e.g., employment or car ownership) related to the emission sources. In one of the few studies that has assessed the impact of air quality regulations, the overall conclusion was that poor people and communities tend to benefit most from air quality improvements.

Including both air pollution and socioeconomic variables in epidemiologic studies can help inform public policy that aims to protect those most vulnerable to air pollution exposure; identify cost-effective, targeted mitigation efforts; ensure equitable protection from health risks; and develop physiologic explanations for the observed associations with SEP. As researchers evaluate how socioeconomic disparities and pollution can affect health and quality of life, their work can benefit through careful consideration of the themes addressed in this article. First, researchers can clearly define their working hypotheses, considering exposures and susceptibilities and both temporal and spatial dimensions. Second, new collaborations can be formed among environmental and social epidemiologists, exposure assessment experts, and other researchers to aid selection of appropriate tools and data sets. Third, research ideas can be developed in collaboration with affected communities and policy makers tasked with environmental and health protection, as well as social and economic policies. Finally, international perspectives and collaborative studies can enhance understanding and improve public health action by showing how the complex interrelationships among SEP, pollution, and health vary across communities and nations.

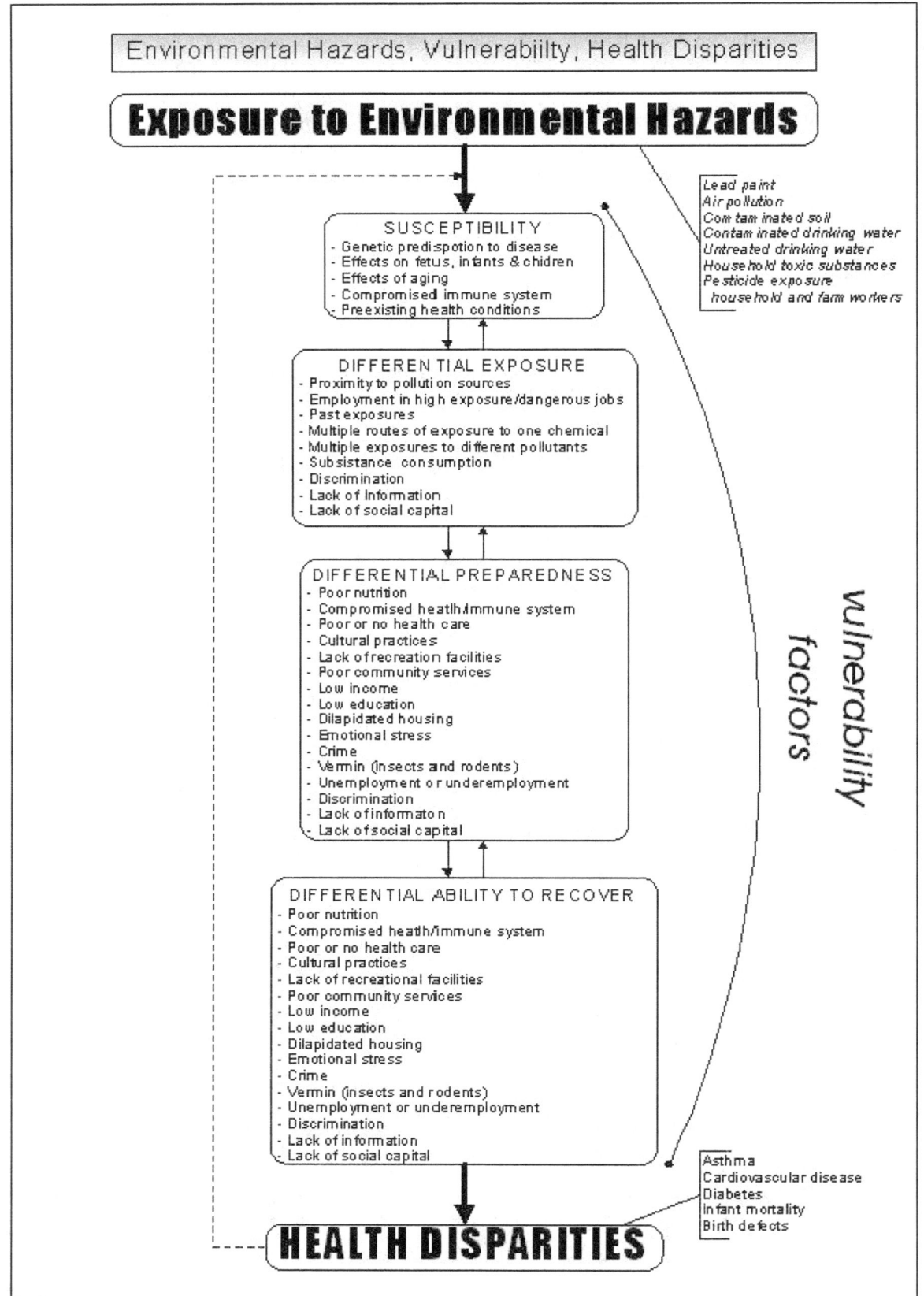

Community-Based Participatory Research:

The premises which gave birth to the Environmental Justice Collaborative Problem-Solving Model are similar to those which gave birth to "community-based participatory research" (CBPR). It is safe to say that this methodology has been utilized in some form or fashion for more than fifty years. A review of case studies in public and environmental health reveals that community-based participatory research principles have been utilized by health care providers, particularly professionals such as social workers and public health nurses. These professionals often worked hand in hand with residents of a community to alleviate public health problems including contagious diseases such as tuberculosis or contaminated water supplies. Assessments of both the affected residents and the community was done utilizing interviews, surveys, and scientific collection of contaminated sources to make a determination of how the individual became ill and what environmental or housing/residential impacts may have contributed to the problem..

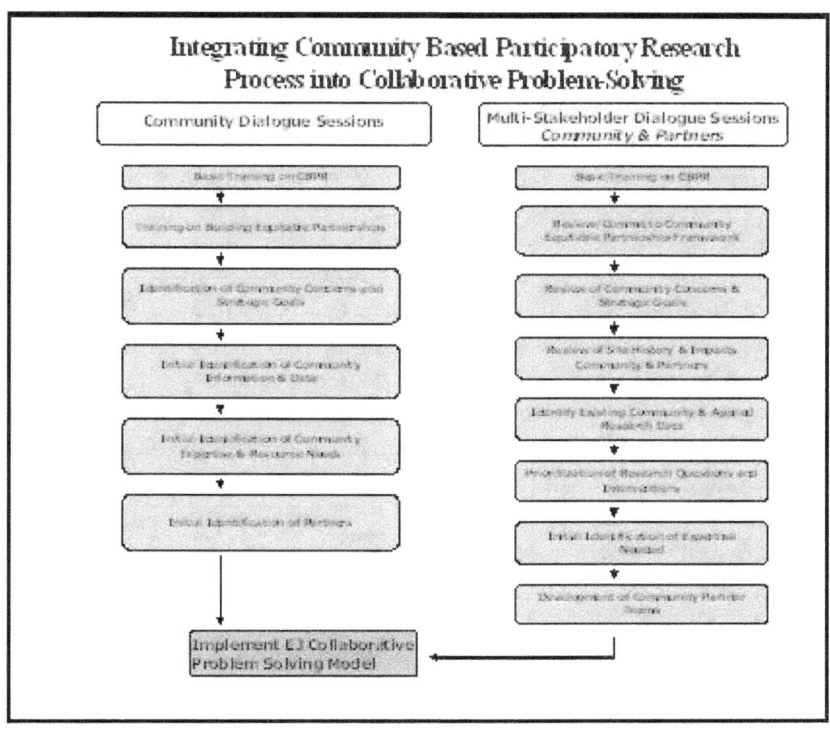

Through use of Community Dialogue Sessions , a foundation of robust community engagement is built. As previously stated, such a foundation is critical to the success of any multi-stakeholder collaborative problem-solving effort seeking to address community environmental justice concerns. These Community Dialogue Sessions provide a structured approach for community residents to obtain training, to analyze the issues at hand, to understand barriers, and to develop appropriate action strategies. This is one way to build community capacity and enable a truly collaborative partnership in which power and resources are shared equitably, as well as a respect for the knowledge that communities bring to the collaborative process. In addition, a similar process of structured engagement between the community and other stakeholders is necessary to ensure that there is a common framework for partnership and problem-solving. Figure 7 above depicts an example of these two processes and their relationship to environmental justice collaborative problem-solving.

In the eyes of community groups, CBPR enables them to promote the following goals:

- Equality of partners;
- Capacity building;

- Validity of community knowledge;
- Fair compensation to community members;
- Bias for action;
- Creation and utilization of language that is clear to all partners;
- Shared research findings;
- Publication of findings with the community as a partner;
- Place-based approaches; and
- Action elements aimed at concrete interventions and improvement in the environment, health, and quality of life of the affected community.

Over the last decade, many people of color, low-income, and tribal communities have become sophisticated advocates in promoting the health of their communities while protecting against further degradation of their environment. The members of these communities gained recognition nationally and internationally by developing expertise in public health assessments, toxicity level monitoring, and regulatory processes influencing siting and permitting of hazardous waste facilities. Those residing and working in impacted communities have gained knowledge through self-education– learning about the federal, state, and local regulatory processes that have allowed for the existence of multiple health risk stressors in communities. Beyond these self-help scenarios, these environmentally overburdened communities now have members who have formal education in health sciences, urban planning and zoning, environmental law, and the biological and environmental sciences. "Home grown" experts who not only personally have experienced cumulative risk stressors during their lifetimes, but return to their communities to improve the health and economic standing of its residents. It is important for EPA and other agencies to recognize this expertise if a meaningful working partnership is to develop in promoting community-based cumulative risk assessments.

CBPR, particularly as related to environmental or public health impacts, cultural or social issues within the community, has been undergoing refinement during the last several years. This research is done with, for, and by community members, sometimes in partnership with scientists or environmental researchers utilizing well accepted research methodologies. Data collected often provides the basis for community health assessments and learning about cumulative health impacts to the community. Such community-based research techniques is recognized by researchers as a legitimate reflection of community knowledge and expertise.

Community-based research attained new significance after being adopted by government agencies and institutions of higher learning, which seek to break out of their traditionally constrained methodologies and partner with community residents. These institutions sought to obtain a grassroots determination of how the community has become overburdened and provide a multi-dimensional picture of cumulative risks and impacts. There are now several community-based research centers in the nation, usually located in institutions of higher learning. In the last few years, they began to create a "network" of such centers. The demand for this type of research has increased because of the recognition of its value in working directly with the community and because of its ability to allow for direct public participation and collaboration. Notably, Canada and the Netherlands presently lead the United States in the development of community-based research institutions and the national research funding that these countries provide to such centers and their respective communities.

The National Institutes of Environmental Health (NIEHS) defines community-based participatory research as "a methodology that promotes active community involvement in the processes that shape research and intervention strategies, as well as the conduct of research studies." CBPR is an important component of NIEHS' Translational Research Program, which was initiated in the early 1990s to link researchers and community residents by encouraging collaborative research projects. The purpose of the program is to refine intervention methods, provide exposure assessment data, study environmental disease etiology, and facilitate the conversion of findings from basic, clinical or epidemiological environmental health science research into information, resources, or tools that can be applied by healthcare providers and community residents to improve public health outcomes in at-risk neighborhoods.

NIEHS endorses the following six principles for effective CBPR:

- *Promotes active collaboration and participation at every stage of research*: CBPR fosters equal participation from all partners. It provides all participants with an equal sense of ownership over the research and the outcomes.
- *Fosters co-learning*: CBPR provides an environment in which both community residents and researchers contribute their respective expertise and where partners learn from each other. Community members acquire new skills in conducting research, and researchers learn about community networks and concerns–information that can be used to inform hypothesis generation and data collection.
- *Ensures projects are community-driven*: Research questions in CBPR are guided b the environmental health issues or concerns of community members. NIEHS recognizes that for research and prevention/intervention strategies to be successful, they must address the concerns of community residents.
- *Disseminates results in useful terms*: Upon completion of CBPR projects, results are communicated to all partners in culturally appropriate, respectful, and understandable terms.
- *Ensures research and intervention strategies are culturally appropriate*: With active participation of community residents from the beginning, research and prevention/intervention strategies are likely to be based in the cultural context of the community in which such work is intended to benefit.
- *Defines community as a unit of identity*: NIEHS Translational Research programs promote collaboration among academic scientists and community partners from underserved communities. In the case of these projects, community is typically characterized by a sense of identification and emotional connection to other members through common interests and a commitment to address shared concerns, such as harmful environmental exposures or environmental injustice.[22]

There are important linkages between the Agency's Cumulative Risk Framework, the Environmental Justice Collaborative Problem-Solving Model, and Community-Based Participatory Research that needs to be systematically developed. CBPR is an important and useful tool in collaborative problem-solving initiatives. It is believed by many to be the missing link of empowerment for affected communities to be able to participate in the decision-making process. It provides the opportunity for community members, experts, and other stakeholders to dialogue separately to identify respective concerns and interests while at the same time allowing the entire collaborative partnership to set priorities together. CBPR research and intervention outputs not only help the affected community, they also contribute valuable information on local environmental and health conditions.

---

[22] O'Fallon, Liam R. and Allen Dearry, "Community-Based Participatory Research as a Tool to Advance Environmental Health Sciences," *Environmental Health Perspectives*, Volume 110, Supplement 2, April 2002.

Proportional Response:

The concept of proportional response is a direct outgrowth of the NEJAC's thinking about conducting cumulative risk analysis in the context of a bias for action and its promotion of a collaborative problem-solving model for addressing cumulative risks and impacts. The idea of proportional response seeks to match the needs of communities and tribes with an appropriate level or type of analysis and action at any given point. In other words, analysis should be commensurate with community needs and the nature of the intervention to be taken. Figure 6, above, attempts to capture the idea of proportional response.

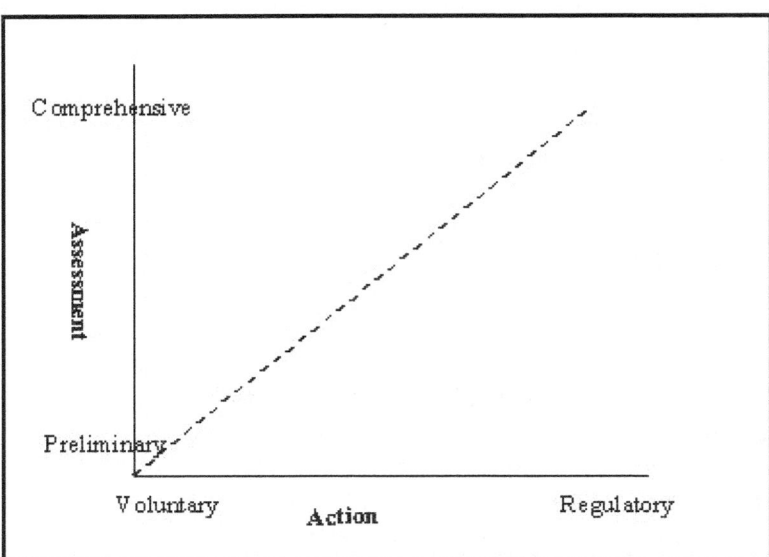

Figure 8: This graph was developed by the NEJAC to illustrated the concept of proportional response, the relationship between the comprehensiveness and rigor of analysis needed and the severity of the action to the taken. The relationship is generally applicable, with the exception of cases involving an imminent threat to public health or safety.

Response also must be proportional to the harm caused. In nearly all communities with environmental justice issues, the adverse effect results from environmental impacts from multiple sources, some large and some small. The key to engaging the sources of impact in collaborative problem-solving and achieving meaningful pollution reduction in the short- and long-term is the expectation of proportional responsibility on the part of all contributors to the harm. Those with the most severe impacts should be held to the most aggressive and significant response. Those with lesser impacts should be expected to contribute their fair share to community improvement. This proportional approach is the most likely to engender immediate, positive response because the causation is clear and the expectation of pollution reduction sensible and achievable.

This proportional response can be contrasted with the "tipping point" approach where a facility needing a permit in an overburdened area becomes the sole target for pollution prevention. Simply because a facility's permit is due for renewal or the facility is seeking siting or expansion, it becomes the enforcement target on the grounds that this new or renewed pollution is the "straw that breaks the camel's back." This kind of approach has many downsides, however. Where the stakes are so high–attainment of a permit to operate–the level of legal and political resistance escalates. Facility lawyers seek every means to avoid facility closure by construing regulatory authority narrowly. Efforts by the facility manager to work with the community to address concerns and recognize community needs take a back seat to litigation over "requirements." Regulators charged with addressing the issues become vulnerable to politicians bemoaning the threat to jobs. Moreover, the other sources of pollution in the area rest easy, confident that they have no responsibility for their own emissions and that the permitted facility will bear the brunt of controversy and attention. The result can impact needed economic development, and it wholly misses the opportunity to engage each contributor of a community burden in the process of making the community whole and healthy.

The proportional approach, in contrast, seeks to identify relative impacts using screening tools, to confront each source of environmental burden with a rough sense of its accountability, to educate the polluting sources about community needs and vulnerabilities, and to build working relationships that lead to overall pollution reduction. Creative alliances can emerge where a large source of emissions can team with smaller sources to cost-effectively reduce the community's burden. These discussions are particularly fruitful where community driven, so that the community members can identify the issues of highest concern and provide insight into ways the polluting sources can reduce their impacts. These dialogues are the best way to appreciate and respond in a holistic way to the aggregation of stressors in a community.

It is important to recognize, however, that not all contributors will be willing to come to the table. Some sources may resist a collaborative problem-solving process, preferring to lie in the weeds and expect other businesses to take care of the problem. Some may continue to narrowly construe their regulatory obligations to protect human health. Some may go further, actively causing environmental deterioration by violating even the terms of their own permits. In some cases, the polluting party is an arm or agent of federal, state or local government, and intergovernmental relations strain the regulatory authority's ability to mandate strict enforcement of environmental controls. In these circumstances, the proportional approach again provides a direction: Those who do not accept their proportional degree of accountability should be subject to a proportional degree of extra enforcement to coerce accountability and pollution prevention where it cannot be encouraged by other means.

In both views of the proportional response, the linchpin is community involvement and multi-stakeholder consensus building. There is no "one size fits all" remedy, but instead the approach must be a search for all applicable legal authorities, an engagement with the community to understand and seek direction on the means to reduce cumulative impacts, and an on-going expectation that all sources of environmental burden will contribute their share to its reduction or elimination.

In the real world context, most communities and tribes, as well as risk assessors, will begin with a description on the multiple stressors that effect a given community. There has not yet been a characterization of the combined effects of these multiple stressors. Being proactive and precautionary is a basic tenet of the collaborative problem-solving model. Hence, impacted communities or tribes should not have to wait until a full characterization is completed before prevention/intervention activities take place. Rather, an initial screening can begin the process of a range of multiple and concurrent activities that include the following: risk reduction efforts to address immediate harms; initiating a dialogue among multiple stakeholders with responsibility for or interest in the community's health; more targeted and in-depth cumulative assessments, and subsequent risk reduction efforts. This concept also recognizes that no matter how many multiple effects may exist, risks must be prioritized and risk reduction is going to take place one by one.

Last, the NEJAC recognizes the importance of strategic planning, scoping, and problem-formulation to operationalize the concept of proportional response. Similarly, the Agency's Cumulative Risk Framework emphasizes the importance of the planning, scoping, and problem-formulation phase of a cumulative risk assessment. Such a process should build on the lessons learned from the growing number of community-based participatory research efforts. A productive partnership with all these parties can lead to a more thorough analysis, the discovery of problems that might otherwise be missed, and a consensus around what issues should be prioritized for action.

Proportional response can be implemented through an iterative-deliberative model, described in two important risk assessment reports: the National Academy of Sciences report, *Understanding Risk*, and the Presidential/Congressional Commission on Risk report.[23] *Understanding Risk* sets out five factors that are crucial to launching and sustaining a deliberative/iterative dialogue:

- Getting the science right – technical experts judge the adequacy of the risk-analytic effort;
- Getting the right science – community interests are being addressed by the scientific work;
- Getting the right participation – get the right parties involved;
- Getting the participation right – make sure parties were adequately consulted during the process; and
- Developing accurate, balanced and informative synthesis – ask parties how well they understood the basis of the decision; whether they perceived bias in the information

The Presidential/Congressional Commission on Risk report emphasizes the importance of a consensus process that links risk assessment with risk management, is iterative in nature, and built on strong multi-stakeholder involvement.

Qualitative Analysis:

As mentioned previously, an integrated analysis of cumulative risk and impacts will require making judgements in both a quantitative and qualitative manner. The NEJAC wishes to note that there exists a body of literature in the area of environmental impacts analysis and cumulative impacts analysis that may prove to be useful to such an integrated analysis. In January 1997, the White House Council on Environmental Quality published a report entitled "Considering Cumulative Effects Under the National Environmental Policy Act."[24] CEQ provides the following eight principles for conducting cumulative effects analysis.

1. Cumulative effects are caused by the aggregate of past, present, and reasonably foreseeable future actions.
2. Cumulative effects are the total effects, including both direct and indirect, on a given resource, ecosystem, and human community of all actions taken, no matter who (federal, non-federal, or private) has taken the actions.
3. Cumulative effects need to be analyzed in terms of the specific resource, ecosystem, and human community being affected.
4. It is not practical to analyze the cumulative effects of an action on the universe; the list of environmental effects must focus on those that are truly meaningful.
5. Cumulative effects on a given resource, ecosystem, and human community are rarely aligned with political or administrative boundaries.
6. Cumulative effects may result from the accumulation of similar effects or the synergistic interaction of different effects.
7. Cumulative effects may last for many years beyond the life of the action that caused the effects.

---

[23] Stern, Paul C. and Harvey V. Fineberg, Ed., *Understanding Risk: Informing Decisions in a Democratic Society*, Washington, DC: National Academy Press, 1996.
The Presidential/Congressional Commission on Risk Assessment and Risk Management. *Framework for Environmental Risk Assessment: Final Report* (Volume 1), Washington, DC 1997.

[24] Council on Environmental Quality, *Considering Cumulative Effects Under the National Environmental Policy Act*, Washington, DC: January 1997.

8. Each affected resource, ecosystem, and human community must be analyzed in terms of the capacity to accommodate additional effects, based on its own time and space parameters.

In addition, the CEQ provides the following list of primary and special methods for implementing cumulative effects analysis.

Primary Methods:
1. Questionnaires, interviews, and panels to gather information about the wide range of actions and effects needed for a cumulative effects analysis.
2. Checklists to identify potential cumulative effects by reviewing important human activities and potentially affected resources.
3. Matrices to determine the cumulative effects on resources, ecosystems, and human communities by combining individual effects from different actions.
4. Networks and system diagrams to trace the multiple, subsidiary effects of various actions that accumulative upon resources, ecosystems, and human communities.
5. Modeling to quantify the cause-and-effect relationships leading to cumulative effects.
6. Trends analysis to assess the status of resources, ecosystems, and human communities over time and identify cumulative effects problems, establish appropriate environmental baselines, or project future cumulative effects.
7. Overlay mapping and GIS to incorporate locational analysis and help set the boundaries of the analysis, analyze landscape parameters, and identify areas where effects will be the greatest.

Special Methods:
1. Carrying capacity analysis to identify thresholds (as constraints on development) and provide mechanisms to monitor the incremental use of unused capacity.
2. Ecosystem analysis to address biodiversity and ecosystem sustainability and usually entails a regional perspective and holistic thinking.
3. Economic impact analysis to analyze the economic well-being of a local community as a result of cumulative effects, and usually involves three primary steps: establishing a region of influence, modeling economic effects, and determining significance of effects.
4. Social impact analysis to address the sustainability of human communities by focusing on key social variables such as population characteristics, community and institutional structures, political and social resources, individual and family changes, and community resources.

A full explanation of both the cumulative effects analysis principles and methods are provided in Appendix D of the report.

Efficient Screening, Targeting, and Prioritization Methods/Tools:

The current regulatory approach for siting and operating various types of facilities or activities is predicated primarily on a risk-based paradigm from a single source or a single pollutant. In many areas, this approach, along with zoning areas for mixed-use, has resulted in the aggregation of sources (clusters) that are within the risk threshold for individual facilities, but cumulatively produce a higher exposure burden to people living in surrounding areas. This issue is critical in addressing the environmental justice concerns of a community or tribe. Short-term assessment tools that identify and characterize the cumulative risks and impacts in communities with undisputed problems is key to putting theory into practice.

In light of this concern, government agencies at the federal and state levels have initiated efforts to develop scientific approaches and tools (models) to evaluate multiple stressors and cumulative risks and impacts. While some of these approaches and tools will take many years to develop because of the complex nature of the models and limitations in the data inputs, many exist which can provide sound baseline information about the multiple stressors in a community. The key impediment to their wide usage is the lack of a clear operational framework within the scientific community, industry, and the impacted communities and tribes as to how best to use them.

Recognizing this inherent delay, the NEJAC concluded that alternate simpler approaches must be adopted. These approaches would identify communities that bear higher pollution burdens as well as other stressors in a shorter time frame so that remedial actions can be initiated. The remedial actions will be site-specific and could include a number of options. Examples include the proper degree of verifiable emissions controls installation in facilities that are primary/high risk drivers through incentives, strengthening enforcement programs, additional siting, and permit and emission requirements for new facilities.

The NEJAC believes one key impediment in the effective utilization of existing assessment tools is the lack of an operational framework for how to understand multiple risks and impacts in environmental justice situations. For this reason, using the matrix illustrated in Table 1 of this report can be an important starting point for discussion and analysis. Another example of such an approach is the "Pollution Burden Matrix for Community Characterization," found in Appendix L of this report. The latter can serve as a conceptual framework for assessing cumulative impacts using a suite of proxy indicators of neighborhood-scale cumulative emissions, exposure, and health effects. In addition, there are many tools using similar principles now in existence, including targeting and prioritization tools.[25] It is safe to assume that, given the complexity of all the factors involved in a comprehensive analysis of community risks and burdens, there should not be a "one size fits all" tool. Moreover, each should be utilized in a way that promotes proportional response, as described earlier in this report.

Unifying Fields of Public Health and Environmental Protection:

A challenge similar to that of statutory, programmatic, and regulatory fragmentation in the nation's environmental protection regime is that of the bifurcation between the fields of public health and environmental protection.[26] For this reason, foresighted individuals and organizations have begun a dialogue to create a vision of environmental health that unifies the fields of public health and environmental protection. One significant event in this dialogue is a workshop sponsored by the Institute of Medicine (IOM) workshop entitled "Rebuilding the Unity of Health and the Environment: A New Vision of Environmental Health for the 21st Century" (June 20-21, 2001) The purpose of the workshop was to raise awareness, promote community-based environmental health, and mold multi-disciplinary partnerships to redefine and improve environmental health. In many respects, such a dialogue provides yet another critical underpinning for a comprehensive approach to

---

[25] Such tools include the following (See Appendix F):
- Environmental Load Profile, EPA Region 2;
- Cumulative Risk Screening Assessment System Using GIS, EPA Region 6;
- Potential Risk Indexing System, EPA Office of Research and Development; and
- Regional Air Impact Modeling Initiative (RAIMI), EPA Region 6

[26] Also highly relevant is the bifurcation of the fields of public health and urban planning. See Greenberg, Michael, Frank Popper, Bernadette West, and Donald Kruekeberg, "Linking City Planning and Public Health in the United States," *Journal of Planning Literature* 8(February)3:235-239 (1994).

community burdens and is integral to efforts to effectively address cumulative risks and impacts.[27] Other key groups involved in this dialogue are the Pew Charitable Trust's support of the development of a national environmental health tracking network and NIEHS' sponsorship of dialogues related to the integration of the social and physical health factors in the built environment. Last, PolicyLink, a national nonprofit research, communications, capacity building, and advocacy organization dedicated to addressing "the continuing question of how to achieve equity in America," has undertaken a community-based analysis of the physical and social factors related to health disparities. [28]

Social Capital:

One concept that is highly relevant to the discussion of how to assess and address cumulative risks and impacts is that of social capital, a complex concept that Harvard University sociologist Robert Putnam defines as the features of social organization, such as networks, norms, and social trust, that facilitate coordination and cooperation for mutual benefit.[29] This is a concept that begins to unify many of the desired goals of a community-based, multi-stakeholder, multi-media, collaborative problem-solving approach to addressing cumulative risks and impacts. These goals include, among other things, a sensitivity to community concerns and stakeholder interests, transparency in the process, the need for confidence in the process, trust among various parties, capacity and resources, consensus building, and a common framework for problem-formulation and prioritization. A central premise of social capital is that social networks have value. Social capital works through multiple channels, including: flow of information, norms of reciprocity (mutual aid), collective action, broader sense of identifies and solidarity. Indeed, social capital is a critical component to moving environmental justice strategies from reactive modalities to proactive problem-solving modalities. On the one hand, it entails the ability to identify, harness, and leverage existing as well as growing new human, technical, organizational, and financial capacities and resources. On the other, it entails building the norms and networks necessary to navigate the complex and contentious relationships inherent in virtually all environmental justice situations.

---

[27] IOM stated: "The goals of environmental health are to maintain a healthy, livable environment for humans and other living species–an environment that promotes well being and a high quality of mental and physical health for its inhabitants... Responsible leadership requires that policy makers, health professionals, industry representatives, and the general public all carry an expanded and enhanced vision of environmental health forward into the 21st century. New approaches towards building environments that actively improve health will be required, including strategies to deal with waste, unhealthy buildings, urban congestion, suburban sprawl, poor housing, poor nutrition, and environmentally related stress." See Institute of Medicine, *Rebuilding the Unity of Health and the Environment: A New Vision of Environmental Health for the 21st Century*. Washington, DC: National Academy Press, 2001. See also Lee, Charles "Environmental Justice: Building a Unified Vision of Health and the Environment," *Environmental Health Perspectives*, V 110, #2, April 2002, pg. 141-144.

[28] See Pew Environmental Health Commission, "America's Environmental Health Gap: Why the Country Needs a Nationwide Health Tracking Network," September 2000. See National Institute for Environmental Health Sciences, "Built Environment–Healthy Communities, Healthy Homes, Healthy People," Research Triangle Park, NC, July 15-16, 2002. See also PolicyLink, "Reducing Health Disparities Through a Focus on Communities," November 2002.

[29] Putnam, Robert D., *Bowling Alone: The Collapse and Revival of American Community*. New York: Simon and Shuster, 2000.

SPECIAL CONCERNS OF TRIBES

American Indian and Alaska Native tribes are sovereign governments recognized as self-governing under federal law. Under its well recognized "trust responsibility" to Indian tribes, the federal government has special fiduciary obligations to protect tribal resources and uphold the rights of indigenous peoples to govern themselves on tribal lands. Many federal laws have delegated authority to tribes in recognition of their sovereign status. The unique legal status of American Indian and Alaska Native tribes creates an important requirement for governmental entities and other stakeholders to understand that the federal government must consult directly with tribal governments when contemplating actions that may affect tribal lands, resources, members, and welfare.[30]

In examining how issues of multiple and cumulative risks and impacts affect American Indian and Alaska Native populations, the NEJAC observes that the question posed at the beginning of this report also applies here. This is the question of what do issues of multiple and cumulative risks and impacts actually look like in the "real life" context of historically disadvantaged, underserved, and environmentally overburdened communities and tribes. (See Section on "Defining the Issue") For tribes, this question cannot be separated from the historical legacy of habitat loss. As mentioned earlier, tribal relationships with the land are paramount to Native American culture. (See Section on "A Native American Health Paradigm") Hence, a proactive approach towards cumulative risks and impacts in a tribal context must include assessments of the ecosystem and pursue the goal of ecological restoration.

EPA has begun to explore issues of cumulative risks and impacts in the Native American context through what are sometimes referred to as" tribal traditional lifeways."[31] The EPA's Indian Program Policy Council has established a Tribal Traditional Lifeways Subcommittee. Among other things, the Subcommittee should examine the paradigmatic conflicts between risk assessment and management methodologies and the Native American reality. Tribes have consistently raised concerns that EPA's programs, risk methodologies and regulatory approaches are generally not sensitive to tribal traditional lifeways, neither do they give a whole or comprehensive view of the health of the people or their environment. Tribes have also called upon EPA to address the environmental impacts which threaten tribal treaty rights, including traditional and customary hunting and fishing areas.[32] The health of the environment is of critical importance to the Native Americans because of their spiritual and cultural connection to the Earth. Tribes traditionally fish, hunt and gather native foods to sustain their way of life and their culture. Without the ability to hunt, trap, fish and gather, opportunities for story telling and sharing experiences that instruct the young are lost–their language, knowledge and skills are lost. Their spirit and culture are irreversibly altered. In addition to adverse long-term changes to the environment, the presence of toxins and pollutants in natural resources has had a severe impact on the ability of tribal people to continue their traditional and cultural practices, including spiritual ceremonies. Tribes point out that pollution

---

[30] See National Environmental Justice Advisory Council, *Guide on Consultation and Collaboration with Indian Tribal Governments and the Public Participation of Indigenous Groups and Tribal Members in Environmental Decision Making.* November 2002. Available at <*http://www.epa.gov/compliance/environmentaljustice/nejac*>.

[31] See Proceedings of EPA Tribal Science Council, Tribal Traditional Lifeways: Health and Well-being Workshop, May 13-15, 2003, <*http://www.epa.gov/osp/tribes/tribal/health.pdf*>. See also Wolfley, Jeannette, 1998, "Ecological Risk Assessment: Their Failure to Value Indigenous Traditional Knowledge and Protect Tribal Homelands," American Indian Culture and Research Journal, Vo. 22, Issue 2, p. 152-169.

[32] Written comments from Jamie Donatuto, Swinomish Tribal Community, LaConner, Washington, on the NEJAC Cumulative Risks/Impacts Draft Report, May 11, 2004.

impacts "the web" or "circle of life" which is critical to maintaining Native American health and culture.

In order to develop a realistic strategy to achieve ecological restoration, the Tulalip Tribe, located in northwest Washington State, has undertaken the following steps: (1) conduct an ecosystem assessment; (2) establish a baseline of historical conditions; and (3) evaluate trends. In addition, there are three major issues that need consideration:

■ There exists a growing shortage of subsistence species upon which tribal diets are dependent, which results in a shift to dependence on processed foods. This shift has been associated with a rise in diseases among Native populations.

■ Native peoples consume and/or use traditional foods or materials which are highly contaminated but uncontrolled. This practice also has resulted in illness and disease among Native populations.

■ Multiple and cumulative risks issues are compounded by the fact that subsistence foods are often contaminated by pollution that is transboundary in nature. This is especially problematic for areas like Alaska and other parts of the Arctic Region.

A good example of the first issue is depicted in the following passage from an article on a Native perspective on risk assessment by members of the Akwesasne Environmental Task Force, in upstate New York. The NEJAC has provided this passage in full because it portrays so well the conflicting assumptions between traditional risk assessment and tribal populations.

Contrary to the conclusions of current risk assessment models, community-based researchers have found that adverse health effects can and do occur even when there is no physical exposure to toxicants. As a striking example, a distinguished toxicologist was invited to speak at Akwesasne about adverse health effects associated with exposure to polychlorinated biphenyls (PCB). She began her talk by noting that many Akwesasne residents, especially women of childbearing age, had virtually eliminated consumption of local fish and wildlife and congratulated Mohawk people for taking such an active role in decreasing the adverse health effects associated with PCB exposure. Much to the surprise of this toxicologist, Mohawk residents did not agree that the solution to contamination issues was to change traditional cultural practices and behaviors to eliminate toxicant exposure. After a long discussion, this speaker was quick to point out that current risk assessment models state that if there is no exposure, then there are no adverse health effects. In Akwesasne, as in many other communities, potentially serious health effects can result when people stop traditional cultural practices in order to protect their health from the effects of toxic substances. When traditional foods such as fish are no longer eaten, alternative diets are consumed that are often high in fat and low in vitamins and nutrients. This type of dietary change has been linked to many health problems such as type II diabetes, heart disease, stroke, high blood pressure, cancer, and obesity.[33]

A good example of the second issue pertains to the plight of the California Indian Basketweavers Association. Herbicides used by forest managers and road crews have contaminated grasses and plants gathered and used by Indian basketweavers to make baskets. As part of the process of making

---

[33] Arquette, Mary, Maxine Cole, Katsi Cook, Brenda LaFrance, Margaret Peters, James Ransom, Elvera Sargent, Vivian Smoke, and Arlene Stairs, "Holistic Risk-Based Environmental Decision Making: A Native Perspective," in *Environmental Health Perspectives*, Vol. 110, Supplement 2, April 2002.

baskets, Indian basketweavers chew the grass, and therefore become exposed to the contaminant.

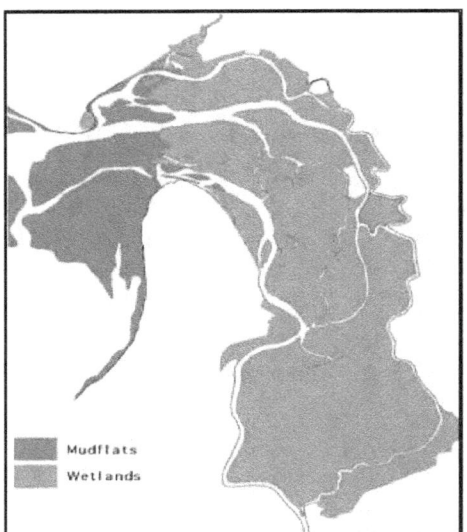

Figure 9: Available ecological resources in the Snohomish River Watershed in 1880s.

EPA convened an interagency group at the federal, state, and local levels to ensure that agencies responsible for land management and the spraying know where Indian basketweavers gather their grasses and prevent them from being sprayed. This example shows the importance of local collaborative and integrated problem-solving, especially when there is a problem of fragmented governmental authorities.[34]

A good example of the third issue are the impacts to the subsistence foods of Alaska Natives by persistent organic pollutants (POP), such as dichlorodiphenyltrichloroethane (DDT), PCBs, and dioxins [35]. These pollutants travel through the environment, in the air, water or by migratory animals, and get deposited in regions such as the Arctic.[36] Once deposited, these contaminants bio-accumulate in the fatty tissues and organs of animals, such as those used by Alaska Natives for subsistence (e.g. seals, whales, fish, and birds).[37]

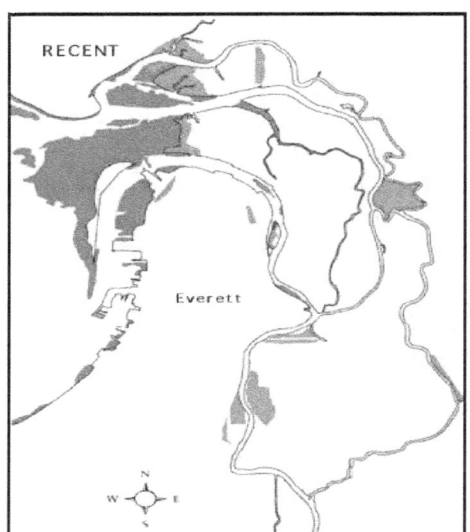

Figure 10: Available ecological resources in Snohomish River Watershed in 1997.

> *"The act and ritual of our subsistence food activities encompass who we are, and all that we are and is a vital source of our spirituality, I emphasize these things because I want you to know how much of an impact the threat of contaminants have on these things which are so sacred to us,"* Sally Smith, Chairperson, Alaska Native Health Board.[38]

POPs are introduced into the environment in a variety of ways, for example, as pesticides for agricultural or pest control purposes (e.g. DDT to kill malaria infected mosquitos) or are used and emitted during industrial or commercial production or manufacturing. The international community recognizes the importance of addressing the serious threats to the environmental and public health from POPs and therefore is working on international agreements

---

[34] Interview with Terry Williams, Tulalip Tribe Environmental Resources Director. Williams also was the first director of the EPA American Indian Environmental Office. See also California Indian Basketweavers Association, http://www.ciba.org.

[35] "Contaminants in Alaska, Is America's Arctic at Risk?," Interagency Collaborative Paper, September 2000.

[36] Ibid

[37] Ibid

[38] Ibid

to reduce and eliminate the use of POPs.[39] In 2001, more than 100 nations met in Stockholm to discuss the concerns posed by POPs and to establish legally binding measures to reduce or eliminate the use or production of POPs.[40]

Assessments performed by the Tulalip Tribe on the Snohomish River Watershed indicates that some 75% of the original vegetation and ecosystem structure has been destroyed.[41] Efforts to restore this habitat have now involved many non-Indian agencies and populations, including state and local governments, and local farmers and recreational users. The partnership that includes the Tulalip Tribe has raised $11 million for ecological restoration of the Snohomish River Watershed. As an outgrowth of the collaboration, state and local government agencies have have matched these funds. The total amount of funds now totals $40 million. The long term implications of this mutual exploration of the ecosystem is significant, particularly in that it builds greater understanding and trust among heretofore antagonistic groups. According to Terry Williams, Tulalip Environmental Resource Program Director, in-depth examination of the issues led to a realization on the part of all parties that they also have a stake in the future ecological viability of the watershed. For example, the reduced ability of the watershed to retain natural water has led to greater runoff of rain water into the Puget Sound, loss of well water, and the lengthening of annual drought periods from two months to four months.[42]   The above story provides testimony to the benefits of the American society gaining valuable lessons from Native American approaches to risk assessment, ecosystems analysis, and habitat restoration.

Tribes concerned about ecological restoration and ecological risk have worked with the EPA to develop a framework for addressing these issues in a way amenable to tribal understandings and culture. This is encapsulated in a tribal traditional lifeways approach to environmental protection, which allows a more comprehensive, inclusive, and holistic approach to EPA's decision-making processes. The tribal traditional lifeways approach takes into consideration the collective and intimate nature of tribal interactions with the environment including the relationship between the environment and the tribes' cultural, social, economical and spiritual ways of life. The goal of such a framework would be to establish a collective, multi-media Agency approach and determine what additional efforts are needed that will allow EPA to adequately consider tribal traditional lifeways when conducting scientific analyses, including assessing risks; developing and implementing environmental programs and regulations; and making decisions that protect human health and the environment in Indian country. It should be noted that this goal is highly compatible with the EPA *Framework for Cumulative Risk Assessment*, which brings attention to the need to address ecological concerns. (See Section on EPA's Framework for Cumulative Risk Assessment)

---

[39] See United Nations Environmental Programme, Persistent Organic Pollutants, http://www.chem.unep.ch/pops/

[40] Ibid

[41] See http://www.pugetsound.org/habitat/reportfolder/r13snohomish.html.

[42] Interview with Terry Williams.

RECOMMENDATION THEMES

The NEJAC has decided to frame its proposed advice and recommendations under the following eight major themes:

- To institutionalize a bias for action within EPA through the widespread utilization of an Environmental Justice Collaborative Problem-Solving Model;
- To fully utilize existing statutory authorities;
- To address and overcome programmatic and regulatory fragmentation within the nation's environmental protection regime;
- To fully incorporate the concept of vulnerability, especially its social and cultural aspects, into EPA's strategic plans and research agendas;
- To promote a paradigm shift to community-based approaches, particularly community-based participatory research and intervention;
- To incorporate social, economic, cultural, and community health factors, particularly those involving vulnerability, in EPA decision-making;
- To develop and implement efficient screening and targeting methods/tools to identify communities needing immediate intervention; and
- To address capacity and resource issues (human, organizational, technical, and financial) within EPA and the states, within impacted communities and tribes, and among all relevant stakeholders.

As such, they also form an implementation framework for Agency to address the issues of environmental justice and cumulative risks and impacts. These eight themes are interrelated. While each is critically important by itself, addressing each (or a few) without all of the others will not be sufficient. They are intended to promote a long-term change in Agency *action*, a change in Agency *thinking*, and a change in Agency *capacity*. **As a start, EPA should incorporate all relevant concepts and recommendations of this report in any and all work growing out of the Agency's** *Framework for Cumulative Risk Assessment* **and the development of Agency cumulative risk guidance.**

TO INSTITUTIONALIZE A BIAS FOR ACTION WITHIN EPA THROUGH WIDESPREAD UTILIZATION OF
AN ENVIRONMENTAL JUSTICE COLLABORATIVE PROBLEM-SOLVING MODEL.

Not only is there a clear and urgent need to address the needs of disadvantaged, underserved, and
environmentally overburdened communities and tribes in a timely and responsible manner, but this is
arguably the most effective way to ensure the maximum benefits from use of EPA's valuable and
limited resources. Not only it is patently unfair to ask long suffering communities and tribes to wait,
but such delay constitutes poor public policy because reducing the environmental risks in such
communities and tribes are likely to be an area where the greatest progress can be made towards
ensuring environmental public health and protection. Further, the sooner those risks are addressed,
the greater the potential cost savings and other benefits in the long-term.

Most importantly, the NEJAC would argue that there exist presently many tools (legal, scientific,
and programmatic) which can be brought to bear to address these environmental risks in the short-
term. Opportunities to make use of these tools are not only abundant in the form of overburdened
communities and tribes, but there exists a considerable array of community-based organizations,
state, local and tribal governments, business and industry, public health practitioners, and federal
agencies, to name a few, which seek to partner together to address these issues.[43] The Environmental
Justice Collaborative Problem-Solving Model makes it possible to integrate these tools.

Hence, there are ample opportunities to combine the EPA's Cumulative Risk Framework with a
community-based collaborative problem-solving model, noted previously as the key finding of this
report. Such a model will enable EPA and its governmental partners, impacted communities,
business and industry, and other relevant stakeholders to act proactively and strategically to address
the needs of environmentally overburdened communities and tribes.

In one sense, all of the themes (and their associated recommendations) of this report serve to help
institutionalize this bias for action within the Agency, both in the short-term and the long-term.
However, in the short-term, the NEJAC recognizes that the Agency must assemble and/or develop a
basic set of tools and skills to fully utilize the opportunities for carrying out risk reduction in areas
that most need it. This entails the development of a set of efficient screening tools to prioritize areas
of greatest need, and to develop a toolkit of practical implementable actions that can be undertaken
in a multi-media manner to bring about such risk reduction. Such implementable actions should be
directed towards those activities which present the highest risks in communities (e.g., diesel

---

[43] It should be noted that during the past several years, attention on the part of different sectors of society, including
state and local government, and business and industry, has been significant. Recently, the American Bar Association
published a 50-state survey of state environmental justice programs. See "Environmental Justice for All: A 50 State
Survey of Legislation, Policy, and Initiatives," ed. Steve Bonorris, American Bar Association – Hastings College of
the Law (Oct. 2003); Available at <*http://www.abanet.org/irr/committees/environmental/statestudy.doc*>. The
National Academy of Public Administrators (NAPA) has published reports entitled *Models for Change: Efforts by
Four States to Address Environmental Justice* (June 2002) and *Addressing Community Concerns: How
Environmental Justice Relates to Land Use Planning and Zoning* (July 2003). The latter focuses on the role of local
government. Finally, the EPA Office of Environmental Justice published Moving Towards Collaborative Problem-
Solving: Business and Industry Perspectives and Practices on Environmental Justice (July 2003). The NAPA and
OEJ reports are available on the OEJ website: <*http://www.epa.gov/compliance/environmentaljustice*>.

emissions reduction, treatment of contaminated groundwater, run-off control, pollution prevention, waste minimization, lead hazard abatement, and product substitution).[44]

To be sure, EPA must pursue an aggressive and comprehensive research agenda on cumulative risks and impacts, particularly as they involve issues of vulnerable communities and populations. However, we will argue that there are many actions which EPA can take before those scientific tools are fully developed. In addition, such research must entail more than basic research alone. Such research also should be conducted in the context of this bias for action. It should involve research on community-based prevention/intervention efforts, community-based participatory research, and translational research.

Last, the NEJAC emphasizes the value of gaining and building on experience as an important vehicle for positive change. Developing a strong experiential base is an important part of capacity building, especially when one is dealing with a set of issues that are technically complex and involve multiple stakeholders. For that reason, we are recommending that EPA initiate a set of pilots in the area of community-based efforts to address multiple, aggregate and cumulative risks and impacts in disadvantaged, underserved, and environmentally overburdened communities and tribes. These pilots should make use of the screening methodology and implementable action toolkit, as well as generate hypotheses for long-term policy and science research in area of cumulative risks and impacts.

---

[44] In the toolkit being suggested, one needs to match types of implementable actions with those activities which are the most critical contributors to risk. See Appendix E for a list of EPA Community-Based Risk Reduction/Healthy Communities Initiatives and Programs and Appendix G for Implementable Risk Reduction Actions.

TO FULLY UTILIZE EXISTING STATUTORY AUTHORITIES.

Communities and tribes with environmental justice issues are frustrated because of the past failure of EPA and the public health community to account effectively for multiple and cumulative risks and impacts. This is an especially important area for the Agency, and one where it can make substantial improvement. The NEJAC believes that the Agency has substantial discretionary authority, and some direct statutory responsibility, for addressing the multiple, aggregate, and cumulative risks and impacts faced by overburdened communities.

These authorities include but are not limited to the following: Construing the nature of the Resource Conservation and Recovery Act (RCRA) permitting authorities, the EPA Environmental Appeals Board[45] found "that when the Region has a basis to believe that operation of the facility may have a disproportionate impact on a minority or low-income segment of the affected community, the Region should, as a matter of policy, exercise its discretion to assure early and ongoing opportunities for public involvement in the permitting process.[46] The Board also found that RCRA allows the Agency to take "a more refined look at its health and environmental impacts assessment in light of allegations that operation of the facility would have a disproportionately adverse effect on the health or environment of low-income or minority populations." Section 404 of the Clean Water Act has comparable discretionary authority to consider disproportionate burdens on minority and low-income communities. The Corps of Engineers must conduct a broad "public interest review" that includes, "among other things, aesthetics, general environmental concerns, safety, and the needs and welfare of the people." The Clean Air Act's Title V operating permits are similarly broad, including "such other conditions as are necessary to assure compliance with applicable requirements of this chapter."

The challenges to rigorous use of the broad authorities described above are considerable, however. There is no one statute providing the "silver bullet" that can be applied to all sources of pollution in communities with environmental justice issues. For example, although RCRA and the Clean Air Act (CAA) have broad discretion to do what it "necessary" to protect health and the environment, the programs that turn that discretion into action are limited in terms of the sources subject to their jurisdiction, the time frames for amending permits, and in many cases the size of the sources agencies have authority to regulate. The Toxic Substances Control Act (TSCA) can require evaluation of cumulative impacts as part of pre-manufacture notices, but this requirement is prospective and does not cover existing risks. Existing risks can be addressed under TSCA's testing authority, but as a practical matter this testing provision has focused on a defined universe of common and toxic chemicals; chemicals added to the agenda will not be evaluated in the short term. The Environmental Response, Compensation, and Liability Act (CERCLA) and the Clean Air Act have "imminent and substantial endangerment" provisions, but both EPA and the states have construed these terms to apply to serious, current emergencies that would not capture impacts with long-term, cumulative impact.

---

[45] The EPA Environmental Appeals Board is the final Agency decision-maker on administrative appeals under all major environmental statutes that the Agency administers. It is an impartial four-member body that is independent of all Agency components outside the immediate Office of the Administrator. The Appeals Board sits in panels of three judges and makes decisions by majority vote. Currently, nine experienced attorneys serve as counsel to the Board.

[46] Chemical Waste Management, Inc., 6 E.A.D. 66, 1995 WL 395962 (1995), See
<*http://www.epa.gov/eab/disk11/*cwmii.pdf>.

Although each of the authorities cited has its limitations in terms of the activities that can be regulated, and who can regulate them, this is not to say that EPA does not have broad authority to address the needs of communities impacted adversely by the cumulative burdens of many sources of pollution. A brief review of the December 1, 2000 memorandum on "EPA Statutory and Regulatory Authorities Under Which Environmental Justice Issues May be Addressed in Permitting" by EPA General Counsel Gary Guzy indicates the opportunities for strengthened legal authority to address cumulative impacts.[47] The memorandum makes clear that there is ample authority under RCRA to require analysis and response where a RCRA-regulated treatment, storage or disposal facility "may have a disproportionate impact on a minority or low-income segment of the affected community." On a permit-by-permit basis, EPA has authority to review:

(a)   Cumulative risks due to exposure from pollution sources in addition to the applicant facility;

(b)   Unique exposure pathways and scenarios (e.g., subsistence fishers, farming communities); or

(c)   Sensitive populations (e.g., children with levels of lead in their blood, individuals with poor diets).

RCRA's corrective action authority appears to afford comparable opportunities for environmental justice and cumulative impact review at RCRA corrective action facilities. Where sewage treatment facilities or underground injection wells are involved, EPA's permit-by-rule obligations under RCRA authorize expanded public participation–to include discussion of cumulative impacts.[48] Where RCRA permits are administered by the states, EPA retains the obligation to review the state-administered permit program and to provide comments on permits inadequately addressing sensitive population risks.[49] EPA also has authority to conduct a "broad public interest review" of Clean Water Act Section 404 permits impacting municipal water supplies, fishery areas, wildlife or recreational areas.[50] Major sources of air emissions can be reviewed broadly for adverse impacts.[51] The General Counsel's memorandum serves as an excellent first step in articulating the specific sources of EPA authority and discretion to assure that cumulative impacts are assessed and redressed. It specifies authorities under which cumulative impacts can be addressed and alludes to gaps where state or local authority may need to be employed to assure full redress of adverse impacts.

The mechanisms to translate this legal authority into action in permitting, enforcement and other contexts has yet to be articulated, however, and this must be done both in terms of individual permits proceedings and area-wide approaches where a permitted facility is but part of the problem. If EPA were merely to issue a directive under one statutory authority to "address cumulative impacts," neither its program offices, the states that implement delegated programs, regulated sources nor the general public would know what actions are mandated by such requirement. Moreover, this general directive is most unlikely to be construed in the absence of specific guidance to cover the many

---

[47] Guzy, Gary. "EPA Statutory and Regulatory Authorities Under Which Environmental Justice Issues May Be Addressed in Permitting," December 1, 2000.

[48] Ibid.

[49] Ibid.

[50] Ibid.

[51] Ibid.

relatively unregulated sources of pollution that add to an disadvantaged and underserved community's cumulative risk.

The NEJAC has a bias for action and tangible results. As a consequence, rather than resorting to an exhortation to the Agency to "maximize its use of discretion" to address cumulative impacts, we have focused on a series of analytic and response steps EPA should undertake in order to make specific and real progress in beginning to reduce cumulative impacts in the near term.

The General Counsel's memorandum is a starting point in this process, but it is only that. More is needed than a dissertation of specific legal authority. EPA also needs to draft information and guidance that can be used to help communities compile inventories of all sources of cumulative adverse impact, not merely those most readily addressed by current legal authority. For this reason, the group also recommends a plan whereby EPA can gather and disseminate comprehensive information on cumulative impacts in order to develop the information base and motivation for broad action to reduce cumulative impacts over the long term. The adverse impacts experienced by communities with environmental justice concerns can be remedied only if all sources of impact are known and all resources for redress are employed.

To address and overcome programmatic and regulatory fragmentation within the nation's environmental protection regime.

Environmental protection in this country has grown by individual pieces of legislation, developed to address a particular environmental media or a pressing problem like abandoned toxic sites. Environmental law has not evolved from a master game plan or unifying vision. As a result, the statutes have gaps in coverage and do not assure compatible controls of environmental releases to all media from all sources.

EPA is both victim and perpetrator of this patchwork approach. At this relatively mature point in environmental regulation, it is difficult to implement the wiser plan, which would be to create a comprehensive statute covering all sources of pollution and respecting the vulnerabilities of communities burdened with past pollution. A framework that properly accounts for multiple, aggregate and cumulative risks and impacts, however, does provide the opportunity to both use current law to its fullest to protect communities from cumulative risk, and to understand the impacts from the more egregious shortfalls in current regulatory obligations.

To address the inadequacies in environmental protection created by the patchwork of existing environmental laws, EPA should use the concepts contained in its Cumulative Risk Framework to define all of the factors that lead to adverse impacts in the community. Key to implementing such an approach is acquiring the collaborative problem-solving and community-based participatory research tools and expertise to conduct planning, scoping and problem-formulation in the context of a Cumulative Risk Framework. This entails involving the impacted communities and tribes, as well as all relevant stakeholders, early in the process. It also entails a focus on communities as the locus of analysis and implementation. Furthermore, it will require multi-media initiatives in which several offices in which several EPA offices, not to mention their federal, state, local, and tribal government agency counterparts, are working together in a collaborative and coordinated manner.

EPA should take make use of the National Academy of Public Administration's (NAPA) considerable work on the fragmentation issue, particularly at the way in which it plays out at the local level.

> *The central dilemmas in environmental management at the local level are typically institutional fragmentation and scientific uncertainty. Environmental problems tend to spill over simple jurisdictional lines to involve many local governments; special purpose districts that may be creatures of either local governments or states; state agencies; local outposts of numerous federal agencies; and a wide variety of non-profit, private sector and community organizations. Each of these institutions is likely to have a different interest in the problem or its management, and few are likely to have reliable or credible technical data.*[52]

The key to success, in NAPA's opinion, is "bringing diverse resources and perspectives together, and holding them together through a period of experimentation and learning." Furthermore, successful local efforts emerge from "a long-term building of civic capacity." In this regard, NAPA sees the following as important:

---

[52] National Academy of Public Administration, *Setting Priorities, Getting Results: A New Direction for EPA*, Washington, DC: National Academy of Public Administration, 2000, p. 111.

- **Strong institutions** in the locality, including non-profit organizations, private firms and business groups, as well as a multiplicity of public agencies, plus mechanisms to bring these institutions together to solve local problems;
- **Shared understandings and experiences**, binding front-line workers and technical experts from these institutions together into an informal "shadow community" that shares an agreement on the technical problems and most likely solutions, and linking these experts with civic leaders in a shared commitment to addressing the environmental issue:
- **Leadership and vision**, with respected individuals leading and driving participants to decisions and with sponsors–political leaders who support collaboration and protect the shadow community as additional technical information becomes known and policies inevitably have to be adjusted.[53]

---

[53] Ibid.

TO FULLY INCORPORATE THE CONCEPT OF VULNERABILITY, ESPECIALLY ITS SOCIAL AND
CULTURAL ASPECTS, INTO EPA'S STRATEGIC PLANS AND RESEARCH AGENDAS.

As previously stated in this report, the concept of vulnerability goes to the heart of the meaning of
environmental justice and disproportionate impacts. Factors related to vulnerability fundamentally
differentiate disadvantaged, underserved, and overburdened communities from healthy and
sustainable communities. The concept is integral to implementation of viable cumulative risk
assessments. It is important to acknowledge and act on the reality that disadvantaged, underserved,
and overburdened communities come to the table with pre-existing physical, biological, and social
deficits, which can exacerbate the effects of environmental pollution. It is imperative that risk
assessors find ways to incorporate measures of vulnerability into their analyses so that they can
distinguish cumulative risk differentials where they exist.

One of the major milestones represented by the EPA's Cumulative Risk Framework is its
acknowledgment of the concept of vulnerability as an important element of cumulative risk
assessment. Moreover, the Framework has defined the concept in a broad sense, to include not only
biologically related susceptibilities and differential exposure, but also social factors that may affect
the way in which contamination impacts individuals or communities.

Presently, analysis of vulnerability as part of cumulative risk assessment is a generally agreed on
conceptual goal, but there is little consensus about how to go about putting this worthwhile principle
into practice. Scientific understanding of the complex physical, biological, and social interactions
that collectively contribute to vulnerability is rudimentary at best. Substantial work remains to be
done on the mechanisms of action that cause vulnerability and the complicated interplay among
them.

While the NEJAC recommends a set of actions to promote the utilization, integration, and
development of this concept in the short-term, the NEJAC also recommends that EPA view this as a
critical interdisciplinary area of scientific inquiry that deserves its own comprehensive research
agenda. For this reason, the NEJAC believes that vulnerability will require systematic development
as an distinct area of inquiry. While this report has provided some ideas about how to think about
key elements of vulnerability, the NEJAC strongly recommends that the Agency develop a plan to
aggressively pursue the full development of a "science of vulnerability" as a critical part of its
research agenda.

Incorporation of the concept of vulnerability into EPA's research agenda will require a
comprehensive community-based approach. This should include but not be limited to a collection of
the relevant questions, array of concepts, body of theory and assemblage of tools that can
characterize the condition of social, political, economic, and environmental vulnerability, its variable
distribution within a population, and its cultural and psychological meaning.

A good starting place for the Agency is to review the extensive public health and social science
literature on "disparity and vulnerability," and elucidate relevant concepts and ideas for cumulative
risk assessment. This review must be informed by the realization that disparity and vulnerability are
interconnected, with health disparities both contributing to vulnerability and being an outcome of
vulnerability. A major goal of this review should be to develop and enhance interagency
partnerships and collaborations with non-governmental organizations (NGO) and affected

communities. The Agency should consider linking efforts to address cumulative risks and impacts with the Nation's efforts to eliminate health disparities by the year 2010.[54]

The NEJAC recognizes that the concepts of vulnerability and health disparities are interrelated. Traditionally, health disparities references to differences in the incidence, prevalence, mortality, and burden of disease among specific susceptible populations. As such, some of the factors that contribute to these disparities include increased risk of disease due to underlying biological or socioeconomic factors, increased exposure to environmental contaminants, or reduced access to health care. The concept of vulnerability then fundamentally differentiates disadvantaged, underserved, and overburdened communities and healthy and sustainable communities.

EPA should make it clear that although quantitative evaluation of vulnerability is precluded in almost all cases by a scarcity of scientific knowledge and understanding, *this is not an excuse to ignore it.* Vulnerability should be an integral part of cumulative risk assessment even if it must be analyzed using qualitative measures.

---

[54] Healthy People 2010 is the national effort to eliminate health disparities along lines of race, ethnicity, income, gender, and other. An effort is underway to link environmental justice and health disparity issues. See Symposium Proceedings of "Building Healthy Environments to Eliminate Health Disparities (May 28-29, 2003)," forthcoming. One recommendation from the symposium is to conduct a comprehensive crosswalk between the Healthy People 2010 Objectives and the EPA Strategic Goals.

TO PROMOTE A PARADIGM SHIFT TO COMMUNITY-BASED APPROACHES, PARTICULARLY COMMUNITY-BASED PARTICIPATORY RESEARCH AND INTERVENTION.

In the past, risk assessment approaches, and environmental protection principles generally, were geared to controlling sources of pollution through technology based regulation. It became evident that these broad national regulations have left uneven results in the form of remaining pockets of higher exposure and adverse impacts. Community groups have often found risk assessment to be mechanical and reductionist, lacking the ability to include social, cultural, and public health concerns into the analysis. To deal with this unaddressed problem, it is becoming necessary to initiate a place-based and population-based approach. In other words, EPA found it necessary to deal on a community by community basis. The EPA Cumulative Risk Assessment Framework represents the beginnings of the Agency's response to deal with this remaining challenge. Addressing this remaining challenge is an issue of environmental justice. More often than not, these remaining pockets of higher exposure and adverse impacts are the "toxic hotspots" in which historically disadvantaged and underserved communities and tribes live, work, worship, go to school, and play.

Because the locus of attention must now include communities and tribes as the center of attention, EPA must promote a paradigm shift to place-based and community-based approaches in its work. An important component of this shift is implementation of a community-based participatory research methodology. This shift should build upon the lessons of and help to further develop a community-based participatory research (CBPR) model. CBPR provides a strong foundation for effective collaborative problem-solving initiatives. In addition, part of the toolkit of implementable actions should include tool development and skills development, for Agency, within communities and tribes, and within all relevant stakeholders, to implement effective community-based efforts.

EPA should undertake an effort to fully document and disseminate success stories and best practices in the conduct of community-based efforts, and to promote their institutionalization. Key among this is the use of the Environmental Justice Collaborative Problem-Solving Model, which promotes clear problem identification, strategic planning and goal-setting. These concepts are key to ensuring successful partnerships and effective implementation of the planning, scoping and problem-formulation phase of a cumulative risk assessment. Also critical are consensus building and dispute resolution tools and skills.

Likewise, EPA should support the use of community-based participatory research, which emphasizes the full utilization of community- and tribal-driven research and action strategies in communities affected by cumulative risks and impacts. Developing partnerships with communities is essential to enhancing the Agency's ability to understand and address the problems confronting highly impacted populations. Community and tribal members often know what the problems are before the Agency scientists and university researchers. In addition, communities and tribes are in the best position to explain the cultural and social factors that influence health and disease. Finally, chances of the ultimate acceptability of any remedy are enhanced if the community is a partner from the earliest stages of decision-making.

Last, EPA should utilize a dynamic evaluation process to assess and improve the effectiveness of its community-based prevention and intervention efforts. The evaluation should include an assessment of whether objectives were met, the quality of the Agency-community partnership, community-capacity building, multi-stakeholder problem-solving partnerships, and institutional change that result in the reduction of social inequality and the increase of social assets.

TO INCORPORATE SOCIAL, ECONOMIC, CULTURAL AND COMMUNITY HEALTH FACTORS, PARTICULARLY THOSE INVOLVING VULNERABILITY, IN EPA DECISION-MAKING.

According to the EPA Framework for Cumulative Risk Assessment, "the goals of the population-based approach were much more useful to decision makers who were dealing with public health or ecological health questions rather than controlling sources of pollution." The NEJAC acknowledges, as does the EPA Cumulative Risk Assessment Framework, that the challenges of such population-based assessments can be daunting, even if only a few of the stressors affecting a population are evaluated together. The NEJAC also notes that while the Agency's Framework acknowledges that a wide-ranging set of stressors may need to be accounted for when one speaks of the "total risk" for a population or community being evaluated, it has yet to fully define all of them.

Moreover, the Agency is particularly deficient, because of its prior technology-based regulatory focus and its own institutional history, in understanding how to incorporate factors which would be key to fully, precisely, and accurately characterizing the risks and impacts involved, particularly social, economic, cultural, and community health factors. These would be most important for communities and tribes where environmental justice issues are involved.

There exist many opportunities to effectively utilize of social, economic, cultural, and community health indicators in the EPA decision-making process. For example, it is possible to describe a community (at the neighborhood, city, metropolitan, county, state and reservation level) by the health of its residents, including access to health care, percent uninsured, rates of illness and mortality, and how people rate their own health, using health statistics routinely collected by the public health infrastructure. This may often exclude reservations. Health disparities between communities can be calculated so that communities most vulnerable to excess illness and death can be identified and prioritized.[55]

Similarly, communities can be characterized and compared by many already-measured social and physical factors that further add to a community's stress, vulnerability and ill health. These include: percent poverty; degree of income inequality and economic isolation; percent racial and ethnic minority; degree of residential segregation; percent distressed, overcrowded housing and vacant land. These public health, social, economic and physical characteristics joined with measurable environmental impacts, such as air toxics, proximity of hazardous waste sites, exposure to pesticide use from agriculture, nearby bus depots/trash transfer stations, and others, provide a fuller picture of the overall health and burden of communities. When combined, they enable EPA to develop a more dimensioned framework of comparison with which to identify communities most burdened and most vulnerable by the complex of factors—social, economic, physical, public health, and environmental—that impact health.

The NEJAC believes that there are two areas where EPA can make substantial progress in this regard: (1) The application and integration of qualitative analysis with quantitative analysis in EPA risk assessment and decision-making is a key component for ensuring that social, economic, cultural

---

[55] For example, the City of Boston's annual Health of the Neighborhoods report is an example of city-wide health indicators that can be utilized to identify vulnerable communities in need of early action control strategies. The report compiles and compares mortality and morbidity data on a neighborhood-by-neighborhood basis. Thus, it is possible to rank neighborhoods by highest to lowest incidence and prevalence of asthma room visits and lead poisoning, and mortality rates by various cancers. An action agenda for disease prevention and health promotion can be guided by this evidence.

and community health factors are properly considered. EPA should make every effort to identify and utilize relevant experience in the use of qualitative methods, including those in the fields of environmental impact assessment, cumulative impact assessment, and social impact assessment. (2) EPA can make efforts to strengthen its capacity to conduct social science and community health analysis in an environmental justice context, including the recruitment of social scientists, community health scientists, and community health representatives (CHR) and persons with community-based experience to the Agency's staff.

TO DEVELOP AND IMPLEMENT EFFICIENT SCREENING, TARGETING, AND PRIORITIZATION METHODS/TOOLS TO IDENTIFY COMMUNITIES NEEDING IMMEDIATE INTERVENTION.

Arguably, utilizing community-based collaborative problem-solving approaches is the quickest and surest way to ensure needed risk reduction in overburden communities suffering cumulative risks and impacts. In order to turn this theory into practice, effective and efficient screening, targeting, and prioritization methods and tools must be developed and implemented. These methods and tools should serve to identify communities needing immediate intervention as well as to prioritize risks and risk reduction efforts within those communities. They should be done in such a way as to promote and institutionalize the bias for action that forms the underpinning of this report.

In the NEJAC's opinion, developing an operational framework for assessing and addressing cumulative risks and impacts is key to ensuring that currently existing screening, targeting, and prioritization methods and tools are most effectively utilized. Although this currently may have to be qualitative in nature, such a framework can allow the Agency to simultaneously bring to bear quantitative single and multi-media methods and tools as well as provide a framework for a dialogue about community risk and use of qualitative methods and tools. In one respect, a matrix of multiple stressors such as the one provided in Table 1 (page 5) serves that purpose.

In addition, much can be gained by focusing on three activities. First, the Agency should inventory and review existing assessment methods and tools to ensure they are addressing the concerns of cumulative risk and impact analysis, including vulnerability factors. Second, EPA should provide guidance regarding minimum criteria for selection and use of a particular tool. This guidance should include a uniform method to be used for screening purposes. Third, the Agency should promote greater cross fertilization among developers and users of various assessment tools; training of developers and users of tools regarding environmental justice, multiple media, cumulative risks and impacts, and vulnerability, and others; and linkage of assessment to cognizable statutory authorities.

TO ADDRESS CAPACITY AND RESOURCE ISSUES (HUMAN, ORGANIZATIONAL, TECHNICAL AND FINANCIAL) WITHIN EPA AND THE STATES, WITHIN IMPACTED COMMUNITIES AND TRIBES, AND AMONG ALL RELEVANT STAKEHOLDERS.

In some ways, this theme is the most difficult to properly articulate because it involves all of the themes heretofore mentioned and is related to the larger question of integrating environmental justice within all policies, programs, and activities of EPA. In addition, capacity building and resource questions must be addressed among multiple groups in order for there to be a proper alignment between all the parties which need to be engaged in a problem-solving paradigm. For example, capacity building for impacted communities refers to the ability of all stakeholders to travel to meetings, have staff capacity to participate, have technical capacity (e.g., computers and access to phones for long distance calls) to communicate with each other, have funds to participate, and have knowledge and information to participate equitably. For government or business and industry, capacity building would include education around how to understand issues of environmental justice, community issues and needs, and how best to engage constructively on these issues. In addition, capacity building involves the development of policies, methods, and tools of relevance to the particular institution, be it a government agency, philanthropy, academic institution, or corporation.

If there is not balanced approach towards capacity building, the first unwanted result will be the inability to impacted communities and tribes to be meaningful involved in risk assessment or prevention/intervention activities. Another unwanted result will be unrealistic expectations and continued frustration on the part of communities when government agencies or industry do not have the tools, skills, or institutional infrastructure to work with the communities and tribes where multiple and cumulative risks and impacts are clearly an issue.

There are two major ways by which the NEJAC will examine this issue. (1) One way of discussing this question would be to discuss the groups for which there must be capacity building around environmental justice and a Cumulative Risk Framework. This pertains to at least three major areas, i.e., EPA and the states, within impacted communities and tribes, and among all relevant stakeholders (e.g., industry, local governments, academia, scientific and public health community). Each of these groups play a vital role in of themselves. However, issues of environmental justice and cumulative risk are so complicated that it will require multiple stakeholders, agencies, and disciplines. Hence, the development of partnerships is of paramount important, as well the ability of the Agency to play a proactive, facilitative role in helping to create and maintain such partnerships. Another key question is the development and implementation of training related to environmental justice, multiple stressors, community-based efforts, and incorporation of such factors in the decision-making process. (2) A second would be to focus on the content of capacity building. This pertains to issues like community-based participatory research, utilization of community- and tribal-based expertise and knowledge, partnership building, community capacity building, consensus building and dispute resolution, special concerns of communities and tribes, effective community-based risk reduction and pollution prevention tools, and community-based evaluation processes. All groups need capacity building. All groups need different types and varying levels of training.

One cannot avoid the fact that financial resources will be needed to make the Agency's vision achieving environmental justice for all people through its Cumulative Risk Framework a reality. For example, EPA's budget must allow for the time and resources to initiate and maintain dialogue with communities and other stakeholders to understand the complexities of vulnerability and cumulative impacts. Resources are needed for EPA's researchers to compile this and all other pertinent data in order to fully develop the scientific analysis to inform the characterization of cumulative risks and to identify the means to reduce them. Beyond these research needs, implementation of cumulative risk reduction will require dedication of resources from a broad array of sources: Federal, state and local officials need to devote resources to understand and address the sources of adverse impact under their control and to incentivize environmental improvement when their jurisdiction is limited. Business must come to the table proactively, appreciating the responsibility to go beyond mere environmental compliance where cumulative impacts are adverse and call upon all to be accountable for environmental improvement. Communities need resources to participate with business and government in there collaborative efforts to reduce adverse cumulative impacts. They need resources in the form of information, training, technical support and the simple resources needed to participate in dialogue, including transportation, technical assistance, administrative support, and other things.

Last, we would like to close with the same issue that was articulated within our opening theme of institutionalizing a bias for action with the Agency. This speaks to the value of gaining and building on experience as an important vehicle for positive change. Developing a strong experiential base is an important part of capacity building, especially when one is dealing with a set of issues that are technically complex and involve multiple stakeholders. The Agency would benefit greatly from a systematic effort to gain and disseminate lessons, models, tools, best practices, skill sets. Again, we want to urge that EPA evaluate where there are gaps in its personnel in its capacity to work effectively within an action oriented cumulative risk context (e.g., social scientists and persons with community-based experience) and develop a strategic plan to fill these gaps.

RECOMMENDED ACTIONS

INTRODUCTION

Recognizing that the eight overarching themes of this report envision significant paradigm changes in the way that the Agency does business and are long-term in nature, the NEJAC is providing the following 12 recommendations on actions which the Agency can take immediately. It is the NEJAC's view that successful implementation of these 12 recommendations will lay the groundwork for the larger changes called for by the eight overarching themes. Successful implementation of these recommended actions will place the Agency in a stronger position to make the transition to being more capable of effectively responding to cumulative risks and impacts in people of color, low-income, and tribal communities. These actions should be part of the Agency's efforts to engage a coherent collaborative problem-solving methodology to ensure risk reduction in disadvantaged, underserved and environmentally overburdened communities and reflect the Agency's bias for action in addressing cumulative risk and impacts.

1. Initiate Community-Based, Collaborative, Multi-Media, Risk Reduction Pilot Projects: EPA should initiate a set of community-based, multi-media, risk reduction pilot projects in low-income, people of color, and/or tribal communities as part of a broad national community-based effort to address risks in such communities. These should be the focus of EPA's bias for action in addressing cumulative risks and impacts. There should be at least one per each EPA Region, as well as attention to tribal populations. Activities should include but not be limited to community-based assessment, partnership building, provision of resources, prevention/ intervention risk reduction efforts and application of the Agency's Environmental Justice Collaborative Problem-Solving Model. In addition, EPA should systematically take the lessons gained from the pilot projects and integrate them into EPA programs as part of the Agency's day-to-day activities. These pilot projects should be part of a short-term and long-term research agenda on community-based, multi-media, collaborative problem-solving approaches to achieve environmental justice and healthy communities. The projects, and its associated research agenda, should:

- include community-based participatory research elements in the selection criteria;
- consider racial, ethnic, economic, and tribal status in pilot selection;
- provide lessons on ways to overcome programmatic and regulatory fragmentation;
- involve other federal agencies, where appropriate;
- document and disseminate information from projects; and
- be incorporated into Headquarters and Regional Environmental Justice Action Plans.

2. Develop Toolkit of Implementable Risk Reduction Actions: EPA should develop a toolkit of early implementable actions to reduce risk and pollution in people of color, low-income, and tribal communities. The purpose of such a toolkit is to "jump start" and support results-oriented processes in impacted communities with proven strategies and methods. The actions should include tools designed for use in large businesses and public facilities, small businesses, schools, mobile sources, surface waters, and homes. Examples of such actions are provided in Appendix C of this report. These actions should include regulatory actions (such as enforcement), incentives for voluntary action, community-based participatory research and collaborative problem-solving. The Agency should ensure that appropriate means exist to disseminate information about and train the public in the use of such tools.

3. Provide Resources for Community-Based Organizations: EPA should ensure that adequate resources are being made available to community-based organizations. EPA should institute new and/or increase the amount of funding available to community based organizations, following examples of past and present grant programs. Additionally, direct support of community-based organizations should be incorporated into other areas where this goal is not a priority. These funds should be complemented by more innovative ways of ensuring that information on such programs are disseminated to community based organizations. Recognizing that community-based organizations require assistance in areas of grant management, the Agency should provide training on grant management. Last, EPA should proactively work with other groups, such as philanthropies, to ensure that resources and technical assistance are provided to community based organizations.

4. Develop and Utilize Tools for Targeting and Prioritization of Communities Needing Urgent Intervention: In the short run, EPA should recommend some methods or tools for screening and prioritization of communities with high cumulative pollution burdens to prioritize Agency activities in those communities. In order to accomplish this task over the next two years. EPA should inventory and review existing screening methods and tools to ascertain: (1) strengths and weaknesses of existing cumulative impact evaluation tools; (2) ways in which these tools can be improved; and (3) recommend specific tool(s) that can be applied to a particular scenario, including guidance regarding minimum criteria for selection and use of a particular tool. In addition to methods and tools available at EPA, this inventory also should include methods used by other federal agencies, states, public health agencies, universities, etc. In the long run, EPA should identify and incorporate appropriate indicators of vulnerability into these screening tools. These development efforts should be done in conjunction with pilot projects and other community based activities (See Recommended Action No. 1), to "truth-test" the accuracy and comprehensiveness of such methods and tools. By "truth testing,"the NEJAC means that such methods and tools should be grounded in community realities. Scientific peer review, which is essential to ensuring sound methodology, should be informed by a robust understanding of community realities. Moreover, the Agency should engage in stakeholder dialogues to ensure that all stakeholders develop a common understanding of the purpose, parameters, and limitations of such tools, as well as ways to use them.

5. Promote Incentives for Business and Industry: EPA should develop an affirmative strategy to incentivize members of business and industry to go beyond compliance to reduce cumulative impacts in overburdened communities. Businesses and industry that reduce their proportional share of the cumulative impacts in such communities should receive appropriate rewards in the form of public recognition for their voluntary efforts and efficient permit processing that facilitates implementation of these pollution reductions. In developing this strategy, EPA should first consider the recommendations made regarding such rewards in the NEJAC's June 2003 report,"Advancing Environmental Justice Through Pollution Prevention." EPA should also evaluate the examples of "regulatory reinvention" projects that have been considered successful by both the impacted community and the business and industry project participants. Three criteria are fundamental to appropriate business and industry incentives: (1) the reductions in impact must go beyond regulatory compliance to tangibly improve community health and quality of life; (2) the level of incentive must be proportional to the degree of improvement and the expectation that the largest contributors to the community burden will make the greatest efforts to reduce negative impacts; and (3) the rewards are developed in the course of collaborative dialogue among impacted community members, business and industry and the regulators. In short, the business and industry incentives must be for voluntary action beyond compliance and reflect a fair acknowledgment of business or industry's actions to reduce environmental exposure and risk, improve community health and the environment.

6. Conduct Scientific and Stakeholder Dialogues in Ways that Enhance Scientific Understanding and Collaborative Problem-Solving Ability: EPA should convene, support, and promote a series of workshops, focus groups, stakeholder meetings, scientific symposia, conferences, and other dialogues to promote greater understanding and consensus around the concepts in this report. Such dialogues are critical to ensuring a sound scientific foundations as well as multi-stakeholder understanding. They are critical to building strategic partnerships–in the private and public sectors and in communities–for the collaborative undertakings called for by this report. In particular, they are critical to bringing diverse perspectives together, and holding them together through periods of experimentation and learning. Such dialogues can be useful catalysts for the long-term building of collaborative problem-solving capacity in the form of strong institutions, shared understandings and perspectives, and leadership and vision.

7. Lay the Scientific Basis for Incorporating Vulnerability into EPA Assessment Tools, Strategic Plans, and Research Agendas: EPA should develop a plan to ensure incorporation of the concept of vulnerability, particularly its social and cultural aspects, into the Agency's strategic plans, research agendas, and decision-making processes. This should begin with an Agency effort to lay the scientific foundations or understanding vulnerability, especially its social and cultural aspects. Issues papers, workshops, case studies and other approaches should be employed in such a foundation laying effort. Additionally, the Agency should initiate and promote dialogue with key partners and stakeholders on the subject. The Agency also should include the concept in its development of screening, targeting, and prioritization methods and tools. The Agency should also direct all offices whose missions relate to policy making, program implementation, regulatory enforcement, and professional and community training, to develop strategic plans for incorporating the concept of vulnerability into their operational paradigm. One vehicle for accomplishing this is each office's Environmental Justice Action Plans. Last, EPA should make it clear that although quantitative evaluation of vulnerability is precluded in almost all cases by a scarcity of scientific knowledge and understanding, this is not an excuse to ignore it. Vulnerability should be an integral part of cumulative risk assessment even it must be analyzed using qualitative measures.

8. Produce Guidance on Greater Use of Statutory Authorities: EPA should inventory, review, and promote the utilization of existing statutory authorities that can increase the capacity of EPA and its state, local and tribal government partners, impacted communities, business and industry, and other stakeholders to address cumulative risk in disadvantaged, underserved, and environmentally overburdened communities. EPA should work on identifying and clarifying existing legal authorities that could be useful in addressing cumulative risks and impacts, especially in disadvantaged, underserved, and disproportionately affected communities. This should build upon the Office of General Counsel's December 1, 2000 memorandum on environmental justice authorities. EPA program offices should translate the authorities into guidance for permitting procedures. In addition, EPA should make cumulative risk reduction as a goal in assessing penalties and authorizing Supplemental Environmental Projects. EPA should explore innovative ways to make use of these authorities to address cumulative risks and impacts, such the combined use of statutory authorities and alternative dispute resolution. In addition, integrated problem-solving approaches that combine multiple regulatory, enforcement, and voluntary emission reduction processes should be explored. Last, EPA should explore a programmatic approach to integrating cumulative risk considerations into permits, rather than one permit at a time.

9. Elevate the Importance of Community-Based Approaches: EPA should develop and implement a systematic plan to elevate the importance of community-based approaches. Such a plan begins with the recognition that the effectiveness of Agency managers and staff, particularly those with a regulatory background, would be enhanced by an understanding of the positive role that community initiative can play in reaching the Agency's environmental and public health goals. This plan should be developed, therefore, around activities in communities that both result in tangible community benefits and demonstrate the success of this approach. All EPA Regional and Headquarter Offices should develop and implement activities to achieve this goal. The second part of this plan should include a systematic process of research, education, training, and dialogue among Agency staff on community-based approaches to environmental protection. These activities should be intended to promote awareness and understanding of the premises, methods, and experience related community based approaches. Areas of examination should include environmental justice, community-based participatory research, collaborative problem-solving, dispute resolution, and others. In addition, special meetings should be convened by offices and groups such as the Innovation Action Council, Office of Environmental Justice, Conflict Prevention and Resolution Center, Public Involvement Improvement Council, and their regional counterparts. As part of this plan, EPA also should facilitate dialogue among its federal, state, tribal, and local governmental partners, business and industry, universities, professional organizations, non-profit organizations, and philanthropies about working togther to promote community-based approaches. Last, the Administrator should provide vision and direction on the importance of community-based solutions in the next generation of environmental protection. Likewise, such direction should be provided by all EPA Assistant Administrators and Regional Administrators.

10. Establish an Agency Wide Framework for Holistic Risk-Based Environmental Decision Making and Incorporation of Tribal Traditional Lifeways in Indian Country: EPA should support the work of the EPA Indian Program Policy Council to establish a collective, multi-media Agency approach and determine what additional efforts are needed that will allow EPA to adequately consider tribal traditional lifeways when conducting scientific analyses, including assessing risks; developing and implementing environmental programs and regulations; and making decisions that protect human health and the environment in Indian country. In addition, EPA should identify examples of successful holistic risk assessment and collaborative problem-solving efforts that abide by the Native American World View of Health and promote ecological restoration in Indian County, and integrate the lessons from such successes into all of the Agency's policies, programs, and activities.

11. Strengthen EPA's Social Science Capacity and Community Expertise: EPA should develop an implement a plan for short- and long-term development of intramural and extramural expertise in the social sciences, community-based work, and collaborative problem-solving. expertise, and collaborative problem-solving skills. As part of this effort, the Agency should conduct a study to identify ways that such expertise can best be utilized and integrated into the Agency's programs. Part of this study should identify larger trends in environmental protection challenges that elevate in the importance of sociology in environmental decision-making and problem-solving. In addition, the study should identify ways to systematically develop the skills of in-house scientists and program personnel in social science areas and community assessment, not the least of which is requiring that program personnel and scientists spend time in communities to understand the real life context of the communities' environmental challenges. EPA also should encourage and support the development of community expertise and social science capacity within its governmental partners, business and industry, universities and the environmental protection field in general. Last, to focus broad based attention on the imperative to overcome the present structural limitations of the environmental protection field and its makeup, the Administrator should issue a policy statement to elevate the importance of the sociology and the social sciences in environmental protection and collaborative problem-solving. One goal of such a policy is to ensure an environmental protection work force that has a built-in bias for action.

12. Integrate the Concepts of NEJAC's Cumulative Risks/Impacts Report into EPA's Strategic and Budget Planning Processes: EPA should ensure that the concepts of this report are integrated into its strategic and budget planning processes. To that end, the Agency can focus on a number of actions. Each EPA (HQ) National Program Manager and Regional Office should update its Environmental Justice Action Plan to address the major actions associated with these recommendations. Using the principles in the Office of Enforcement and Compliance Assurance's (OECA) environmental justice targeting strategy as a model, each EPA (HQ) National Program Manager should identify the priority areas for application of this report's major concepts and action items into its operating plans. Each Regional Office should incorporate the major action concepts and action items of this Report into its Regional Strategic Plans. Last, the Assistant Administrator, OECA, Director, OEJ, and the Office of the Chief Financial Officer should work together to incorporate these concepts and action items into the next update of EPA's Strategic Plan.

CONCLUSION

Over the past 18 months, the National Environmental Justice Advisory Council, through its Cumulative Risks and Impacts Work Group, has conducted a process of extraordinary engagement to develop this report and its recommendations. This process has involved all stakeholders, including communities, business and industry, state and local government, tribes, and public health practitioners. In addition, the NEJAC has conducted focus group discussions with communities, tribes, industry, and state officials. The NEJAC also devoted a public meeting to this issue (New Orleans on April 13 through 16, 2004) during which six EPA Deputy Assistant Administrators or Deputy Regional Administrators took part. The meeting included many hours of public comment on this issue.

Cumulative risks/impacts is an incredibly complex and difficult issue. To begin with, cumulative risks/impacts is intellectually challenging – difficult to define and scientifically complex. The issue requires that one understand both the conditions and processes of impacted communities and tribes. It necessitates the involvement of multiple stakeholders, which requires that one address issues of communications, trust, and divergent interests and differing definitions of success. Consideration of cumulative risk/impact involves legal and policy questions. Lastly, it requires an examination of fragmentation in our Nation's environmental protection regime and the very structures and processes of governance in current American society.

In a very real sense, the fact that the NEJAC is addressing the issue of cumulative risks and impacts represents the maturation of environmental justice issues. The NEJAC's involvement with the issue of cumulative risk and impact did not start 18 months ago when this Work Group was formed.. It has been an issue that has been an explicit and implicit part of the environmental justice dialogue ever since it rose to national prominence in the 1980s.

For these reasons, the concepts and recommendations of this report are testaments to the greater ability of all sectors of American society to understand and address the issues of environmental justice. The NEJAC believes that the concepts and recommendations of this report provide a solid foundation for the Agency to be able to better address the issues of cumulative risks and impacts. The report places the Agency in a better position to make the transition to a new era of environmental protection, one that is characterized by place-based, collaborative and integrated problem solving. Finally, the Agency will be able to address systematically the "toxic hotspots" where disadvantaged, underserved, and environmentally overburdened communities and tribes have yet to reap the full benefits of our Nation's environmental progress.

The issue of cumulative risks/impacts is a unifying one, because it is a vehicle through which the impressive array of tools now available to ensure pollution prevention and risk reduction can be brought together and applied in new, innovative, and more effective ways. Exciting new approaches, partnerships, and models will surely emerge. Ensuring that these new possibilities will blossom will require a critical appraisal of past Agency policies and practices. Ensuring that this new day in environmental protection will come to pass will require committed individuals willing and able to provide foresight, analysis, and leadership.

Ensuring Risk Reduction in Communities with Multiple Stressors: Environmental Justice and Cumulative Risks/Impacts

Appendices

APPENDIX A:

EPA CHARGE TO NEJAC ON CUMULATIVE RISKS AND IMPACTS

In May 2003, the Agency will be issuing the "Cumulative Risk Assessment Framework." In that document, the Agency described various features of a cumulative risk assessment as follows: (a) multiple stressors; (b) consideration of how stressors act together, rather than individually; and (c) a population-focused assessment which means that the characteristics of that population needs to be defined and multiple stressors are assessed with regard to impact on that population, although not every individual will see the same (or all) effects.

The Agency, therefore, is asking the NEJAC to provide advice and recommendations on the following questions:

> (1) How should the Agency proactively address the issue of using the various existing statutory authorities and their implementing regulations relating to cumulative risks which were identified by the Environmental Law Institute in their November 2001 research report entitled, "*Opportunities for Advancing Environmental Justice: An Analysis of U.S. EPA Statutory Authorities*"?

> (2) What factors should the Agency consider when conducting a cumulative risk assessment of vulnerable minority, indigenous, and/or low-income communities disproportionately exposed to environmental harms and risks, and cumulative impacts? These may include, but should not be limited to: (a) multiple durations, pathways, sources, or routes of exposure; (b) multiple effects or impacts; (c) nonconventional stressors or risk factors (e.g., lifestyles, access to health care); and (d) quantification of risks. In addition, what short-term actions should the Agency take to ensure that it can proactively respond to community concerns about the above-stated factors, in parallel with Agency efforts to develop adequate scientific methodology for conducting cumulative risk assessments?

> (3) How should the Agency ensure that vulnerability of certain segments of the population are incorporated into the cumulative risk assessment? In addition, what short-term actions should the Agency take to ensure that it can proactively respond to community concerns related to vulnerability, in parallel with Agency efforts to develop adequate scientific methodology for incorporating this factor in cumulative risk assessments?

> (4) How can the Agency promote more effective participation by vulnerable minority, indigenous, and/or low-income communities disproportionately exposed to environmental harms and risks, and cumulative impacts to improve community health through cumulative risk assessment, particularly during the planning, scoping, and problem formulation phase of a cumulative risk assessment?

> (5) How can the Agency partner with an affected community to more effectively use the results of a cumulative risk assessment to develop appropriate intervention and prevention strategies, including use of models of conducting cumulative risk assessment that promote communities and technical experts working and reaching decisions together?

In sum, in order to ensure environmental justice for all communities and tribes, what short-term and long-term actions should the Agency take in proactively implementing the concepts contained in its Cumulative Risk Assessment Framework (i.e., using the concepts of cumulative risk to determine: (a) disproportionate exposure to multiple stressors; (b) the resulting cumulative impacts; and (c) developing appropriate intervention and prevention strategies)?

APPENDIX B:

COMMUNITY MULTIPLE STRESSORS MATRICES

Multiple, Aggregate, and Cumulative Risks and Impacts (Stressors) in Laredo, Texas

Demographics:	Border city with population over 180,000, 97% Latino primarily Mexican American. It is the fastest growing border community (growing by 45% 1990-2000) and is one of the ten (10) fastest growing metropolitan areas in the US. Ranks at the top in commercial and border crossings with over 60% of the nations product and goods passing through its four (4) international bridges between Mexico and Latin American into the U.S. and Canada. The World Trade Bridge is completely commercial with over 11,000 trucks and trailers crossing daily. Finally it is a semi-arid mostly hot area, its primary source of potable water is the Rio Grande (an international body of water). Poverty and unemployment is twice the state rate and the population is younger than that of Texas in general. 50% of the population is either uninsured or underinsured.
Social/ Cultural Conditions:	Laredoans are resilient and have excelled as well made great strides in economic, social, education and health as well in developing industry to improve living standards and the quality of life. Two major universities and one local junior college as well multiple training services by both city and private entities have played a major role in the standard of living and progress of the city. Yet there are still some challenges. Laredo with a population of over 180,000, grows by another 100,000 daily by persons who work and travel into Laredo and when it comes to health, commerce and travel, we also incorporate an additional 700,000 persons from Nuevo Laredo Mexico. Poverty, unemployment, young population with over 50% in school age, old housing, and lack of infrastructure are additional factors. The population is young with a 26-year average and with over 60% of the population in pre-school or school age. Even though unemployment and poverty is high it is less than other areas in Texas because the growing and booming industry which continues to flourish. Wal-Mart in a given day does the highest gross selling than any other in the US. The low income and underdeveloped area in this community and other border communities also can make border communities more vulnerable to environmental contaminants. The cultural and social conditions may also pose more risks since the general health status is not optimum.
Pollution Sources:	Untreated waste water sometimes drains into the cities' water source (international body of water -Rio Grande) by Mexico on daily basis, two railways separate the city and add to traffic congestion, 11,000 commercial trucks and trailers cross through one bridge on a daily basis, illegal dumping of both household and commercial contaminants, abundance of improperly disposed tires (100,000/year), unregulated warehouses that store both declared and non-declared potential toxic materials, lack of potable water, runoff and frequent contaminated water exposure.

Unique Exposure Pathways:	Water contamination through raw sewerage, potentially toxic materials through inappropriate storage in over 2000 warehouses, spills of potential chemical and toxic material through daily commerce and transportation of both regulated and unregulated trucks and trailers. Two railroads that divide the city into 3 parts that sometimes impede efficient and timely access to health and emergency facilities. Potential air contamination because of automobile and trailer travel and commerce in a city that is the number one international crossing area for the nation, possible agricultural exposure from pesticides and runoff, natural occurring and manmade contamination (arsenic, mercury, lead), old landfills, agricultural areas, old military base, underdeveloped areas (Colonias) and exposure from natural gas companies that produce emissions. General health status may also predispose persons to an inadequate response or the exposure impact such as an important multi drug resistance problem for Tuberculosis. A concern for environmental contaminant impacts on persons who may be compromised because of general health, nutritional status, social and economic factors.
Existing Health Problems & Conditions:	Laredo has made great strides in public health, sanitation, health care prevention, disease control and primary care however there are still several challenges Unincorporated rural or semi rural subdivisions (Colonias) with substandard housing and sanitation cause a higher incidence of many communicable diseases. Lack of access to health care and health care facilities and being federally classified as medically underserved poses a serious concern to adequate health care. Over half of the population lacks the appropriate resources to seek health, preventive and medical care and is either underinsured or uninsured. Wellness and preventive health care is lacking as well as proper nutrition for a good immunological response. Adequate prenatal care is inaccessible for some posing a threat to maternal and child health. Critically important health issues are both infectious and noninfectious as well emerging diseases and environmental health concerns. Hepatitis A and Tuberculosis in adults is higher than the state rate as well neural tube defects, food borne infectious and vector borne (West Nile virus and dengue) are important public health concerns as well rabies control. Chronic and emerging diseases such as breast, cervical and stomach cancer, diabetes, obesity, substance abuse and mental health behavior pose a current and future challenge to health care and the health care delivery system. Bi-national issues in prevention, disease control and environmental health pose a challenge but one that is being addressed through cooperation and dual services. Other environmental and occupational issues are: CDC designated high exposure area for childhood lead exposure, pesticide, household poisoning, naturally occurring metals exposure (arsenic and mercury), air contaminants exposure and high levels of asthma in children as well newly found former Laredo air force base environmental contaminants.

Community Infrastructure & Capacity/ Social Capital:	Laredo is a major international thoroughfare for business and commerce. Over the last five (5) years it has also become a center for highly developed technology, education and trade and is quickly becoming a center for biomedical services and research. Several public health issues are directly related to basic infrastructure for sanitation, water and waste water treatment. There are over 2000 warehouses and two railroad systems that divide the city into three (3) isolated sections that further divide our community. This division further restricts access to vital municipal, public health, emergency and medical care services which continue to place our community at risk for possible contamination. The older sections of town divided by the railroad also have an increased incidence of lead exposure to children with 6 of the 10 cases for 2003 living in that area. In addition the social structure of the amount of travel and commerce constantly put our community at risk of what is stored and managed by the railroad, warehouses, trucks, trailers and new industrial growth on both sides of the border. We have 12 major "maquiladoras" (U.S. companies in Mexico such as Sony, General Motors, Delphi) and about 40 smaller ones in Nuevo Laredo, Mexico; our sister city produces important amounts of industrial waste which needs to be managed and disposed appropriately. The industry of tires being taken to the border also poses an environmental threat. Yet these entities are needed to help the economic development and existence of our community and many other border communities. For Laredo our research and economical development serves as an opportunity to improve living standards and health conditions however this cannot be accomplished without true partnerships which is what we have been doing for years. In addition there is a large investment in education, community training, outreach and extended services to support better prevention and intervention and to improve the quality of life.
Programmatic & Regulatory Fragmentation:	Border communities have been resilient to coordinate and partner to create a safe environment and to promote the public health well being. However state and federal programs and regulations many times challenge local efforts causing fragmentation of services and enforcement. Some of the issue revolves on who has responsibility for the action and enforcement. Federal, state and local guidelines on environmental health, hazardous materials, water and air monitoring, vector control, agricultural inspection are some of the areas of concern as well dedicated funding which only allows for focused and dedicated services (at times joint inspections are a challenge because of divergent statutory rules, regulations and enforcement); who has authority, where each entity begins and ends their program and regulatory responsibilities and if there are human resources for enforcement are the problems. For example the state is responsible for radiation enforcement but only has one person for 11 counties, local authorities have not program and enforcement capability and yet we need to address the issue if there is a spill or exposure. Another issue is water contamination where we are dealing with state, federal and international regulations of two countries. When any issue of contamination on our water source (Rio Grande) occurs, multiple entities with varying rules, regulations and enforcement need to be consulted posing a real challenge to response efficiently and quickly to protect and safeguard health and the environment. An addition issue with water is the rules for potable water safety. We had a cryptosporidiosis and the state environmental agency, the private utilities that used federal standards all had a diverse interpretation and guidelines which made our job more difficult because we couldn't agree on one standard level to proceed to protect human health. Finally landfill issues are also a challenge because there are different rules as to who has authority between state, and local entities for disposal of certain items such as tires in our area. A coordinated effort and similar rules and programs where we were working from the same rules and enforcement would be a great assistance to local communities.

EXCERPTS FROM
CHELSEA CREEK COMMUNITY-BASED COMPARATIVE RISK ASSESSMENT

See: *http://www.epa.gov/region01/eco/uep/boston/bprogress.html* for full text of report.

I. Chelsea and East Boston: The need for the Chelsea Creek Comparative Risk Assessment
Both East Boston and Chelsea are low to moderate-income, diverse communities, with a large immigrant base. Both have been disproportionately impacted by industrial development and suffer from a disproportionately low percentage of open space and green space as compared to other communities in the Greater Boston region. The Chelsea Creek runs between Chelsea and East Boston. The Creek is a Designated Port Area, which requires that development along the Creek be reserved for marine industrial uses. The designation does not generally allow for public access or recreational use of any waterfront area; instead, the Creek is host to polluting industry, parking lots, a multi-ton salt pile, and fuel storage for industrial and commercial enterprises. There are also numerous 21E hazardous waste sites along the Creek and abandoned or contaminated property. These all contribute to the negative environmental and public health impacts of Chelsea and East Boston.

The Chelsea Creek Action Group (CCAG), local residents, and other community organizations lack easy access to the scientific information or data that is necessary to validate their claims of environmental pollution and public health threats; and have no access to data on the cumulative impact of the pollution emitted by all of the industries. This data is key when advocating to local, state, and federal agencies to address these problems. CCAG and the EPA sponsored the Chelsea Creek Community Based Comparative Risk Assessment so the East Boston and Chelsea communities could learn more about the environmental, public health, and social concerns they identified as community priorities and to develop strategies to address these issues.

II. The Chelsea Creek Community Based Comparative Risk Assessment (CRA)
CCAG, the East Boston Ecumenical Community Council, and U.S. EPA Region I sponsored a two-year community based Risk Assessment which gave residents of East Boston and Chelsea the opportunity to identify and make recommendations for the improvement of issues of greatest concern in the following three categories: environment, public health, and social issues. Risk Assessments typically inventory pollution and other sources of degradation that impact the quality of life or health of a community. The community based Comparative Risk Assessment that CCAG and the EPA sponsored was unique and innovative because rather than following the technical protocol, residents led the process and determined what they feel are the worst issues in those categories. Community members listed all of their concerns and then narrowed the entire list down to six priorities (three environment concerns, two public health concerns and one social concern): ambient air quality, water quality, open/green space, asthma and respiratory ailments, noise, and traffic. These six areas of concern were examined in a broad context, with attention focused on gathering and analyzing available data, and determining action steps to address some of the problems. With the guidance of residents, a committee of technical experts assessed the issues identified by the community and gathered existing information on each to develop a holistic look at the Chelsea Creek area in Chelsea and East Boston. The experts analyzed the risk of exposure, potential health impacts, and how local, state, and federal agencies and regulations could improve the environmental and public health for Chelsea and East Boston residents.

III. Goals of the Comparative Risk Assessment (CRA)

There were several goals of the Chelsea Creek CRA: 1) to engage local residents and provide them with a baseline of information on potential exposures and risks from targeted environmental, public health, and social issues in East Boston and Chelsea; 2) to serve as a tool to help residents and community organizations understand environmental risks and use the information to prioritize action steps - community groups in East Boston and Chelsea have worked to mitigate environmental health risks for many years; the results of the Chelsea Creek CRA will compliment existing efforts and may also play a role in helping to determine future actions and citizen campaigns; and 3) to engage and inform government agencies (federal, state, and local) about the area and resource needs with the hope that these agencies will dedicate more resources (financial, technical, and staff) to the area.

APPENDIX D:

CUMULATIVE EFFECTS ANALYSIS

Table 1-2. Principles of Cumulative Effects Analysis
(a) **Cumulative effects are caused by the aggregate of past, present and reasonably foreseeable future actions.** The effects of a proposed action on a given resource, ecosystem, and human community include the present and future effects added to the effects that have taken place in the past. Such cumulative effects must also be added to effects (past, present and future) caused by all other actions that affect the same resource.
(b) **Cumulative effect are the total effect including both direct and indirect effects, on a given resource, ecosystem and human community of all actions taken, no matter who (federal, nonfederal or private) has taken the actions.** Individual effects from disparate activities may add up or interact to cause additional effects not apparent when looking at the individual effects one at a time. The additional effects contribute by actions unrelated to the proposed action must be included in the analysis of cumulative effects.
(c) **Cumulative effects need to be analyzed in terms of the specific resource, ecosystem and human community being affected.** Environmental effects are often evaluated from the perspective of the proposed action. Analyzing cumulative effects requires focusing on the resource, ecosystem and human community that may be affected and developing on adequate understanding of how the resources are susceptible to effects.
(d) **It is not practical to analyze the cumulative effects of an action on the universe; the list of environmental effects must focus must focus on those that are truly meaningful.** For cumulative effects analysis to help the decisionmaker and to inform interested parties, it must be limited through scoping to effects that can be evaluated meaningfully. The boundaries for evaluating cumulative effects should be expanded to the point at which the resource is no longer affected significantly or the effects are no longer of interest to affected parties.
(e) **Cumulative effects on a given resource, ecosystem and human community are rarely aligned with political or administrative boundaries.** Resources typically are demarcated according to agency responsibilities, county lines, grazing allotments, or other administrative boundaries. Because natural and sociocultural resources are not usually so aligned, each political entity actually manages only a piece of the affected resource or ecosystem. Cumulative effects analysis on natural systems must use natural ecological boundaries and analysis of human communities must use actual sociocultural boundaries to ensure including all effects.
(f) **Cumulative effects may result from the accumulation of similar effects or the synergistic interaction of different effects.** Repeated actions may cause effects to build up through simple addition (more and cor of the same type of effect), or the same or different action may produce effects that interact to produce cumulative effects greater than the sum of the effects.
(g) **Cumulative effects may last for many years beyond the life of the action that caused the effects.** Some actions cause damage lasting for longer than life of the action itself (e.g., acid mine drainage, radioactive waste contamination, species extinctions). Cumulative effects analysis needs to apply the best science and forecasting techniques to assess potential catastrophic consequences in the future.
(h) **Each affected resource, ecosystem, and human community must be analyzed in terms of its capacity to accommodate additional effects, based on its own time and space parameters.** Analysts tend to think in terms of how the resource, ecosystem, and human community will be modified given the action's development needs. The most effective cumulative effects analysis focuses on what is needed to ensure long-term productivity or sustainability of the resource.

Table 5-3. Primary and Special Methods for Analyzing Cumulative Effects			
Primary Methods	**Description**	**Strengths**	**Weaknesses**
1. Questionnaires, Interviews, and Panels	Questionnaires, interviews, and panels are useful for gathering the wide range of information on multiple actions and resources needed to address cumulative effects. Brainstorming sessions, interviews with knowledgeable individuals, and group consensus building activities can help identify the important cumulative effects issues in the region.	■ Flexible ■ Can deal with subjective information	■ Cannot quantify ■ Comparison of alternatives is subjective
2. Checklists	Checklists help identify potential cumulative effects by providing a list of common or likely effects and juxtaposing multiple actions and resources; potentially dangerous for the analyst that uses them as a shortcut to thorough scoping and conceptualization of cumulative effects problems.	■ Systemic ■ Concise	■ Can be inflexible ■ Do not address interactions or cause-effect or relationships
3. Matrices	Matrices use the familiar tabular format to organize and quantify the interactions between human activities and resources of concern. Once even relatively complex numerical data are obtained, matrices are well-suited to combining the values in individual cells of the matrix (through matrix algebra) to evaluate the cumulative effects of multiple actions on individual resources, ecosystems, and human communities.	■ Comprehensive presentation ■ Comparison of alternatives ■ Address multiple projects	■ Do not address space or time ■ Can be cumbersome ■ Do not address cause-effect relationships
4. Networks and System Diagrams	Networks and system diagrams are an excellent method for delineating the cause-and-effect relationships resulting in cumulative effects; they allow the user to analyze the multiple, subsidiary effects of various actions and trace indirect effects to resources that accumulate from direct effects on other resources.	■ Facilities conceptualization ■ Address cause-effect relationships ■ Identify Indirect relationships	■ No likelihood for secondary effects ■ Problem of comparable units ■ Do not address space or time
5. Modeling	Modeling is a powerful technique for quantifying the cause-and-effect relationships leading to cumulative effects, can take the form of mathematical equations describing equations describing cumulative processes such as soil erosion, or may constitute an expert system that computes the effect of various project scenarios based on a program of logical decisions.	■ Can give unequivocal results ■ Addresses cause-effect relationships ■ Quantification ■ Can integrate time ans space	■ Need a lot of data ■ Can be expensive ■ Intractable with many interactions
6. Trends Analysis	Trends analysis assesses the status of a resource, ecosystem, and human community over time and usually results in a graphical projection of past or future conditions. Changes in the occurrence or intensity of stressors over the same time period can also be determined. Trends can help the analyst identify cumulative effects problems, establish appropriate environmental baselines, or project future cumulative effects.	■ Addresses accumulation over time ■ Problem identification ■ Baseline determination	■ Need a lot of data in relevant system ■ Extrapolation of system thresholds is still largely subjective
7. Overlay Mapping and GIS	Overlay mapping and geographic information systems (GIS) incorporate locational information into cumulative effects analysis and help set the boundaries of the analysis, analyze landscape parameters, and identify areas where effects will be the greatest. Map overlays can be based on either the accumulation of stressors in certain areas or on the suitability of each land unit for development.	■ Addresses spatial pattern and proximity effects ■ Effective visual presentation ■ Can optimize development options	■ Limited to effects based on location ■ Do not explicitly address indirect effects ■ Difficult to address magnitude of effects

Table 5-3. Primary and Special Methods for Analyzing Cumulative Effects			
Primary Methods	**Description**	**Strengths**	**Weaknesses**
8. **Carrying Capacity Analysis**	Carrying capacity analysis identifies thresholds (as constraints on development) and provides mechanisms to monitor the incremental use of unused capacity. Carrying capacity in the ecological context is defined as threshold of stress below which populations and ecosystem functions can be sustained. In the social context, the carrying capacity of a region is measured by the level of services (including ecological services) desired by the populace.	■ True measure of cumulative effects against threshold ■ Addresses effects in system context ■ Addresses time factors	■ Rarely can measure capacity directly ■ May be multiple thresholds ■ Requisite regional data are often absent
9. **Ecosystem Analysis**	Ecosystem analysis explicitly addresses biodiversity and ecosystem and ecosystem sustainability . The ecosystem approach uses natural boundaries (such as watersheds and ecoregions) and applies new ecological indications (such as indices of biotic integrity and landscape pattern). Ecosystem analysis entails the broad regional perspective and holistic thinking that are required for successful cumulative effects analysis.	■ Uses regional scale and full range of components and interactions ■ Addresses space and time ■ Addresses ecosystem sustainability	■ Limited to natural systems ■ Often required species surrogates for system ■ Data intensive ■ Landscape indicators still under development
10. **Economic Impact Analysis**	Economic impact analysis is an important component of analyzing cumulative effects because the economic well-being of a local community depends on many different actions. The three primary steps in conducting an economic impact analysis are (1) establishing the region of influence, (2) modeling the economic effects, and (3) determining the significance of the effects. Economic models play an important role in these impact assessments and range from simple to sophisticated.	■ Addresses economic issues ■ Models provide definitive, quantified results	■ Utility and accuracy of results dependent on data quality and model assumptions ■ Usually do not address nonmarket values
■ **Special Impact Analysis**	Social impact analysis addresses cumulative effects related to the sustainability of human communities by (1) focusing on key social variables such as population characteristics, community and institutional structures, political and social resources, individual and family changes, and community resources; and (2) projecting future effects using social analysis techniques such as linear trend projections, population multiplier methods, scenarios, expert testimony, and simulation modeling.	■ Addresses social issues ■ Models provide definitive, qualified results	■ Utility and accuracy of results dependent on dataquality and model assumptions ■ Social values are highly variable

EPA COMMUNITY-BASED AND PROGRAMMATIC INITIATIVES ADDRESSING COMMUNITY MULTI-MEDIA CONCERNS

EXAMPLES OF EPA-SPONSORED COMMUNITY PROJECTS ADDRESSING MULTIMEDIA CONCERNS

St. Louis Communities Mobilize to Address Environmental Concerns

St. Louis elected itself for cutting-edge community-based environmental management. Through sessions sponsored by EPA Region 7, they identified a number of key environmental matters. The number one issue, identified by nine of ten participants, was the need for healthy air. That was the genesis of three cross-cutting projects. While these projects have a basis in ambient (outdoor) air quality, each project has uniquely integrated health, ambient air, indoor air, pollution prevention, household hazardous waste, water, lead-poisoning and other key environmental health concerns. The projects are complementary to a holistic approach in St. Louis. This results from project leadership that recognizes the assets and challenges of their communities. They have found ways to work in this environmental justice community through obstacles of economics and education. These are innovative leaders that realize, invigorate and reward the community's assets to overcome complex environmental challenges. They have found local 'environmental evangelists' to spread the empowerment for local environmental stewardship. Region 7 is proud to be one of the agents who helped make St. Louis successful in these efforts.

The St. Louis Community Air Project (CAP) is managed by the St. Louis Association of Community Organizations (an community organization that works for neighborhood development, both in its people and housing). The CAP is a coalition of community partners -- individuals, neighborhoods, businesses, industry and government -- whose motto is "Our Goal is Healthier Air for St. Louis." With EPA assistance, this group established health benchmarks and conducted air monitoring for hazardous air pollutants. They determined six chemicals of concern from the air monitoring effort. The CAP is implementing an action plan that has three tiers of effort -- personal (such as choosing appropriate household cleaners or reducing unnecessary car usage), community(working with neighbors or industry to gain voluntary pollution reduction efforts) and public (the traditional regulatory controls). Early on, the CAP realized youth were underutilized resources and change agents. Emily Andrews, the CAP's 'managing partner,' developed materials that could be taken into the classroom to work with students to help them understand how their family activities affected air quality. Inner-city students at Roosevelt High School's Communication Career Academy developed a 13-minute performance art video entitled The Importance of Clean Air. Over 150 copies of this video are in circulation, teaching young (and older) people how they can improve air quality. Ms. Andrews took this video to another partner, the public library system, to establish an education program whose outcome included a bookmark contest. Here students illustrated what actions they believed needed to be taken to create healthier air for St. Louis. The library printed and distributed 5000 copies of the winning bookmarks. The St. Louis CAP is pioneering new ways for people to achieve healthier air for their community.

The North Side Clean Air Project (NSCAP) has taken a different path than most to addressing air quality. They are managed by Grace Hill Neighborhood Services, a local community organization that provides social and health services in severely stressed St. Louis neighborhoods. NSCAP entered this process recognizing that their community did not have the capacity to manage a air monitoring program. They needed to have a hard-hitting, quick results program. Doug Eller, Grace Hill's project manager, has built a unique team that builds upon the assets of this community. Under his guidance, AmeriCorps had developed and operates a river front trail. The Trail Rangers are helping trail visitors and other community groups understand the how human behaviors influence air quality and what actions individuals can take in their homes or in their community to gain healthier air. Residents in these neighborhoods have some of the highest asthma rates and blood-lead levels in the nation. NSCAP is working through local health and day-care providers to help residents reduce their environmental risks. One very creative tools they are using is local entrepreneurship. They are creating a cottage industry that produces an environmentally-safe all purpose cleaner. The cleaner is sold at a price that undercuts the local dollar store and residents will get a free refill – both on product and on environmental education/empowerment.

The Missouri Botanical Garden has a global reputation for environmental stewardship. The charter of this private institution includes education and program development. As EPA was working with the CAP and NSCAP, these partners realized that accessible educational activities about airborne toxics did not exist. The Garden undertook a charge from EPA to provide readily available materials for educators. These materials help students of all ages understand what is in the air and how behaviors impact the air quality and health. Increased knowledge of these issues will influence future decision-making of students and adults, as well as remove misperceptions about the causes of air pollution. All materials are based on research and have received national peer review. Kindergarten to grade 12 modules are correlated to national and Missouri education standards. Each module will include a teacher/leader guide, one lead activity and three or more connecting activities. These activities may be used individually or taught sequentially as a thematic unit. Every module emphasizes how our choices impact human health, using multi-media aspect(connections among air, water and soil). In one lesson, someone might explore brownfield concepts while another explores household hazardous wastes. In the very near future, the modules will be available to the public at no charge. The educational materials were developed with the understanding that while few students go onto to be scientists or engineers, all of us need to become responsible stewards of our environment. Glenda Abney, the Garden's project manager, assembled an outstanding team of educators who created materials that allow a student/adult to explore environmental health concepts through dynamic, engaging reading, art and social science activities.

South Phoenix Multi-Media Toxics Reduction Project

South Phoenix has a history of mixed-use development creating a patchwork of industrial facilities, residential housing, landfills, and commercial enterprises, representing numerous pollution sources. The area, informally identified as south of downtown Phoenix, has a strong African-American heritage. Today the area reflects a predominately Hispanic culture. Key community issues include risks and exposure from chemical fires, air pollution and hazardous waste storage. Region 9's Air Division has targeted the area to pilot a multi-media toxics reductions project.

The South Phoenix Multi-Media Toxics Reduction project responds to OAR's interest in transferring the *Cleveland Air Toxics Project* to other urban areas and applying the new *Guidance For Local Areas to Reduce Toxics Levels*. Region 9 was selected to receive $270 K, secured from OAR and OSWER, to implement a community-based pilot project in South Phoenix, utilizing the above referenced model approaches. These funds have been granted to ADEQ, the lead agency for the multi-media toxics reduction project.

The project builds upon past and ongoing efforts in the area including: permit reviews for PCB facilities; joint state/EPA RCRA compliance inspections for over 40 sites; the Joint Air Toxics Assessment Project including a one-year air toxics monitoring effort in South Phoenix; and other projects related to pollution prevention and TRI enforcement. South Phoenix is also considered a strategic priority for environmental justice.

ADEQ, also has been focusing on South Phoenix as part of their South Phoenix Environmental Initiative. The multi-media toxics reduction project represents the next logical step for Phase II of their work.

In partnership with ADEQ, efforts are underway to initiate a stakeholder process which will:
1) Develop an inventory of toxics sources and set priorities for reduction planning;
2) Identify and implement early reduction activities (e.g. anti-bus idling, lead outreach);
3) Identify actions to reduce toxics (emissions and exposures) as part of community toxics reduction plan;
4) Implement actions utilizing an array of tools (P2, EMSs, technology, compliance, regulation, etc.) that will result in reduced toxics emissions from air, water and waste.

ADEQ, in collaboration with the City of Phoenix, Maricopa County, AZ Department of Health Services has submitted a detail work plan, outlining the goals, objectives and strategic approaches to ensure a comprehensive, inclusive process for toxics reduction planning.

To better coordinate EPA's activities and technical assistance, a cross-divisional group has been formed. Representatives from Air, Waste (RCRA and P2), Superfund, Cross-Media Division, and OPPA (Children's Health) participate on this group. EPA Headquarters is also engaged in the project with representatives form OAR (ORIA, OTAQ, OAQPS) and OPPTS coordinating with Region 9 on monthly conference calls.

Concurrently with this project, the JATAP has initiated a one-year air toxics monitoring pilot in the greater South Phoenix area and will have data available in the spring of 2004.

Chelsea Creek Community-Based Comparative Risk Assessment

The Chelsea Creek Action Group (CCAG), the East Boston Ecumenical Community Council, and EPA New England's Urban Environmental Program led a two-year effort to conduct a first of its kind community-based comparative risk assessment to engage, inform and involve residents of East Boston and Chelsea, MA to understand and address the greatest multi-media environmental, public health, and social issues of concern. A grant from EPA provided $100,000 to implement the project. The Chelsea Creek Community-Based Comparative Risk Assessment was unique and innovative because rather than following a standard risk assessment process, residents and nonprofit groups had input and involvement into identifying the key issues of concern and worked with technical experts to gather data, analyze results, and identify next steps for action. A public process engaging hundreds of local residents and volunteers surveyed community concerns and public meetings narrowed the list of concerns down to six priorities for the project: 3 environmental concerns (ambient air quality, water quality, and open/green space); 2 public health concerns (asthma/respiratory disease and noise); and 1 social issue (traffic). These six issues were examined in a broad context by a Resident Advisory Committee (comprised of 10 resident volunteers from East Boston and Chelsea) and a Technical Advisory Committee (comprised of 10 scientific and technical experts from academia, local, state, federal government, and health professionals) with effort focused on gathering and analyzing available data, identifying greatest public health concerns for residents, mapping available data, identifying current projects addressing the issue on a neighborhood level, and making a set of recommendations on how to address problems and concerns identified. The overall goals of the project included: (a) engage local residents and provide a baseline of information on potential exposures and risks from targeted environmental, public health, and social issues in East Boston and Chelsea, MA; (b) serve as a tool to help residents and community organizations understand environmental risks and use the information to prioritize action steps through local nonprofit groups; and (c) engage and inform government agencies (federal, state and local) about the area, issues, and resource needs with the hope of securing additional investments to service community needs. Each chapter of the Community-Based Comparative Risk Assessment yielded specific data results, but a few general themes emerged as summary findings: (1) Data on environmental and public health issues in Chelsea and East Boston is insufficient; (2) Even when local data exists, the quality is unacceptable; (3) Current federal, state, and local regulations do not adequately protect the health of urban residents or the quality of the local environment; (4) Actions are needed from local, state and federal government agencies to address data gaps, information quality, and making measurable progress on all issues; and (5) Actions are needed from local residents to hold government agencies accountable for their roles and to make improvements on issues. As a result of this effort, the Chelsea Creek Action Group has secured a commitment from EPA New England to convene a multi-agency stakeholder group representing federal, state and local government to coordinate government actions and resource investments to improve the quality of life for residents in East Boston and Cheslea related to the Chelsea Creek.

EXAMPLES OF INNOVATIVE EPA PROGRAMMATIC INITIATIVES
TO ADDRESS MULTIMEDIA COMMUNITY CONCERNS

<u>Urban Environmental Program</u>

The Urban Environmental Program (UEP) was first initiated as a regional pilot program in EPA New England in 1995, and was expanded into a full regionally-designed program by Administrator Robert Varney in 2002. In urban areas throughout New England, local residents are exposed to significant environmental and public health hazards every day and these conditions create cumulative, disproportionate, and inequitable health risks - especially high risks and sensitive populations including children and the elderly. The mission of the UEP is to improve the environment and enhance the quality of life for urban residents throughout New England, with a special emphasis on servicing the needs of urban residents in Massachusetts, Rhode Island, and Connecticut. Since this is a regional program, it is only operational in EPA New England and there are no counterparts across the country in other EPA regions. UEP Program Goals are to: (1) Build community capacity to assess and resolve environmental problems; (2) Achieve measurable and sustainable improvements in urban communities; and (3) Restore and revitalize neighborhoods for urban residents. The UEP strategy for improving environmental quality and public health is the UEP Community Development Pyramid, which outlines a five-phase model to develop an infrastructure and community capacity for achieving long term results. The five phases are: (1) Understanding the problem and identifying stakeholders; (2) Building community capacity and developing local partnerships; (3) Leveraging public resources to improve public health and the environment; (4) Effective Partnerships; and (5) Healthy Communities. The target issues for the UEP include: (1) Environmental Health (childhood lead poisoning, asthma, indoor air quality, children's health and sensitive receptors/populations); (2) Urban Toxics in Air, Water and Soil (lead, PCBs, dioxin, mercury, petroleum, combined sewer overflows/bacteria, Cr6, particulate matter, and ozone); and (3) Urban Development & Redevelopment (vacant lots, urban agriculture, smart growth, transportation, open space/green space). The program strategy and goals are achieved through a package of UEP services that are available to communities in targeted urban areas. UEP Program Managers are dedicated staff which serve as community liaisons and resource brokers to bring EPA New England services and resources (technical resources, expertise, funding, etc.) to targeted urban areas. UEP Program managers are responsible for implementing the UEP Community Development Pyramid through partnerships and coalition-building, building community capacity and consensus, public awareness and education, environmental revitalization, improving public health, problem-solving, facilitation, conflict-resolution, and grant/project management. The UEP also runs an annual, competitive grant program to identify and fund eligible applicants to complete projects in target urban areas across New England. For more information about the program, please visit our website at www.epa.gov/region01/eco/uep or read the "Agents of Change: Making the Vision a Reality" Urban Environmental Initiative Five Year Report, 2001.

<u>Community Action for a Renewed Environment (CARE)</u>

Many cities, towns and neighborhoods continue to express concerns about their exposure to toxic pollutants from multiple sources. While EPA's regulatory programs have significantly reduced the overall exposure to toxic pollutants across the country, there is still more to be done to reduce risks at the local level in communities.

CARE is a proposed multi-media effort designed to reduce toxic pollutants in communities through community-based projects similar to those underway in Cleveland, St. Louis, and South Phoenix. As these projects demonstrate, community-based approaches are an effective way of addressing diffuse sources of toxic pollutants and cumulative risk by addressing issues comprehensively, and by targeting solutions to the specific characteristics and needs of the community. CARE will encourage and support communities' efforts to focus resources on the greatest risks and build consensus to mobilize local resources to reduce exposures to toxic pollutants. CARE will build on the wide range of current Agency efforts designed to address community concerns such as Diesel Retrofits, Brownfields, the National Estuary Program, Design for Environment, Environmental Justice Revitalization Projects, Tools for Schools, and RGI, improving their effectiveness by working to integrate them to better meet the needs of communities

The proposed CARE program will provide competitive grants to state, tribal and local governments, NGOs, and community organizations. Two categories of competitive grants will be awarded. In the first category, EPA will provide smaller grants ($50-$100k) to communities to help them assess their toxic-exposure problems and begin to identify potential solutions. EPA will help work with the grantees to create environmental toxic reduction partnerships, assess the sources of exposure to toxic pollutants, and estimate the most significant sources of human health and ecological risks in the community. The expectation is that after completing the grant the community would have developed the capacity to select and carry out their highest priority activities to reduce risks.

The second category of larger grants ($300-$500k) will help the communities go beyond planning and start to reduce risks. The grants will provide seed money to implement community-based projects that show actual risk reductions. Communities receiving these grant will have identified and will understand the sources of exposure to toxic pollutants in the community and have the organizational capacity to begin implementing risk reduction activities. Many of the communities that will be eligible for these grants are already working in partnership with EPA through other place-based programs. We hope that over time many of the communities that develop capacity with the first set of grants would become eligible for this second set of grants.

The initiative will be managed by a central team that will provide analytic tools and models to assist communities in identifying, prioritizing and reducing risks. It will also conduct training and hold conferences, as needed, to educate community members and share lessons learned. Finally, the team will collect and aggregate results provided by the specific projects and conduct program evaluations to assess the resulting benefits and lessons learned. The Regions will have teams that work directly with the communities to provide needed support and information.

Environmental Justice Collaborative Problem-Solving Grant Program

The Environmental Justice Collaborative Problem-Solving Grant Program provides financial assistance to community-based organizations to undertake community-based efforts to proactively and strategically address environmental justice issues through collaborative problem-solving methods. The program was initiated in in FY2003 by the EPA Office of Environmental Justice (OEJ) with a Request for Applications from community-based organizations, of which 15 have been selected for financial assistance in the amount of $100,000 each. Another round of 15 will be selected in FY2004.

The concepts behind this grant program were developed over the past several years through the Federal

Interagency Working Group on Environmental Justice demonstration projects. Through these projects, OEJ developed the concept of an environmental justice collaborative problem-solving model, which describes community-based, multi-agency, and multi-stakeholder efforts to achieve environmental justice and healthy, sustainable communities. The model is based upon a set of premises which includes but is not limited to the following: (1) Seeking proactive, strategic, community-based solutions to environmental justice issues, building on community visioning and planning processes; (2) Promoting an asset-building approach to building community capacity and social capital, particularly for disadvantaged and underserved communities; (3) Incorporating consensus building and dispute resolution principles and methods, including the "Mutual Gains Approach to Negotiations"; (4) Utilizing community-based participatory research methodologies; (5) Establishing multi-stakeholder partnerships to leverage human, organization, technical, and financial resources; (6) Fostering an integrated approach to addressing environmental, health, social, and economic needs; (7) Promoting multi-agency coordination to effectively utilize resources of all relevant federal, state, tribal, and local government agencies; and (8) Integrating an evaluation framework and promotes replication of lessons learned and best practices.

One community-based effort which has provided much insight for the development of this model is the the ReGenesis Revitalization Project in Spartanburg, South Carolina. The ReGenesis Project has transformed the focus in a poor, African American community in Spartanburg from one that focused primarily on negative environmental impacts to a vision for broad community revitalization. As of August 2003, the project has leveraged more than $5 million in public and private sector funding.

APPENDIX F:

EPA SCREENING AND ASSESSMENT TOOLS FOR
ADDRESSING COMMUNITY CONCERNS

Tool	Description
Regional Air Impact Modeling Initiative (RAIMI)	The U.S. Environmental Protection Agency (EPA), Region 6, established the Regional Air Impact Modeling Initiative (RAIMI) to evaluate the potential for health impacts as a result of exposure to multiple contaminants from multiple sources, at a community level of resolution. It is a practical approach for implementing cumulative type assessments on a localized scale. Often when evaluating permitting and enforcement actions, EPA needs to consider the bigger picture as opposed to the traditional source-by-source, program-by-program approach. Such an approach has blindly focused on selective units, often located among a "forest" of others impacting the same receptor neighborhoods. As a result, goals of RAIMI focused on developing the capability to conduct localized assessments in a timely enough manner so as to actually be useful in day-to-day permitting and enforcement activities, that would obviously support cross-program participation, and that would provide results at a level of resolution and traceability that serve as an asset to stakeholders needing to evaluate and implement solutions. Contact Jeff Yurk at yurk.jeff@epa.gov.
Cumulative Risk Index Analysis	Region 6 has developed a multi-purpose environmental screening tool using data from all EPA's major databases and our regional Geographic Information System (GIS) technology. The system is used to compare human health, ecological, and regulatory related risks. The system has also proven to be very effective at identifying cumulative risks. Approximately 90 environmental criteria have been developed for the Region's risk screening system. Forty-five of these criteria have been used to identify multi-media inspection targets. The enforcement targeting application has significantly contributed to inspection success rates of 70 to 100 percent in the past two years. The Comparative Cumulative Risk System has been used for more than 6,500 environmental justice (EJ) analyses in our Region, and has become a standard for communicating EJ information. All our cumulative risk evaluations include EJ and can include approximately 20 other related socio-economic criteria. The system is routinely used in the National Environmental Policy Act (NEPA) program as a environmental screening tool evaluating possible ecological stressors, sources of pollutants impacting human health, cultural resource concerns, populations who are vulnerable for socio-economic reasons (income, education, language), and regulatory compliance issues (inspections, fines, violations). Contact Gerald Carney at carney.gerald@epa.gov.

Tool	Description
Environmental Load Profile	Through the use of geospatial software and environmental databases, EPA Region 2 has advanced the concept of an Environmental Load Profile (ELP). The ELP provides a representation of the environmental load (i.e. relative burden) within a selected community. Further, it serves as a screening tool for identifying communities that may bear disproportionate environmental loads on a statewide level. The product serves to identify salient characteristics (e.g., indicators of air quality, environmental well-being) that would serve as indicators of environmental burden, and further provide the user with a consistent basis for comparison. Specifically, the indicators of a community are compared to statewide-derived benchmarks in deciding whether a selected community bears more of an environmental load than the rest of the state. Currently, the ELP consists of the following derived indicators: TRI Air Emission; Air Toxics; and Facility Density. As additional indicators are developed, they will be incorporated into the ELP. While the product is useful as an initial start in identifying areas experiencing environmental concerns, the user should note that a more detailed investigation for a community's actual burden should, where appropriate, be conducted at the local level. Finally, the tool further allows the user to obtain a summary report of all the indicator values calculated for a specific community. These summary reports open through an Internet-based browser (e.g., Netscape 6.2) Although the ELP tool is a stand-alone product, it can be particularly useful as it compliments the efforts/results obtained when performing an EPA Region 2 environmental justice analysis using another Region 2 GIS application titled, Environmental Justice Demographic Screening Tool. Contact Roland Hemmett at hemmett.roland@epa.gov.
Community Air Screening How To Manual	EPA's Office of Pollution Prevention and Toxics has developed a step-by-step guide to help communities complete all of the tasks needed to understand and improve local outdoor air quality. The Manual explains how to form a partnership, clarify goals, develop a detailed local source inventory, use a risk-based screening process to identify priorities, and develop options for reducing risks from priority sources and concentrations. Communities using the How To Manual will get the education and the consensus building process they need to mobilize local resources for voluntary actions that can be used to supplement statutory requirements to address community concerns. The How To Manual is a tool designed to support the Agency's new community-based initiatives to address toxics concerns at the local level. The Manual can help communities address concerns about aggregate ambient air concentrations resulting from multiple sources, both stationary and mobile. Environmental justice communities with concerns about air quality may find this Manual especially helpful. The Community Air Screening How To Manual has now completed both internal and external peer review and will be published in the spring, 2004. Contact David Lynch at lynch.david@epa.gov.

Tool	Description
Risk Screening Environmental Indicators (RSEI)	RSEI is a screening tool that compares toxic chemicals released to the environment from industrial sources. RSEI allows communities to examine rankings and trends, and set priorities for further action. Information can be sorted in numerous ways such as by chemical, media, geographic areas, etc. RSEI is a fast and effective tool that uses risk concepts to quickly and easily screen large amounts of data, saving time and resources. RSEI users can perform, in a matter of minutes or hours, a variety of screening-level analyses. Previously, such activities would have taken days, weeks, or even months to organize the relevant information, evaluate that information, and perform the complex and sophisticated analyses that are necessary to provide a risk-related perspective. RSEI is particularly useful for examining trends to measure change, ranking and prioritizing chemicals and industry sectors for strategic planning, conducting risk-related targeting, supporting community-based projects, and investigating environmental justice issues. Considerable resources can be saved by conducting preliminary analyses with the model to identify risk-related situations of high potential concern, and which warrant further evaluation. Contact Richard Engler at engler.richard@epa.gov.
Environmental Justice Geographic Assessment Tool	The Environmental Justice Geographic Assessment Tool is an innovative access tool, which offers a new approach to assessing and addressing potential allegations of environmental justice. Through an extensive Geographic Information System (GIS) interface, this easy-to-use application provides community-specific information that are available nationwide. Developed jointly by the EPA Office of Environmental Information and Office of Environmental Justice, the tool provides information relevant to any area in the continental United States with potential or existing environmental justice concerns. Once fully developed, the tool will provide information necessary to conduct a robust preliminary analysis of EJ-related factors in any area of concern, with the goal of taking action (whether programmatic or regulatory in nature) to address any environmental justice concern that may arise. This tool is meant to serve as a module to be incorporated at the front end (e.g., screening) of all appropriate Agency assessments. The tools is an online resource system that (1) allows for interactive mapping, zooming and viewing locations of regulated facilities, environmental monitoring sites, bodies of water, as well as land use, community demographics, streets, schools, and hospitals; (2) obtains and catalogs information from several sources such as EPA, USGS, U.S. Census, CDC, and NCHS; and (3) combines environmental, social, economic, and health indicators in a profile that provides a table of calculated statistics of the selected area of interest. Contact Charles Lee at lee.charles@epa.gov.

APPENDIX G:

EXAMPLES OF AVAILABLE RISK AND POLLUTION REDUCTION PROGRAMS AND APPROACHES

Program Type	Program Description	Web Site or Point of Contact
For Large Community Businesses and Public Facilities	**Identifying Pollution Prevention Opportunities** Encourage large chemical, refining, and manufacturing facilities to institute voluntary pollution prevention programs. Encourage companies to conduct audits to identify pollution prevention opportunities. Identify national industry sector leaders to use as benchmarks for local companies. Organize a community team with independent expertise to help facilities identify pollution prevention opportunities.	http://cfpub.epa.gov/clearinghouse/index.cfm http://www.epa.gov/compliance/assistance/sectors/index.html http://www.epa.gov/opptintr/p2home/resources/index.htm
For Small Community Businesses	**Design for Environment Program** EPA partnership program working with individual industry sectors to compare and improve the performance and human health and environmental risks and costs of existing and alternative products, processes, and practices. DfE partnership projects promote integrating cleaner, cheaper, and smarter solutions into everyday business practices. Partnership programs include auto refinishing, printing and publishing, and dry-cleaning businesses.	http://www.epa.gov/dfe/projects/auto/index.htm http://www.epa.gov/dfe/projects/flexo/index.htm http://www.epa.gov/dfe/projects/gravure/index.htm http://www.epa.gov/dfe/projects/litho/index.htm http://www.epa.gov/dfe/projects/screen/index.htm http://www.epa.gov/dfe/projects/garment/index.htm
	Environmental Results Program An innovative program designed to assist businesses to improve their performance and address environmental problems. In the Environmental Results Program communities and regulating agencies can combine resources to educate businesses about their environmental impacts and obligations, help them to certify their compliance, and track them to evaluate their environmental performance.	http://www.epa.gov/permits/masserp.htm http://www.epa.gov/compliance/incentives/innovations/programresults.html

Program Type	Program Description	Web Site or Point of Contact
	Greenbusiness Program Organize a program like the Bay Area Green Business Program, a partnership of community organizations, environmental agencies, professional associations, waste management agencies, and utilities to work together to recognize and assist businesses that operate in an environmentally friendly manner.	http://www.abag.ca.gov/bayarea/enviro/gbus/gb.html
	Businesses for the Bay Create a voluntary organization of businesses, like the Businesses for the Bay organization in the Chesapeake Bay watershed, committed to helping each other implement pollution prevention in daily operations and reduce releases of chemical contaminants and other wastes to your watershed.	http://www.chesapeakebay.net/b4bay.htm
	Stationary Source Pollution Prevention Fact sheets for Communities and Small Businesses Multiple fact sheets on topics such as metal operations, electroplating, autobody paint shops, and printers. Includes information designed to help communities identify pollution prevention and reduction opportunities for small businesses. Designed to provide concrete assistance to help small shops implement easy pollution prevention measures and reduce releases of air toxics. Fact sheets now in final production.	Contact Amanda Aldridge at Aldridge.Amanda@epa.gov
For Schools	**Tools for Schools** EPA voluntary, easy-to-use resource kit to help schools identify, remedy, and prevent indoor air quality problems in a cost effective manner. Schools implement a range of specific guidelines emphasizing reduced pesticide exposure use, safe chemical storage, proper ventilation, and more.	http://www.epa.gov/iaq/schools/
	Clean School Bus USA Brings together partners from business, education, transportation, and public health organizations to work to reduce pollution from public school buses. Includes policies and practices to eliminate unnecessary idling, retrofit buses with newer control technologies, and replace older buses.	http://www.epa.gov/otaq/schoolbus/
For Mobile Sources	**Voluntary Diesel Retrofit Program** Develop a program to retrofit older diesel engines with modern emission control technology. Enlist private and/or public fleets for participation.	http://www.epa.gov/otaq/retrofit/

Program Type	Program Description	Web Site or Point of Contact
	Anti-Idling Campaigns Develop education campaign and administrative policies to discourage vehicle idling in areas where people congregate.	
	Vehicle Engine and Maintenance Campaigns Sponsor a campaign to encourage proper vehicle and engine maintenance. Could involve a "tune your car today: at a local garage; checklists and parts giveaways for do-it-yourselfers, etc.	
For Community Surface Waters	**Fish Consumption Surveys and Advisories** Perform surveys to determine whether there should be more fish/wildlife consumption advisories. Make advisories widely available to the public by print, radio, or television in multiple languages with an emphasis on subpopulations with high expected consumption.	http://www.epa.gov/waterscience/fish/
	Watershed Protection A Watershed Protection Approach is a strategy for effectively protecting and restoring aquatic ecosystems and protecting human health. This strategy has as its premise that many water quality and ecosystem problems are best solved at the watershed level rather than at the individual waterbody or discharger level. Major features of a Watershed Protection Approach are: targeting priority problems, promoting a high level of stakeholder involvement, integrated solutions that make use of the expertise and authority of multiple agencies, and measuring success through monitoring and other data gathering.	http://www.epa.gov/owow/watershed/index2.html
	Mercury Reduction in Hospitals Help hospitals comply with new requirements by providing information and assistance. Encourage hospitals to eliminate mercury sources such as thermometers. Conduct education programs for citizens and hospital staff about mercury reduction.	http://www.noharm.org/mercury/issue
	Household Mercury Thermometer Exchanges Sponsor a trade-in program that provides citizens with new, non-toxic thermometers in exchange for mercury thermometers to reduce risk of mercury contamination in homes and to reduce the risk of water contamination and outdoor air pollution due to improper disposal.	http://www.noharm.org/mercury/issue

Program Type	Program Description	Web Site or Point of Contact
	National Estuary Program The National Estuary Program is designed to encourage local communities to take responsibility for managing their own estuaries. Each NEP is made up of representatives from federal, state and local government agencies responsible for managing the estuary's resources, as well as members of the community -- citizens, business leaders, educators, and researchers. These stakeholders work together to identify problems in the estuary, develop specific actions to address those problems, and create and implement a formal management plan to restore and protect the estuary.	http://www.epa.gov/owow/estuaries/about2.htm
	Coastal America Coastal America is a unique partnership of federal agencies, state and local governments, and private organizations. The partners work together to protect, preserve, and restore our nation's coasts.	http://www.coastalamerica.gov/
For Community Homes	**Develop a Community Campaign using Home*A*Syst** Home*A*Syst is an environmental risk assessment guide for the home that helps homeowners identify risks and take actions to protect health and the environment. Organize a community education campaign using the Home*A*Syst program and materials.	http://www.hud.gov/offices/lead/helpyourself/index.cfm
	Radon "Test and Repair" Campaigns Enlist citizens to test their home for radon and provide information and assistance to correct the problem if radon levels are unacceptably high.	http://www.epa.gov/iaq/radon/
	Home Consumer Products Education Campaigns Educate citizens in practices they can adopt such as proper solvent storage, vehicle operation tips, landscaping and yardcare options to minimize use of pesticides and polluting equipment, use of lower toxicity home products, etc.	

Program Type	Program Description	Web Site or Point of Contact
	Low Emission Gas Can Exchanges Emissions from portable fuel cans present a significant source of exposure to gaseous toxics such as benzene, especially if the can is stored inside a dwelling or attached garage. Encourage citizens to exchange their old-style containers for new ones meeting higher standards.	http://www.arb.ca.gov/msprog/spill con/gascanfs/gascanfs.htm
	Campaign for a Lead Safe America Protect community children with an education and testing program to reduce exposure to lead in homes and soil.	http://www.hud.gov/offices/lead/ou treach/communityoutreach.cfm#lea dsafehome
	Lead in Drinking Water Campaigns Approximately 20% of human exposure to lead is attributable to lead in drinking water. Provide education about ways to reduce exposure to lead in drinking water.	http://www.epa.gov/OGWDW/Pubs /lead1.html
	National Asthma Public Education and Prevention Campaigns Conduct an education campaign in schools and homes to reduce asthma and to increase the asthma awareness and asthma triggers.	http://www.epa.gov/asthma/
	Integrated Pest Management Programs Integrated pest management (IPM) uses habitat modification, biological controls, and chemical controls. IPM protects people from noxious pests and toxic pesticides. Conduct a community Integrated Pest Management (IPM) Education Campaign.	http://schoolipm.ifas.ufl.edu/ http://www.epa.gov/pesticides/
	Household Hazardous Waste Collections Exposure to hazardous household materials can be significantly reduced by collecting old and unused products and disposing of them properly. Conduct a neighborhood drive to collect pesticides, coolants, lubricants, solvents, and other hazardous products, some of which are now banned due to their toxicity.	http://www.epa.gov/epaoswer/non- hw/muncpl/hhw.htm
	Smoke Free Homes and Cars Campaigns Making homes and cars smoke-free are an easy and proven ways to protect nonsmokers from secondhand smoke exposure. Conduct a smoke-free campaign using existing materials, including television, radio, and print PSAs, smoke-free home brochures, and the toll-free pledge number, and other materials.	http://www.epa.gov/smokefree/inde x.html

APPENDIX H:

IMPACTS OF ECONOMIC, RACIAL, AND
SOCIAL INEQUALITY ON HEALTH

The following was prepared by H. Patricia Hynes and Russ Lopez (Boston University School of Public Health) in December 2003.

ECONOMIC

Poverty results in greater illness, injury and mortality. The stresses and health impacts of being poor, which are particularly suffered by pregnant women, infants, children and the elderly, are well documented in public health literature.

Economic disparities or the degree of economic inequality has significant impact on health, and may be more significant that absolute poverty, according to the studies assembled by Richard Wilkinson in *Unhealthy Societies*. The reasons given for why increases in income inequality result in increased health disparities are three-fold:

1. **Growing inequality** results in **increased poverty**. A major study of industrialized countries found strong correlation between income inequality and rates of child poverty, with the United States being highest in both.

2. **Greater inequality** is associated with a **shift of resources** (through tax rates and tax breaks) from the poor to the better off, resulting in fewer social services and benefits for the poor. The consequence is that the poor get poorer and sicker.

3. A seeming counterintuitive finding in a number of studies is that societies that have higher economic inequality also have higher mortality rates among the wealthy classes as well as among the poor. For example, the degree of income inequality among U.S. states is the best predictor of mortality rate, a better predictor than absolute poverty. Homicide rates correlate with economic inequality in U.S. states.

4. **Economically unequal** societies and communities have **weaker social cohesion**, a precursor to increased illness and death. They are more vulnerable by way of being less prepared and less able to recover from crises.

If we don't understand this, we concentrate on poverty and don't look at the power structure. The economist and Nobel Prize winner Amartya Sen argues that, historically, growth has not resulted in better health for the poor. Reducing disparities has.

Economic Isolation: Associated with growing inequality is an increasing isolation of the poor. The phenomenon of communities opposing multi-family housing and affordable housing joined with suburbanization and the growth of gated communities have combined to place poorer people further away from the non-poor. This allows a concentration of risk and reinforces the consequences of poverty outlined above. Furthermore, some sociologists such as Douglas Massey theorize that the isolation of the poor allows the non-poor to ignore the problems of poverty or even to deny the existence of the poor. Neighborhoods with high percentages of poor people have higher levels of infant mortality, increased risk of avoidable deaths associated with crime and violence, and a greater chance that they will bear a disproportionate burden of the environmental costs of contemporary society. (See also Diez-Roux)

RACE

Race, independent of poverty, is also a determinant in health. Racial disparities in health exist throughout the United States and have been measured (or can be) for the following illnesses and health indicators: lead poisoning, asthma prevalence and emergency room visits, life expectancy, and specific diseases.

Racial segregation is also implicated in higher rates of illness, greater exposure to toxic substances, poorer services and fewer resources. More highly segregated African Americans tend to live in higher poverty census tracts with lower quality of medical care, more discriminatory care, and greater social inequality all of which are associated with higher stress and higher blood pressure (Polednak). A study of 1990 exposures found that African Americans were breathing air with higher total modeled air toxics concentrations than Whites in every large metropolitan area in the United States; moreover, the more highly segregated the area, the higher the air toxics levels (Lopez). In an update using 2000 data, this relationship between segregation and air toxics exposure was found to extend to Hispanics and Asians as well as Blacks, and to describe a pattern of disproportionate exposure by race and ethnicity in metropolitan areas regardless of size.

Some public health studies on the health status of minority groups, such as Multicultural Health: The Health Status of Minority Groups in Connecticut, have been conducted and others are in progress. They are important for revealing health disparities within local populations and can be combined with census data and measures of vulnerability such as income inequality and racial segregation to reveal those communities most vulnerable by factors of injury, illness and death; poverty; minority status; segregation and isolation.

SOCIAL INEQUALITY AND HEALTH DISPARITIES

There is a rich literature on the social determinants of health that makes a compelling case for the role of social factors in significantly affecting the health of a community. These social factors include poverty, unemployment, poor nutrition, housing and transportation, deprivation in early childhood, lack of control over one's life, and poor social relations. Researchers in the field have concluded that health disparities within populations are most commonly caused by environmental factors, where environment includes the social (e.g., gender, income, race, status in work/unemployment and status in society, etc.); built (e.g., housing, proximity to locally undesirable land uses) and physical (e.g., proximity to pollution).

Examples of findings from studies collected and undertaken, in some cases, by Marmot and Wilkinson include the following. The longer the time that people live in poverty and in isolated, disadvantaged circumstances (such as highly segregated and marginalized communities), the more likely they are to have a range of health problems, particularly heart disease. Life expectancy is lower for people who are poorer, lower in the workplace hierarchy, less educated, suffer more stress, have less control over their lives, and experience discrimination such as racism. Health, they conclude, follows a social gradient; and policy initiatives to improve health and healthful living conditions must strive to reduce the burden of inequality.

CONCLUSION

Linking these public health and social science findings to the *science of vulnerability*, we conclude that people and communities which are disproportionately exposed to and burdened with a host of social, environmental, and health inequalities, including poverty, discrimination by race and ethnicity, unemployment, toxic exposures, and health disparities are excessively exposed (in the present and past), more susceptible to future exposures, less prepared to ward off the health consequences, and less able to recover from the debilitating effects. The greater and longer duration of the burdens, the more vulnerable—by every aspect of vulnerability—are individuals and communities to a host of diseases and lower life expectancy.

DATA SOURCES

The **census** provides data on income levels, race, gender and ethnicity, housing, and food security at all geographic areas of interest (very local to regional and national levels). **Federal, state and local public health agencies** collect health data on a regular basis through numerous **surveys, registries**, such as the cancer registry, through birth and death certificates, and through **surveillance** programs, such as state lead programs and emerging asthma programs. We acknowledge the shortcomings of the census and public health data, particularly for Native Americans, immigrant, homeless and very poor people. Local pilot projects and studies, undertaken by trusted community organizations in partnership with the EPA and public health regional offices, may be a better source of this information.

Indices

Income inequality is measured by the **GINI Index** on a scale of 0 to 100. This measure of economic inequality is available at different geographic levels from country to state and metropolitan areas, using standard databases such as the census and UN economic data. It is possible to incorporate the GINI Index into a screening tool at the national level to identify states and metropolitan areas most unequal by income and to join this score with others such as racial dissimilarity (discussed in next section) in order to identify vulnerable metropolitan areas (that is, vulnerable by weakened ability to cope with and recover from crises, such as pollution, natural disasters, loss of services, etc.)

Racial segregation is measured by the **Dissimilarity Index** on a scale of 0 to 100. The DI can be described as the proportion of a group that would have to move in order to achieve complete integration. There is an extensive literature on the Dissimilarity Index and it has been calculated, at least for African Americans, since the 19th Century in some large metropolitan areas. Used usually to characterize residential segregation, it is also used to describe school segregation. (See Massey and Denton)

Application for a Screening Tool for Cumulative Risk

Methods involving color coding or qualitative ranking (high, medium, low) from scores could be used in a screening process to identify the communities within EPA regions most burdened by low income and extreme income inequality, racism, racial segregation. The EPA databases on air pollution and hazardous waste and national and regional public health data would be combined with the social indicators of inequality to capture the communities within regions with the highest cumulative risk.

Alternatively, these indices could be combined into an overall measure of disparity in a methodology that uses mean values and standard deviations from the mean and that allows differences in scale to be accommodated. The scores would be joined with EPA data and public health data to identify areas of highest overall risk.

SOURCES

Ana Diez-Roux. Invited Commentary: Places, People, and Health. *American Journal of Epidemiology*. March 15, 2002 . Volume 155, Number 6, Pages 516-9.

Russell Lopez. Segregation and Black/White Differences to Air Toxics in 1990. Environmental Health Perspectives. April 2002. Volume 110 Supplement 2, Pages 289-295.

Douglas Massey. The Age of Extremes: Concentrated Affluence and Poverty in the Twenty-First Century. *Demography*. Population Association of America. November 1996. Volume 33, Number 4, Pages 395-412

Douglas Massey and Nancy Denton. American Apartheid: Segregation and the Making of the Underclass. 1993. Harvard University Press. Cambridge, MA.

Multicultural Health: The Health Status of Minority Groups in Connecticut. 1999. Connecticut Department of Public Health. Prepared by Margaret Hynes et al.

Anthony Polednak. Segregation, Discrimination and Mortality in U.S. Blacks. *Ethnicity and Disease*. Winter/Spring 1996. Volume 6, Pages 99-105.

Richard Wilkinson. Unhealthy Societies: The Afflictions of Inequality. 1996. Routledge. London.

Richard Wilkinson and Michael Marmot, Eds.. Social Determinants of Health: The Solid Facts. 2003. World Health Organization.

APPENDIX I:

CASE STUDY OF COMMUNITY-BASED STUDY OF VULNERABILITY
(WEACT-COLUMBIA UNIVERSITY PARTNERSHIP)

The following discussion was prepared by Darryl Hood (Meharry Medical College) and extracted, in part, from an article entitled, "The Challenge of Preventing Environmentally Related Disease in Young Children: Community-Based Research in New York City" The authors are Frederica P. Perera, Susan M. Illman, Patrick L. Kinney, Robin M. Whyatt, Elizabeth A. Kelvin, David Evans, Mindy Fullilove, Jean Ford, Rachel L. Miller, Ilan H. Meyer, and Virginia A. Rauh of Columbia Center for Children's Environmental Health, Mailman School of Public Health, Columbia University; and Peggy Shepard, West Harlem Environmental Action, Inc.

The Columbia Center for Children's Environmental Health (CCCEH) studied the health effects of exposure to several common urban air pollutants in a cohort of over 500 African-American and Dominican (originally from the Dominican Republic) mothers and children residing in three low-income neighborhoods in New York City: Washington Heights, Harlem, and the South Bronx. The center's mission is to identify prenatal and postnatal exposures that increase children's risk for asthma and other respiratory disorders, neurocognitive and behavioral disorders, and cancer risk, so that the most harmful exposures can be reduced or eliminated.

Molecular epidemiologic methods were used to study the correlation between levels of exposure effects found in personal and indoor/outdoor air monitoring samples, biologic samples (i.e., maternal blood and urine, umbilical cord blood, meconium, and children's blood at 2 years of age), neurodevelopmental assessment results, and questionnaire responses. Psychosocial stressors and nutritional deficits were measured as potential effect modifiers. This comprehensive data collection, repeated at regular time intervals from in utero through 3 years of age, afforded CCCEH researchers the ability to determine prenatal and postnatal levels of exposure that may increase children's risk of the outcomes under study.

The center measured exposure to a range of air contaminants that are common in Washington Heights, Harlem, and the South Bronx: particulate matter < 2.5 • m in aerodynamic diameter (PM2.5), polycyclic aromatic hydrocarbons (PAHs), diesel exhaust particulate (DEP), nitrogen oxide, nonpersistent pesticides (NPPs), home allergens (dust mite, mouse, cockroach), environmental tobacco smoke (ETS), and lead and other metals such as mercury. These two Northern Manhattan neighborhoods and the South Bronx are located in a densely populated metropolitan region that has in recent years exceeded the annual PM10 (particulate matter < 10 • m in aerodynamic diameter) standard of 50 • g/m3. In addition, these lower-income neighborhoods contain substantial local sources of combustion-generated pollution. Infants and young children in urban areas also spend a large part of time indoors where irritating and allergenic substances (i.e., gaseous and particulate emissions from gas stoves, space heaters, cigarettes, pest populations, and NPPs) may increase susceptibility to allergic sensitization, respiratory symptoms, and eventually, the development of asthma.

Their study described the unique susceptibility of the fetus and infant as well as additional contributing risk factors, including environmental exposures and disease rates in the three neighborhoods from which the study cohort was derived and the CCCEH's innovative research methods and preliminary results. They also described a community education campaign called "Healthy Home Healthy Child," which involved a partnership of 10 community-based direct service health and environmental advocacy organizations whose health educators informed neighborhood residents about how to protect themselves from unnecessary risk.

Special Vulnerability of the Fetus and Infant

There is mounting evidence that the fetus and infant are significantly more sensitive to a variety of environmental toxicants than adults because of differential exposure, (See Figure 1) physiologic immaturity, and a longer lifetime over which disease initiated in early life can develop. For example, experimental and human data indicate that the fetus and young child are especially vulnerable to the toxic effects of ETS, PAHs, particulate matter, nitrosamines, pesticides, polychlorinated biphenyls (PCBs), metals, and radiation (1-5)

Genetic damage/potential cancer risk.

Several studies suggest that the fetus clears toxicants less efficiently than the adult and may be more vulnerable to genetic damage and the resultant risk of cancer. For example, given experimental evidence that the amount of PAH crossing the placenta and reaching the fetus is less than one-tenth of the dose to the mother (10,11), the levels of PAH-DNA adducts measured in rodent fetal tissue are higher than expected (12,13). Similarly, their research in Poland has shown that PAH-DNA adduct levels in the white blood cells of newborns actually exceeded those in paired maternal samples, despite the estimated 10-fold lower dose of the parent compound to the fetus (13,14). In addition, plasma cotinine and aromatic DNA adduct levels in the Polish newborns were higher than in paired maternal samples, suggesting reduced ability of the fetus to clear cigarette smoke constituents (13,14). Increased adducts in the fetus relative to the adult could result from lower levels of phase II (detoxification) enzymes and decreased DNA repair efficiency in the fetus (3,14-16).

Respiratory disease

With respect to respiratory disease, there are critical windows in both prenatal and postnatal development during which exposure to irritants and other toxicants can modify the formation and maturation of the lung. The complete development of the human lung occurs through the sixth to eighth years of life (17). There is recent evidence from the CCCEH study of pregnant women and children that in utero sensitization to specific allergens can occur independent of maternal sensitization, possibly putting the child at higher risk of asthma (18). Children have been identified as a sensitive population to particulate matter, especially in those with respiratory symptoms (19).

Neurologic development

The exquisitely sensitive process of development of the human central nervous system has been reviewed by Faustman (20). This process involves the production of 100 billion nerve cells and 1 trillion glial cells, which then must follow a precise stepwise choreography involving migration, synaptogenesis, selective cell loss, and myelination (20). A mistake at any one step can have permanent consequences. Experimental studies of prenatal and neonatal exposure to chlorpyrifos have reported neurochemical and behavioral effects as well as selected brain cell loss (21,22). The behavioral and morphologic effects of developmental toxicants are highly dependent on the timing as well as on the dose and duration of exposure. This is illustrated by both rodent and human studies showing that the effect of irradiation on brain malformation is heightened during a window of susceptibility of fetal development (20).

Susceptibility Factors in Addition to Young Age

The enhanced susceptibility of the fetus and newborn is likely to be compounded by cofactors including nutritional deficits, genes, and social stressors.

Nutrition. Deficits in antioxidants have been strongly implicated in asthma. These micronutrients can moderate the effect of oxidants on lung function, reducing oxidative stress and resultant tissue damage and airway inflammation (23-25). With respect to growth and development and cancer, antioxidants remove free radicals and oxidant intermediates, thereby inhibiting chemical-DNA binding that has been associated with decreased weight, length, and head circumference at birth (9) and also with cancer (26). In addition, essential fatty acid status contributes to observed variations in cognitive and motor function and to low birth weight and reduced head circumference (27-29). Nutritional deficits are associated with poverty, although there is interindividual variation in nutritional status within socioeconomically disadvantaged populations.

Genetics. Genetic susceptibility can take the form of common polymorphisms that affect the toxicity to the individual. For example, there are two genes that can increase an individual's vulnerability to organophosphates (OPs) such as chlorpyrifos by reducing the reservoir of functioning protective enzymes (30). The first gene has a prevalence of 4% and results in a poorly functioning form of the enzyme acetycholinesterase; the second gene results in a relatively inactive form of the enzyme, paraoxonase (prevalence of 30-38%) (20,30). Other examples of gene-environment interactions involve the gene coding for the -ALA enzyme that affects lead metabolism and storage (30), and the P450 and glutathione-S-transferase genes that play a role in activation and detoxification of PAH and influence PAH-DNA damage (30). Genetic susceptibility may vary by race and ethnicity.

Individual- and community-level psychosocial stressors

The notion that community-level conditions can produce profound effects on host susceptibility to disease is derived from the long-standing existence of strong social class gradients in health (31). Recent studies have shown that women who live in violent, crime-ridden, physically decayed neighborhoods are more likely to experience pregnancy complications and adverse birth outcomes, after adjusting for a range of individual level sociodemographic attributes and health behaviors (32,33). Other studies have suggested that the stresses of racism and community segregation are associated with lower birth weight (34,35). Several studies have shown that the effects of individual poverty on birth outcomes are exacerbated by residence in a disadvantaged neighborhood (36).

Disproportionate Exposure in Minority Populations

Children in the United States suffer from unacceptably high rates of developmental disorders, asthma, and cancer (30,37-42). Rates of asthma and behavioral disorders have increased in the past decades (30). Although improved detection and reporting have contributed, environmental factors are known or suspected to play a role. The rates of these diseases are disproportionately high in underserved, minority populations such as those in New York City where CCCEH is located. African Americans and Latinos in Northern Manhattan and the South Bronx represent high risk groups for asthma, adverse birth outcomes, impaired development, and some types of cancer (43,44)

Washington Heights, a low-income community in northern Manhattan, has a large Latino population. According to 1990 census data (45), the median household income in 1989 was $22,175, with 29.4% of the population living below the poverty level (46). Two-thirds (66.9%) of residents were Latino, with 65.2% being Dominican. Central Harlem is also a low-income minority community that was 91.9% African American in 1990 (45). The median household income in 1989 was $13,861, and 38.9% of the population lived below the poverty level. The South Bronx is another low-income minority community made up largely of Latinos (57.2%) and African Americans (31.4%). The median household income in 1989 was $12,088, and 45.8% of the population lived below the poverty level.

PM2.5, diesel exhaust particulate, and PAHs.

Harlem, Washington Heights, and the South Bronx are at the center of a large sprawling metropolitan region that in recent years has been out of compliance with the National Ambient Air Quality Standard for particulate matter, exceeding the annual PM10 standard of 50 g./m3 (47). The regional influx of polluted air is augmented by substantial local sources of combustion-generated pollution. Ambient PM2.5, DEEP, and PAH levels result from region-wide pollution emissions upwind of New York City, as well as from local sources such as diesel bus depots, waste incinerators, industrial operations, and a network of commuter highways.

Foremost among the local combustion sources are the cars, trucks, and buses using the highways and the commercial truck and bus routes that surround and interlace Harlem and Washington Heights. Two of the major north/south avenues passing through the center of these communities--Broadway and Amsterdam Avenues--are the principal truck routes for moving goods in and out of Manhattan. In addition, diesel bus depots, waste incinerators, and a multitude of small industrial operations release substantial amounts of airborne particulate and gaseous pollutants in these areas. Diesel engines emit 30-100 times more particles than are emitted by gasoline engines that have contemporary emission-control devices (48). Sources of diesel particulate located in northern Manhattan include six Metropolitan Transit Authority bus garages, each one housing from 200 to 400 diesel buses, a large marine transfer station, and a commercial bus terminal.

The South Bronx is similarly congested, with local pollution point sources such as a sewage waste treatment plant, traffic from seven bridges feeding into the area, as well as excess trucks and buses passing through regularly en route to the Harlem River Yards, bus depots, Hunts Point Terminal Food Distribution Center, and the New York Post printing plant. Commerce from the Hunts Point Market alone brings roughly 7,000 diesel trucks and tractor-trailer trucks into the neighborhood daily (49). The majority of the borough's waste facilities and transfer stations located in the South Bronx process 21% of the city's commercial waste and pelletize 70% of the city's sewage sludge (49). The South Bronx is located beneath the takeoff and landing corridors of LaGuardia Airport and a mile from two power plants, which are the second and fourth dirtiest in New York State (50). Residents are justifiably concerned about the potential health impacts of the many ambient pollution sources on children growing up in these communities.

The impact of diesel bus and truck traffic (DEEP) on the spatial variability of fine elemental carbon particle concentrations in Harlem was demonstrated in a community-based pilot study conducted by CCCEH scientists along with high school interns from West Harlem Environmental Action (WE ACT), the center's lead community partner (51). Over a 5-day period, researchers wearing backpacks containing personal ambient air monitors that collected information on fine particle (PM2.5) and elemental carbon concentrations in the air they breathed counted trucks, buses, cars, and pedestrians at four intersections in Harlem between 1000 and 1800 hr. This study showed that reflectance measurement of the "blackness" of the particulate sample on the filter is highly correlated with elemental carbon concentration ® = 0.95) and may be used as a surrogate for diesel exposure (51). Results also showed that diesel traffic density varied widely at the four locations, with 8-hr PM2.5 concentrations ranging from 22 to 69 μg/m3. For comparison, the annual fine particle standard proposed by the U.S. Environmental Protection Agency (EPA) in 1998 is 15 μg/m3 (52).

Environmental tobacco smoke. Recent research indicates that ETS exposure is more prevalent among African Americans and Hispanics than whites (53-55). In addition, there is evidence that minorities are more susceptible to the chemicals in tobacco smoke. Higher levels of cotinine and a tobacco-specific carcinogenic nitrosamine have been reported in black smokers than in white smokers, after controlling for self-reported amount of smoking (55-57). In a recent study, African-American children had 2-fold higher cotinine levels than white children as a result of exposure to 1 cigarette/day (58). Similarly, after adjusting for cigarette dose, cotinine levels in pregnant women were higher in African Americans than in whites, while the rate of decrease in infant birth weight per nanogram of maternal cotinine was similar in the two groups (59). These findings point to the possibility that cigarette smoking may have a more deleterious effect on fetal development among African Americans than among whites (59).

Pest allergens. Goldstein et al. (60) reported levels of airborne cockroach allergen in Harlem apartments that were orders of magnitude higher than those seen in previous studies in New Orleans, Louisiana, and Rochester, Minnesota. Sarpong et al. (61) found that African-American race was a predictor of higher allergen exposures. As will be discussed below, 85% of the homes of pregnant women studied by the CCCEH had detectable cockroach allergen levels.

Poorer Health Outcomes in Northern Manhattan and the South Bronx

The context for our research is the high rates of neurodevelopmental disorders, asthma, and cancer in children in the United States (30). Although improved detection and reporting have contributed to marked increases in some of these disorders over the past decade, environmental factors are known or suspected to affect these increases. The rates of neurodevelopmental disorders, asthma, and cancer in children are disproportionately high in the underserved, minority populations of Washington Heights, Harlem, and the South Bronx (43,44,48).

Asthma. Pediatric asthma is a serious and growing public health problem in the United States (62). New York City is one of four metropolitan areas in the country with the highest annual increase in asthma mortality (34). Asthma rates vary markedly within New York City. Five of the seven New York City zip code areas with the highest asthma hospitalization rates are located in Harlem (42). In the South Bronx in 1994, prevalence of asthma among children < 17 years of age was 17.9% in Hispanics, 11.6% among non-Hispanic blacks, and 8.2% among whites (41). A recent study of pediatric asthma rates suggested that material and behavioral characteristics associated with poverty, such as parental smoking, air pollution, housing conditions, and allergens, may contribute to the disparities (63). Early life wheezing, especially in the presence of atopy and sensitization to environmental allergens, appears to be a good predictor of persistent wheezing and asthma (64-66).

Impairment of fetal growth and child development. Low birth weight is the second leading predictor of infant mortality in the United States as well as a major cause of delayed development (67,68) and a risk factor for childhood asthma (26). As a whole, the largely minority population in our three target communities is at elevated risk for low birth weight and subsequent cognitive delay compared to other U.S. populations, but here, too, rates vary. In 1997, the incidence of low birth weight was 13.5% in central Harlem, 10.5% in the South Bronx, and 7.7% in Washington Heights, compared to 7.1% in whites in New York City (69). Children are also at elevated risk of subsequent cognitive delay compared to other populations: 68% of elementary school children in Washington Heights and 74% in central Harlem are reading below grade level, compared with 46% city-wide (38).

Cancer and other outcomes. Nationally, African Americans continue to exceed white Americans in deaths from diseases with known or suspected environmental components, including cancer (70,71). Early life exposures may be important determinants of risk. It has been estimated that for genotoxic carcinogens, as much as one-half of total lifetime cancer risk may be accrued before the age of 6 years (72).

Community Outreach

The CCCEH was modeled on the premise that the challenge of prevention requires an interdisciplinary, community-based research strategy to identify preventable risk factors and act upon that information. It incorporates both molecular epidemiology and multilevel analyses (84,85). Molecular epidemiology using biomarkers is a relatively new and useful tool in defining environment-susceptibility relationships, when used in conjunction with reliable monitoring and epidemiologic methodologies to provide individual estimates of exposure, dose, biologic response and susceptibility to pollutants (86-93). The center's research also follows the paradigm of the Chinese box described by Susser and Susser (85) in that it aims to integrate multiple levels of organization (individual/molecular and community/ecologic) in design, analysis, and interpretation, nesting the individual level analysis within the overarching environment of the community.

Within the center's study area of northern Manhattan and the South Bronx, there is considerable variation in exposure, susceptibility factors, and risk belying the stereotype of a uniformly disadvantaged population. This allows the Center to study dose-response relationships as well as community impacts on individual outcomes. They anticipated that this multilevel approach would provide a more complete understanding of the complexity of the disease process, permitting the development of a variety of independent and complementary approaches to intervention at the individual and macro levels. These interventions might include education regarding lifestyle changes, regulations to control involuntary exposure to toxic pollutants, and even broader social policy changes.

The center has an active group of advisors on its Community Advisory Board (CAB). WE ACT is the center's lead community partner and has advocated for improved environmental conditions in Harlem for over a decade. Directors of nine additional health service and environmental advocacy organizations that are well-established in Washington Heights, Harlem, and the South Bronx also serve on the CAB: Alianza Dominicana, Best Beginnings, Community Association of Progressive Dominicans, E.C.H.O. for Sustainable Development, Harlem Dowling West Side, Heart of Harlem, Northern Manhattan Perinatal Partnership, St. Mary's Episcopal Church, and The South Bronx Clean Air Coalition. For several years, these organizations have provided direct health services to community residents, advocated for improved care as well as better access to care, and worked steadily toward improving environmental conditions in these communities.

In collaboration with its CAB, the center developed a community education campaign called "Healthy Home Healthy Child." The campaign worked to increase local residents' awareness of environmental health threats and preventive techniques to reduce pollution exposure to themselves, their families, and, in particular, their children. Focus groups were established with residents of Washington Heights, Harlem, and the South Bronx to help identify environmental issues that were of special concern to these communities. Additionally, 555 young mothers were surveyed in public places to gauge awareness of environmental hazards. The center's scientists combined their knowledge of current research findings with community concerns to target seven environmental hazards--air pollution, cigarette smoke, nutrition, pesticides, lead poisoning, drugs and alcohol, and garbage management--in the "Healthy Home Healthy Child" campaign.

Written materials on each topic were developed in collaboration with WE ACT to ensure that the literature incorporated local cultural values and were at an appropriate reading level for the community. The materials aim to educate community parents about sources of environmental hazards, their health consequences, and how to take steps to prevent or at least diminish everyone's exposure to toxic pollutants. The literature is distributed at health fairs, various community events, and through the 10 CAB organizations' regular activities. A WE ACT health educator delivers presentations to parents at day care centers, distributing campaign materials throughout Washington Heights and West Harlem. The

CCCEH is currently collaborating with the full CAB to train health educators on staff at each organization to deliver presentations on the seven environmental health topics. The effort will expand the reach of the campaign into more neighborhoods, including those in the South Bronx, and improve its sustainability.

The center and CAB have also hosted community events including an environmental health fair attended by over 300 study cohort mothers and children as well as local residents, and a large national conference called "The Health of Our Children in the Urban Environment: A Dialogue among Scientists, Community Leaders and Policymakers" held 27 March 2000. At this conference, David Satcher, U.S. Surgeon General, and Kenneth Olden (National Institute of Environmental Health Sciences, Research Triangle Park, NC) addressed an audience of 500 local residents and professionals in environmental health-related fields about the need for exactly the kind of research combined with community outreach that the center is conducting. CAB members participated in the panel discussions addressing the intersection of scientific research with community health and public policy.

The CAB is invaluable for its counsel and is a necessary stepping stone toward building a larger communication network within local neighborhoods and changing perceptions that have previously inhibited a better and more substantial working relationship between community members and scientific researchers. The center's partnership with its CAB helps to dissolve some of the barriers to better health care and at-home prevention practices by opening lines of communication with community leaders who may have had no former relationship with the university. With that contact, multiple opportunities arise for education of local residents who have established relationships with these community-based organizations on which they depend for health services and advocacy. Ultimately, a larger segment of the community is reached in the dissemination of important health findings and preventive methods for reducing risk.

Conclusion

The health of a society can be judged by the health of its children. As a society we can and must do better in preventing harm to this vulnerable group. This will entail the early identification of preventable risks and the prompt translation of this knowledge into protective policies and interventions. There is a need to better understand the interactions between multiple exposures and susceptibility factors that may disproportionately affect children, particularly those in certain social and ethnic groups, putting them at greater risk from toxic pollutants.

Clearly, the CCCEH has been working to understand the health risks from early life exposures to environmental contaminants in combination with susceptibility factors and is attempting to address these threats through education, policy-relevant research, and the timely dissemination of research results.

EPA HUMAN HEALTH RESEARCH STRATEGY

For Immediate Release
November 3, 2003

EPA Announces Human Health Research Strategy to Address Needs for Science
Contact: Suzanne Ackerman, 202-564-7819

Dr. Paul Gilman, EPA Assistant Administrator for Research and Development and EPA Science Advisor, announced today the release of a long-term plan for research to further the Agency's mission to protect public health. The *Human Health Research Strategy* identifies and prioritizes the research that will be conducted over the next five to 10 years to improve the scientific foundation for EPA's human health risk assessments and to evaluate risk management decisions.

The plan provides a strategic approach to address research needs in several recent initiatives by the EPA's Office of Research and Development: computational toxicology, children's health, aging, asthma and the cumulative risk of exposure to multiple environmental contaminants.

"This plan provides a roadmap for EPA scientists to follow over the next decade to improve the science needed by decision makers to protect the public health and environment, " said Gilman. "Explorers into unknown territory use global positioning systems or GPS to keep them on course. This strategy will be our guide to exploring the unknowns in environmental science," he said.

The plan focuses on improving the integration of environmental science disciplines at EPA and improving the links in the various fields of science to understand how we are exposed to environmental contaminants, what dose is needed to obtain an adverse health effect and what health effects occur from exposure.

"Building stronger connections between, exposure, dose, and effect research, will improve our ability to make sound human health risk assessments," Gilman said.

The *Human Health Research Strategy* emphasizes the need for EPA to partner with other local, state, Tribal and federal organizations, public health organizations, and industry to conduct human health research.

The *Human Health Research Strategy* is posted on EPA's Web page at http://www.epa.gov/ord/htm/researchstrategies.htm. A limited number of print copies are available from EPA's National Service Center for Environmental Publications (NSCEP). To obtain copies, please contact NSCEP at 1-800-490-9198 and reference EPA document number 600/R-02/050.

**United States
Environmental Protection
Agency**

FACT SHEET: *Human Health Research Strategy*
A Focus on EPA's Research

The mission of the U.S. Environmental Protection Agency (EPA) is to protect public health and safeguard the environment. Risk assessment is an integral part of this mission in that it identifies and characterizes environmentally related human health problems. The *Human Health Research Strategy* presents a conceptual framework for future human health research by EPA's Office of Research Development (ORD) over the next 5-10 years. This research strategy outlines ORD's core research effort to provide broader, more fundamental information that will improve understanding or problem-driven human health risk issues encountered by EPA's Program and Regional Offices. ORD's human health program will address two strategic directions, including research to improve the scientific foundation of human health risk assessment and research to enable evaluation of public health outcomes from risk management decisions. An important consideration in the development of this strategy was to ensure that EPA human health research supplements and expands on other federal agency efforts.

BACKGROUND: Human health risk assessment provides a qualitative and quantitative characterization of the relationship between environmental exposures and effects observed in exposed individuals.

Risk assessment is also the primary scientific input to the risk management process, which involves the recognition of a potential new risk and development, selection, and implementation of EPA actions to address the risk. Based on input from Regional and Program Office risk assessors and ORD scientists, future human health research in ORD will focus on ways to improve the scientific foundation of human health risk assessment, including approaches to

---

Four-Step Process for Risk Assessment

1. Hazard identification,
2. Dose-response assessment,
3. Exposure assessment, and
4. Risk characterization.

---

harmonizing the use of mechanistic data in human health risk assessments, predicting the effects of aggregate and cumulative exposure, and protecting susceptible subpopulations such as children, older adults, and those with preexisting disease or genetic predispositions for different responsiveness to environmental pollutants. Future ORD research on human health will also address the increasing need to estimate public health benefits of EPA regulatory decisions and rule making.

SUMMARY: Research to improve human health risk assessment is based on the assumption that major uncertainties in risk assessment can be reduced by understanding and elucidating the fundamental determinants of exposure and dose and the basic biological changes that follow exposure to pollutants leading to a toxic response.

ORD's human health research program, as detailed in the *Strategy*, will address disparate approaches for the risk assessment of cancer and noncancer health effects. This research will lead to a common set of principles and guidelines for drawing inferences about risk based on mechanistic information. ORD's research on aggregate/cumulative risk will address the fact that human are exposed to mixtures of pollutants from multiple

---

Objectives of Human Health Risk Assessment Research

- Harmonizing human health risk assessments
- Predicting aggregate/cumulative risk
- Protecting subpopulations.

---

sources. This program will develop the scientific support for decisions concerning exposure to a pollutant by multiple routes of exposure or to multiple pollutants having a similar mode or mechanism of action. ORD's research on susceptible subpopulations (i.e., children, older adults, genetically predisposed, or those with preexisting health problems) will focus on developing a scientific understanding of the biological basis for differing responsiveness of subpopulations within the general populations, including factors associated with their differential exposures.

The *Strategy* specifically addresses research needs in several recent initiatives by the EPA/ORD: computational toxicology, children's health, aging, asthma and the cumulative risk of exposure to multiple environmental contaminants.ORD will also provide the scientific understanding and tools to EPA and others in evaluating the effectiveness of public health outcomes resulting from risk management decisions.

EPA/ORD has prepared the *Human Health Research Strategy* to strengthen the scientific foundation of EPA's risk assessments and risk management decisions. ORD research strategy documents provide a framework of needs and

---

Focus of Human Health Risk Assessment Research

- Identifying, discovering, or developing the most effective methods and models;
- Determining how models can be integrated into a decision making framework to assess impact of risk management actions on public health;
- Developing a framework for accurately quantifying changes in public health.

---

priorities to guide its programs over the next five to ten years. They form the basis for more detailed plans, such as the *2003 ORD Human Health Research Multi-Year Plan*, which describes anticipated goals and performance measures over a 5-10 year period. Each Laboratory and Center within ORD is also responsible for developing its own approach to linking specific projects and tasks to the *2003 ORD Human Health Multi-Year Plan* and the themes described in the *Human Health Research Strategy*.

DOCUMENT AVAILABILITY: The primary method for document availability will be via ORD's Web site at **http://www.epa.gov/ORD** . A limited number of paper copies and CD-ROMs are available from EPA's National Service Center for Environmental Publications (NSCEP). To obtain copies, please contact NSCEP by telephone (1-800-490-9198 or 513-489-8190), by facsimile (513-489-8695), or by mail (P.O. Box 42419, Cincinnati, OH 45242-0419). Please provide your name and mailing address and the title and EPA number of the document requested (Human Health Research Strategy, EPA 600/R-02/050).

CONTACT: Hugh Tilson, U.S. EPA, Office of Research and Development, National Health and Environmental Effects Research Laboratory, Research Triangle Park, NC; 919-541-4607; Fax: 919-541-1440; email: tilson.hugh@epa.gov

APPENDIX K:

STATUTORY AUTHORITIES

INTRODUCTION

EPA administers our national federal environmental protection regime and the statutes that underlie it. This chapter examines ways in which the Agency can proactively use existing statutory authorities and their implementing regulations to address cumulative risks and impacts. Useful background information in addressing this question has been identified by the Environmental Law Institute (ELI) in its November 2001 research report, "Opportunities for Advancing Environmental Justice: An Analysis of U.S. EPA Statutory Authorities." To adequately address cumulative risks and impacts, one must also identify the authorities available to state and local public health officials that can be used to assessing cumulative risks and reducing or eliminating cumulative impacts. This chapter reviews the ELI report and summarizes state and local authorities that are responsive to these questions. There is an immediate need to determine how to maximize the use of these legal tools to help impacted and overburdened communities and tribes in their quest to improve the health and welfare of their members. Presently, EPA and state and local government utilizes only a handful of the authorities available to it.

Together, EPA and state and local agencies can effectively marshal the combination of these legal authorities to protect and improve health outcomes. An agency-wide unified strategy is needed so that the federal, state and local governments proactively apply legal tools. This coordination can lead to environmentally protective decisions that integrate the status of community and tribal health with the impacts of the totality of the environmental burdens affecting communities.

OVERVIEW OF THE ELI REPORT

The ELI report identifies statutory authorities for furthering environmental justice goals in EPA's regulatory programs. It reviews in detail ten federal statues (and their regulatory programs):

- The National Environmental Policy Act, or NEPA
- The Federal Water Pollution Control Act, or the Clean Water Act or CWA
- The Clean Air Act, or the CAA
- The Resource, Conservation and Recovery Act, or RCRA
- The Comprehensive Environmental Response, Compensation, and Recovery Act, or CERCA or Superfund
- The Federal Insecticide, Fungicide and Rodenticide Act, or FIFRA
- The Federal Food, Drug, and Cosmetic Act, or FFDCA
- The Safe Drinking Water Act, or the SDWA
- The Toxic Substances Control Act, or TSCA, and
- The Emergency Planning and Community Right-to-Know Act, or EPCRA

These statutes were chosen because, according the report, taken together they encompass most of EPA's mandate to protect public health and the environment by controlling pollution and regulating the manufacture, use and disposal of specific substances.

To begin its analysis, the ELI report points out that the laws provide the Agency with considerable discretion to address environmental justice concerns, which include cumulative risks and impacts, even if not directed to do so in specific statutory language. This capacity is based in EPA's general discretionary authority to interpret and implement the statutes that contain broad admonitions to "protect human health and the environment." Inherent in this language is the obligation to assure that environmental justice communities receive protection of health and the environment equivalent to communities with fewer sources of pollution and/or fewer vulnerabilities to adverse impact. Although agencies are granted considerable leeway by courts in choosing how to exercise their inherent authorities, this leeway has been challenged recently, and many agencies are becoming more cautious and less aggressive construing their statutes. This highlights the need for clear, workable approaches to cumulative risks and impacts that can withstand challenge in court.

The ELI report notes three overarching sources that support implementation of environmental justice throughout federal programs. According to the report, NEPA speaks broadly to the goals of environmental justice through its policy objectives, which emphasize assuring health and welfare for all Americans. NEPA's statutory language obligates EPA to administer all of its programs in accordance with national environmental policy, through environmental impact assessment or other means. NEPA specifically refers to the need to consider cumulative effects, including "the interrelated cultural, social, occupational, historical, or economic factors that may amplify the natural and physical environmental effects of the proposed action. NEPA's implementing agency the Council on Environmental Quality (CEQ) has issued guidance specifying the consideration of environmental justice under NEPA and providing a focus for the response to adverse cumulative impacts. Title VI of the Civil Rights Act, while only touched upon in the ELI report, is a second source of legal authority to mandate environmental justice. EPA's current draft guidance to the states on implementing Title VI discusses a place-based, cumulative approach to reducing adverse impacts in environmental justice communities. That fledgling initiative on addressing cumulative risks and impacts could be much expanded. Finally, Executive Order 12898 requires that environmental justice be considered in the federal government's regulatory processes. The order states that each federal agency must make environmental justice part of its mission "by identifying and addressing, as appropriate, disproportionately high and adverse human health or environmental effects of its programs, policies and activities on minority populations and low income populations." Explicit in this analysis should be evaluation of the way in which each major rulemaking evaluates and addresses the need to avoid adverse cumulative risks and impacts in environmental justice communities.

In its analysis of various statutory authorities, the ELI report first analyzes EPA's authorities by function, discussing standard setting and rule making; permitting; program delegation; enforcement; information gathering; financial assistance; and public participation. The report next provides a statute-by-statute review of the authorities potentially useful for environmental justice. This NEJAC Working Group report reviews ELI's functional analysis as important background for its recommendations and conclusions to the NEJAC.

ELI'S FUNCTIONAL REVIEW OF ENVIRONMENTAL AUTHORITIES

Standard Setting and Rule-Making

Generally, EPA's statutory authorities grant broad rule making powers so that it can promulgate regulations that are necessary to carry out its statutory mandates. The various environmental statutes contain at least four categories of standards; (1) technology based standards; (2) design and practice standards; (3) harm based standards; and (4) standards for regulating substances.

Items (1) and (2), technology based standards and design and practice standards, are keyed to the control measures available or achievable to control pollution, or to a specific method of managing waste. The relationship between these types of standards and cumulative risk and impacts is particularly challenging where the standards are premised on eliminating exposure to toxics to the extent feasible or practicable. Relying as they do on cost and the limits of technology, the standards rarely consider cumulative risk (as contrasted with a harm-based standard, where control requirements vary based on risk regardless of cost or particular technologies). Nevertheless, cumulative risks and impacts can be utilized in these types of standard setting to protect highly burdened and impacted communities. For example, under the Clean Water Act, EPA has the authority to take cumulative and synergistic effects into consideration when listing pollutants, and setting effluent guideline limitations, thus overriding cost considerations to secure adequate health protection. Under the CAA's toxics program and in setting Maximum Contaminant levels under the SDWA, EPA can make discretionary judgments to incorporate cumulative risk and impact information. Even in the cases of uniform design requirements (like installation of a double liner or purchase of a certain kind of tank), EPA can use its discretion in evaluating the total of permitting conditions at an entire facility to increase protection where demanded by cumulative risks and impacts.

According to the ELI report, harm based standards "establish the allowable concentrations of pollution in the environment necessary to protect public health and environmental quality with an 'ample' or 'adequate' margin of safety." In most cases, harm based standards are based upon an assessment of risks. Therefore, an evaluation of cumulative risks and impacts is directly relevant to establishing harm-based standards. Regulation under the CAA is perhaps the clearest example of how harm based standards can be enhanced by cumulative risks and impacts information and application of the Framework. The Agency's program for its primary National Ambient Air Quality Standards (NAAQS) are set at a level necessary to protect public health with an adequate margin of safety. This language has been interpreted to mean that EPA must protect not only the average healthy individual, but also sensitive people – those with conditions that render them especially susceptible to air pollutants. This language provides a strong invitation to apply the cumulative risk principles embodied in the Framework to protect overburdened and highly impacted communities and tribes.

Standards for regulating substances, such as the ability to add to the number of substances it regulates, or change the reportable quantity of a substance, also provides the agency with considerable discretion to address cumulative risks and impacts. As EPA proceeds to consider new hazardous waste or hazardous substances listings or new chemicals for testing, its procedures should include evaluation of the potential for adverse cumulative impacts. In determining its research agenda for chemicals, EPA could consider the constituents whose occurrence most contributes to cumulative risk, and could elevate those constituents in its study agenda.

Permitting

The ELI report notes that permits and permitting procedures are at the core of EPA's powers under most major pollution control statutes. As noted at many NEJAC meetings, permitting has long been a focus of environmental justice debates. The report also points out that much of the discussion of EPA's permitting authority centers on two related questions. First, can the Agency deny a permit on environmental justice grounds? Second, can the Agency place conditions on a permit that specifically address environmental justice concerns?

For facility siting, EPA often has little chance to weigh in. Most siting decisions are local, land use planning or zoning issues. Still, there are areas where the Agency has authority to address siting issues, such as wetlands and coastal zones. For example, under section 404 of the Clean Water Act (CWA), EPA has considerable ability to consider and address disproportionate impacts and cumulative risk and impacts. Similarly, under NEPA (which applies to major federal actions significantly affecting the quality of the environment) the Environmental Impact Statement process allows the Agency opportunities for dealing with the disproportionate impacts.

In the realm of operating permits, EPA can exercise even more substantial discretion when administering these programs. EPA's grant of authority often takes the form of general provisions that give the Agency discretion to decide what measures are necessary or appropriate to protect public health and the environment. These provisions are found in RCRA, the CAA (Title V operating permits) and the Clean Water Act (section 402(a)(1)), among others.

The ELI analysis of operating permit authority indicates that there are substantial opportunities to consider cumulative risks and impacts to protect overburdened and highly impacted communities and tribes. The information generated in a cumulative risk analysis, as described in the Framework, could be incorporated into the permitting process.

Program Delegation

Federal environmental laws provide for delegation of programs for permitting, monitoring and enforcement to state and tribal government. Delegation serves two purposes. First, it recognizes the important role that states and tribes play in environmental protection regimes. Second, it provides for national standards to be developed and implemented. There is a deliberate tension in this process. In delegated programs, states or tribes have primary responsibility to implement the purposes of federal environmental laws, but EPA has the ultimate oversight.

Program delegation offers several opportunities for considering cumulative risks and impacts. During the program delegation process, EPA can consider environmental justice issues, including cumulative impacts. This analysis can extend to the states' or tribes' ability to carry out the delegated program. After a program is delegated, EPA has the power to exercise oversight, although this is often politically difficult. Thus, EPA could review or disapprove certain program decisions based on failure to consider adequately cumulative risks and impacts. Last, EPA has the authority to revoke delegated authority if the program is not appropriately implemented. This is an action of last resort, however, and is not usually invoked. Nevertheless, the authority to revoke can be persuasive to ensure the cumulative risks and impacts are considered.

Enforcement

The ELI report observes that EPA has the obligation to assure compliance with environmental standards, whether through enforcement activities such as issuing an administrative order, seeking an administrative fine, revoking or withholding a permit, bringing a court action, or pursuing criminal charges. In selecting which actions to pursue, EPA has discretion to consider a variety of factors, including the consequences for public health. It is within the Agency's discretion to give priority to actions that penalize or halt conduct that has a disproportionate impact on environmental justice communities. The Framework could be useful in identifying the hazards faced by these communities and help shape the actions that could be brought.

There are several points along the continuum of the enforcement process where EPA can act to promote environmental justice. First, in case selection, EPA could use the "imminent and substantial endangerment" provisions (contained in several environmental statutes) to prioritize cases based on cumulative risks and impacts. It is also possible, according to ELI, for EPA to initiate enforcement actions based primarily on environmental justice considerations. Risks to a sensitive or overburdened population could establish the necessary proof for a substantial endangerment argument. Under the enforcement provisions of some statutes, such as section 504 of the Clean Water Act, EPA can consider combined effects. Statutory authority to consider combined sources and effects gives the Agency flexibility in evaluating cases for enforcement. EPA could decide to place a greater priority on bringing enforcement actions based on cumulative impacts or risks. However, because proof of substantial endangerment is generally more difficult to obtain than proof needed for a simple violation of a standard, this approach may have limited utility.

Second, in case resolution, EPA often has authority to shape penalties to the nature and severity of the harms at issue, the economic gain by the violator and other circumstances. EPA's broad authority to tailor penalties to the individual facts of any case could mean that cumulative risks and impacts are used in penalty calculations or in shaping the terms of the remedy. An approach to calculating penalties that recognizes cumulative risks and impacts could also have a deterrence effect on other potential violators.

The vast majority of enforcement actions are resolved via settlement, which creates opportunities for crafting creative remedies. The Agency has developed a policy that promotes the incorporation of environmental projects, called supplemental environmental project or SEPs, into settlement activities. This policy encourages SEPs in communities where environmental justice concerns have been raised in the course of enforcement. The Agency could use this policy, and the inherent flexibility of its enforcement authority, to reach settlements that can address health issues associated with overburdened and impacted communities and tribes. SEPs provide the opportunity to look holistically at the impacted community and to bring resources to bear on the harms the community identifies as most in need of remedy.

Third, in criminal cases, environmental justice considerations could influence sentencing following a conviction. Sentencing guidelines generally call for a factual evaluation of the particular harm, and harms to the health of overburdened and highly impacted communities may be an enhancing factor in calculating punishment.

Finally, citizen suits can be an effective way to protect overburdened and highly impacted communities and tribes, as well as develop and bolster legal theories of cumulative risks and impacts. Congress (and many state legislatures) has added provisions to many environmental laws that allow private citizens to act as "attorneys general" in bringing actions against violators.

Information Gathering

EPA has authority to undertake a wide variety of information gathering activities. This authority has been given to EPA so that it can meet the technical and scientific challenges that are inherent in environmental decision-making. EPA could use these authorities to assist in addressing environmental justice issues and begin to answer the questions that highly impacted communities and tribes have been asking.

In research, the Agency could take several actions that would assist in decoding the links between public health and cumulative risks and impacts. First, EPA could seek to improve the scientific knowledge base in this field by shaping its research agenda around cumulative risks and impacts. Specific statutory language in the Clean Air Act authorizes EPA to research air pollution issues particularly relevant to communities of color and low-income communities, such as cumulative risks. Second, under certain statutes (such as the CAA) the Agency can impose research requirements on regulated entities. This authority provides another opportunity to foster research on cumulative risks and impacts. Finally, federal environmental law could be used to support efforts to involve communities in Agency research activities.

EPA's monitoring programs can also be a source of information that has direct use for the study of cumulative risks and impacts. EPA has extensive authority to require monitoring by regulated facilities and the Agency also has authority under certain statutes to carry out its own monitoring. These authorities could be of utility to communities wishing to learn more about the emissions that confront them.

Reporting by facilities is another source of information that could be useful to highly impacted and overburdened communities. These reporting requirements often afford EPA discretion, so the Agency could design their nature and scope to be relevant to cumulative risks and impacts.

Financial Assistance

EPA awards hundreds of millions of dollars each year in grants, contracts and assistance agreements. Awards to States and tribes account for the bulk of these funds, but non-governmental entities also receive support. EPA can further environmental justice goals by targeting funding to highly impacted and overburdened communities, and the groups that are working with them. EPA could make environmental justice considerations a part of the award decision for grant making, or design a series of proposal requests specifically for issues such as cumulative risks and impacts. The ELI report points out that federal financial assistance is the mechanism that triggers federal civil rights legislation, which requires that financial assistance recipients serve and protect people equally without regard to race, color or national origin.

EPA could also consider tying the award of funds to state and tribal entities with environmental justice principles by establishing grant conditions that adequately address environmental justice concerns. The Agency also has the ability to assist communities to participate in regulatory decision-making by making awards to community groups to participate in regulatory actions. Where these grants are made, EPA could make a condition of receipt consideration of cumulative risk analysis or reduction, as appropriate.

Public Participation

According to the ELI report, all of the major environmental statutes provide discretionary authority and, in many cases, explicitly require EPA to involve the public when implementing statutory mandates. EPA has considerable authority to involve overburdened and highly impacted communities and tribes in its activities. Above all, EPA has general discretionary authority under most of its statutes to involve affected communities early in decision-making. This authority could greatly benefit the Framework, which calls for an active citizenry and community responsiveness.

Several environmental statutes, such as Superfund and the Clean Water Act, emphasize public participation. EPA has developed regulatory programs for citizen involvement across all programs, and most Agency initiatives attempt to expand public participation requirements into true public involvement. EPA is required to engage in "notice and comment" prior to taking certain actions, and it is during this period that the most common form of public participation takes place. New initiatives expand notice and comment to include informal public meetings, facilitated on-going interaction with the public, and better responsiveness to public input. EPA could use all of these forums as an opportunity to explicitly solicit information about cumulative risks and impacts.

Several statutes, such as the SDWA, establish mechanisms (such as Advisory Councils) for involving the public in a more direct manner than notice and comment. EPA could actively solicit participation from highly impacted and overburdened communities for these advisory bodies as a way to enhance opportunities to raise environmental justice issues. In addition, EPA hosts a number of databases and information clearinghouses that could be sources for data about cumulative risks and impacts. Finally, several statutes, including EPCRA, allow for citizen petitions.

OTHER AUTHORITIES

In addition to federal environmental laws, there are other federal statutes that could be useful to communities and tribes seeking to evaluate cumulative risks and impacts, and reduce or eliminate the health effects linked to them. A thorough review of these laws is beyond the scope of this report and the charge to the Working Group. Because they could be useful to environmental justice communities, they are summarized here.

The Federal Public Health Service Act

The federal Public Health Service (PHS) Act is the major authority supporting activities of the Department of Health and Human Services, including activities at CDC, FDA, and NIH. The focus of the PHS Act is the coordination of state and federal health policy. The PHS Act contains provisions relating to generating and upholding international agreements, policies and programs; conducting medical and biomedical research; sponsoring programs for disease prevention and control, and administration of health research; providing resources and expertise to states in planning and direction of health-related services; and enforcing laws to ensure drug safety, protect against impure foods, faulty medical equipment and radiation-producing products.

The PHS Act differs from environmental laws in several ways. It is an organic act, while environmental laws are media-specific. It contains no citizen suit provisions and few, if any opportunities for public participation and citizen involvement in decision-making. Finally, it is focused on information gathering, technical support to states and tribes, and dissemination of information and research. Despite these differences, the federal agencies and departments that practice public health and carry out biomedical research under the PHS Act could be powerful and effective allies for EPA as it seeks to improve health outcomes in tribes and communities that are highly impacted by environmental pollution.

State Health Laws

State public health laws can also be a tool for helping communities and tribes that are heavily impacted and overburdened. State authorities can potentially be very powerful and flexible because States have plenary power to regulate the environment and public health, as well as delegated programs from the federal government. In addition, state tort law claims (e.g., negligence, strict liability) can be used to seek redress for environmental harms that fall outside the scope of the regulatory arena.

REFERENCES TO CUMULATIVE RISKS/IMPACTS
Opportunities to Advance Environmental Justice:
An Analysis of USEPA Statutory Authorities
Environmental Law Institute

Introduction Defining activities which further EJ goals	*Identifying fully the impacts of agency actions and decisions on communities of color and low-income communities.* One prominent issue in the national dialogue on environmental justice has been the need for EPA to consider adequately the environmental and health impacts of its decisions on communities that are already heavily burdened by polluting facilities and activities. Incinerators, waste and wastewater treatment facilities, transfer stations, refineries and factories are often disproportionately represented in these communities. As Richard Lazarus and Stephanie Tai have noted: "One of the major lessons of environmental justice is that EPA's past failure to account for **aggregation of risks and cumulative impacts** has caused EPA's existing standards to fail to protect human health and the environment in certain communities." Richard Lazarus & Stephanie Tai, *Integrating Environmental Justice into EPA Permitting Authority*, 26 ECOLOGY L.Q. 617, 642 (1999). Measuring the **cumulative and synergistic impacts** of multiple sources – and not simply the effects of individual pollutants or individual facilities – involves a host of technological and scientific complexities. A central goal of environmental justice has been to focus regulatory action on preventing and addressing these impacts. (Introduction/Defining Activities Which Further Environmental Justice Goals, p. iii)
Chapter 2: Standard Setting	EPA can use its discretionary power to address impacts on communities of color and low-income communities at any of these stages. For example, pollutant listings could take into account **cumulative and synergistic effects**, impacts on sensitive populations, and other relevant concerns. Clean Water Act effluent limitation guidelines can be revised to address environmental justice considerations if EPA deems those considerations "appropriate," a term that confers substantial discretion. The agency also can establish more stringent effluent limitations pursuant to "any" state or federal law or regulation, which presumably includes NEPA and Title VI of the Civil Rights Act. Environmental justice impacts also might be taken into account in decisions to grant or deny variances from technology-based standards. [Chapter 2, p.8]
Chapter 2: Standard Setting Standards for regulating substances	Finally, EPA has considerable discretion to regulate certain chemical substances under its pollution control authorities, even where the substances are not expressly designated in the statutes. As noted above, the agency may bring additional pollutants under the technology-based performance standards of the Clean Air Act and Clean Water Act. Similar authority for EPA to add to the number of substances it regulates is found in RCRA, which contains an expansive definition of "hazardous waste" and allows EPA to consider numerous factors in determining whether the definition is met, 42 U.S.C. §§ 6903(5), 6921. In addition, CERCLA provides the agency with authority to designate as hazardous any substances that "may present substantial danger to the public health or welfare or the environment." 42 U.S.C. 9602 (a). Each of these provisions afford discretion for the agency to consider **cumulative and synergistic effects**, impacts on sensitive populations, and other environmental justice issues when designating substances for regulation. [Chapter 2, p. 11]

Chapter 3: Permitting and other Approvals	Much of the discussion of EPA's permitting authority centers on two related questions: (1) whether the agency may deny a permit on environmental justice grounds; and (2) whether it may place conditions on a permit that specifically address issues of concern to low-income communities and communities of color. Lazarus & Tai at 619. Arguments for taking such actions are based on the full range of environmental justice issues, including **disproportionate impacts, cumulative or synergistic impacts, effects on sensitive populations, unique exposure pathways, and cultural and socio-economic considerations.** Along with outright denial of permits or bans on particular substances or practices, the conditions that have been proposed as falling within EPA's authority include site-specific mitigation measures, heightened monitoring requirements, advanced pollution prevention and best management practices, specialized control technology, enhanced public participation procedures, information disclosure, and community inspections. NEJAC Permitting Report at 24-30. [p. 13]
Chapter 3: Permitting and Other Approvals Cumulative impacts and siting considerations Statutory authorities.... p. 15	Siting of industrial facilities and other potentially polluting activities raises important environmental justice questions. To the extent that claims of disproportionate impact rest upon the concentration of sources within a geographic area or their proximity to sensitive populations, siting decisions become crucial to ensuring that no single community bears more than its fair share of the impacts. Since most land-use and zoning decisions are made at the state and local levels, EPA has comparatively little opportunity to weigh in on siting issues generally. However, the agency has considerable authority over a number of important issues carved out by the federal environmental statutes. Specifically, the agency has authority to address siting decisions that involve: (1) geographic areas where the federal government has specialized jurisdiction, such as wetlands and coastal zones; (2) concentrations of pollutants, such as non-attainment areas under the Clean Air Act; (3) heavily regulated facilities, such as waste disposal sites and incinerators; and (4) the federal government's own activities that impact the environment. Within these realms, EPA has broad discretion and numerous opportunities to consider and address environmental justice issues in siting decisions. Its authority to do so often is based on language that requires an "assessment" of the health or environmental impacts – which may include **cumulative impacts** – of siting an activity or facility, or an analysis of "alternatives" to a proposed project, which may include alternative sites or forgoing the project entirely. [p. 15]
Chapter 3: Permitting and Other Approvals	Through a detailed public notice-and-comment procedure, the Corps and EPA must consider whether a project has "practicable alternatives" that would have less adverse ecological impact; whether it would threaten water quality or endangered species, or cause "significant degradation" to drinking water supplies and fish and wildlife habitat; whether the proponent has taken all "appropriate and practical steps" to minimize and mitigate impacts at the proposed site; and whether the project would contribute unacceptably to **cumulative impacts** in the surrounding area. 40 C.F.R. §§ 230.10, 230.11. This Section 404 process provides ample opportunity for considering and addressing disproportionate impacts and other environmental justice issues, as well as a public forum in which the affected communities can express their concerns. Hill & Targ at 27-36. Similar requirements govern EPA's and the Corps' determination of ocean dumping sites under the Marine Protection, Research, and Sanctuaries Act. OGC 2000 Memorandum at 9-10. [p. 16]

Chapter 3: Permitting and Other Approvals	RCRA's omnibus provision has its counterparts in Clean Air Act Section 504(a), which provides that Title V operating permits "shall include . . . such other conditions as are necessary to assure compliance with applicable requirements of this chapter," 42 U.S.C. § 7661c(a); in Clean Water Act Section 402(a)(1), which in certain circumstances allows EPA to impose on discharge permits "such conditions as the Administrator determines are necessary to carry out the provisions of [the Act]," 33 U.S.C. § 1342(a)(1); and in Safe Drinking Water Act regulations, which authorize underground injection permit conditions "necessary to prevent the migration of fluids into underground sources of drinking water," 40 C.F.R. § 144.52(a)(9); *Envotech*, 6 E.A.D. at 281. Though similarly worded, each of these broad provisions must be interpreted in light of their respective statutory goals and framework, which are analyzed in the individual chapters. But as a general matter, the statutes' common mandate for protecting human health and the environment, read with the discretion afforded by the *Chemical Waste Management* and *Envotech* decisions, gives EPA ample authority to consider in the permitting process **cumulative impacts, sensitive populations, unique exposure pathways, and other environmental justice concerns** where the agency is the permitting authority. [p. 18]
Chapter 3: Permitting and Other Approvals	In order to make these determinations, EPA is authorized to collect substantial amounts of data from the parties proposing to manufacture or use a chemical substance or pesticide. FIFRA applicants must supply detailed information about the pesticide's chemical makeup and effects, and can be required to supplement this information even after registration through an EPA-initiated "data call-in." 7 U.S.C. § 136a(c)(2)(B). TSCA pre-manufacture notices must be accompanied by any test data the party knows about or could reasonably ascertain. 15 U.S.C. § 2604(d)(1). Under either statute, EPA could consider the need to include data on a substance's persistence in the environment and its **cumulative and synergistic impacts**, as well as demographic and other information useful for determining its impacts on low-income communities and communities of color. *See* Memorandum from Howard F. Corcoran, U.S. EPA Office of General Counsel, Environmental Justice Law Survey (Feb. 25, 1994) [hereinafter "OGC 1994 Memorandum"]. [p. 19-20]
Chapter 5: Enforcement	These directives to federal agencies apply to EPA as it decides which enforcement cases to pursue, and what relief to seek in those that it pursues. For example, the NEPA language requiring agencies to take "presently unquantified environmental amenities and values" into consideration provides a basis for the agency to fully examine the **cumulative impacts** of emissions on low-income communities and communities of color when prioritizing inspection and enforcement decisions. Similarly, the admonition to employ not only environmental sciences but also the social sciences in decision-making gives EPA a clear basis to examine the effect of existing emissions on members of identifiable groups and sub-populations, not just average healthy individuals. Going even further, EPA could consider the impact of emissions on the continuing integrity and vitality of these very groups, whose ability to survive as sustainable ethnic or cultural communities may be jeopardized by discharges that threaten their subsistence or the health of their members to such an extent that group identity and cohesion is lost. EPA can include all these factors as it decides the most effective use of its enforcement powers. [p. 28]

Chapter 5: **Enforcement**	Another central issue is the **cumulative or synergistic effects** of exposure to a number of emissions from numerous facilities. EPA has authority to consider these **cumulative effects** in enforcement. As discussed above, Section 504 of the Clean Water Act authorizes EPA to take action "upon receipt of evidence that a pollution source *or combination of sources* is presenting an imminent and substantial endangerment to public health or welfare." 33 U.S.C. § 1364 (emphasis added); similarly, CAA Section 303 provides that EPA may bring suit to immediately restrain any person causing *or contributing to* pollution that presents an imminent or substantial endangerment. 42 U.S.C. § 7603. This statutory authority to consider combined sources provides EPA with considerable flexibility in evaluating cases for enforcement action. For example, there may be only one or two facilities that are out of compliance but whose emissions, when added to those of complying facilities, may create conditions of endangerment. EPA could place a greater priority on bringing enforcement actions against the violators than would exist in the absence of **cumulative impacts**. EPA also could consider bringing action against a larger group of dischargers whose aggregate impact on ambient conditions endangers public health, even though no single facility exceeds regulatory standards. In such cases, EPA might seek a remedy that imposes requirements more restrictive than the standards that obtain in the absence of **cumulative effects**. [p. 31]
Chapter 5: **Enforcement** Citizens suits	Citizen suits can be an effective vehicle for community participation, as well as for developing substantive **legal theories of cumulative harm and protection of sensitive populations** that are important for addressing environmental justice issues. In addition, community control of the legal action helps ensure that enforcement decisions, as well as settlement decisions, will be reviewed fully by those presumed to be best able to reflect the community's goals and expectations. On the other hand, technical requirements and the need for expert witnesses may prove difficult challenges, and legal fees for long and hard-fought cases can be steep. EPA could support citizen suits by developing a program to provide assistance for those suits that are designed to advance issues of concern to low-income communities and communities of color. For example, EPA can support access to records and documents, access to its inspectors and experts and other litigation support, or even direct financial support of citizen plaintiffs. In appropriate cases, the agency can provide significant direct assistance by choosing to intervene in citizen suits using the authority provided in its statutes. [p. 37-38]
Chapter 6: **Information** **Gathering**	The need for research into health and environmental issues of concern to people of color and low-income communities has long been a focus of the national dialogue on environmental justice. Discussion about research to promote environmental justice issues has centered on both the substance of the research and the manner of conducting the research. It is widely believed that a greater understanding is needed of how to gauge the health effects of pollution on overburdened communities: **cumulative and synergistic effects** of pollutants, as well their effects on people who may be particularly sensitive because of underlying medical conditions such as asthma, or socio-economic conditions such as limited access to health care, poor nutrition, etc. In addition, research into medical conditions that are more prevalent in communities of color, such as asthma or lead poisoning, can also further efforts to ensure environmental protection for those communities. The process for conducting research from the development of research projects to the research itself and the evaluation of the results has also been the subject of much discussion. Communities of color and low-income communities, which historically have had limited input into the regulatory decision-making process, have similarly been excluded from decisions about scientific and technical research priorities. *See generally*, NATIONAL ENVIRONMENTAL JUSTICE ADVISORY COUNCIL, ENVIRONMENTAL JUSTICE AND COMMUNITY-BASED HEALTH MODEL DISCUSSION (Meeting Report, May 2000). [p. 39-40]

Chapter 6: Information Gathering	EPA also has authority to require regulated entities to undertake research. Perhaps the most prominent example is the chemical testing program under the Toxic Substances Control Act. 15 U.S.C. § 2603. EPA can take environmental justice concerns into account in determining which existing chemicals will be subject to testing by chemical manufacturers and processors. In addition, TSCA Section 4(b)(2), which sets out the types of effects for which EPA may prescribe testing standards, specifically includes "**cumulative or synergistic effects**, and any other effect which may present an unreasonable risk of injury to health or the environment," giving EPA broad authority to research the types of health effects of concern to communities of color and low-income communities. 15 U.S.C. § 2603(b)(2). [p. 41]
Chapter 9: NEPA	The Council on Environmental Quality oversees not only the federal government's compliance with NEPA, but also federal agencies' compliance with Executive Order 12898, "Federal Actions to Address Environmental Justice in Minority Populations and Low-Income Populations," issued on February 11, 1994. As such, CEQ has issued a guidance document to assist federal agencies with their NEPA procedures to ensure that environmental justice concerns are both identified and addressed. See Council on Environmental Quality, Environmental Justice: Guidance under the National Environmental Policy Act (Dec. 10, 1997) [hereinafter "CEQ EJ Guidance"], *available at* http://ceq.eh.doe.gov/nepa/regs/ej/ej.pdf (last visited Nov. 13, 2001). In its guidance document, the CEQ suggests that federal agencies consider six principles as they incorporate environmental justice into the NEPA process.

(2) Agencies should consider relevant public health and industry data concerning the potential for **multiple exposures or cumulative exposure** to human health or environmental hazards in the affected population, as well as historical patterns of exposure to environmental hazards, to the extent that such information is reasonably available.

(3) Agencies should recognize "the interrelated cultural, social, occupational, historical, or economic factors that may amplify the natural and physical environmental effects of the proposed action." These factors should include the physical sensitivity of the community or population to particular impacts, the effect of any disruption of the community structure associated with the proposed action, and the nature and degree of the impact on the community's physical and social structure. [p. 70-71] |
| **Chapter 9: NEPA** Preparation of Environmental Impact Statement (Scoping) | Upon determining that a proposed action may significantly affect the environment, a federal agency must prepare an EIS. This process begins with scoping – "an early and open process for determining the scope of issues to be addressed and for identifying the significant issues related to a proposed action." 40 C.F.R. § 1501.7. To determine the scope of an EIS, an agency must consider three types of impacts: direct, indirect, and **cumulative**. 40 C.F.R. § 1508.25. [p. 78] |
| **Chapter 9: NEPA** | *Cumulative Impacts.* According to the CEQ regulations, "effects" can be "ecological . . . aesthetic, historic, cultural, economic, social, or health, whether direct, indirect, or **cumulative**." 40 C.F.R. § 1508.8. The regulations define "**cumulative impact**" as "the impact on the environment which results from the incremental impact of the action when added to other past, present, and reasonably foreseeable future actions regardless of what agency (Federal or non-Federal) or person undertakes such other actions. **Cumulative impacts** can result from individually minor but collectively significant actions taking place over a period of time." 40 C.F.R. § 1508.7. Thus, where EPA does prepare an EIS, the agency has authority to consider fully the adverse environmental and health impacts of a proposed activity on already overburdened communities. *See generally* DANIEL R. MANDELKER, NEPA LAW AND LITIGATION 10.12 (1999) [hereinafter "Mandelker"] (discussion of case law addressing consideration of **cumulative impacts**).

The Council on Environmental Quality has provided a guidance document on addressing **cumulative impacts** that emphasizes the importance of analyzing such impacts during all |

	phases of the EIS process, from scoping through the development of alternatives and mitigation measures. Council on Environmental Quality, Considering Cumulative Effects Under the National Environmental Policy Act (January 1997), *available at* http://ceq.eh.doe.gov/nepa/ccenepa/ccenepa.htm (last visited Nov. 13, 2001). The guidance states the general principle that "additional effects contributed by actions unrelated to the proposed action must be included in the analysis of **cumulative effects**." Id. at Table 1-2. The guidance also a lists a number of examples of **cumulative effects** issues that could arise in a proposed activity, including: social, economic or cultural effects on low-income communities or communities of color resulting from ongoing development; long-term containment or disposal of hazardous wastes; and air emissions resulting in degradation of regional air quality. Id. at Table 2-1. EPA's guidance underlines the importance of considering **cumulative impacts**, stating that "analysts need to place special emphasis on other sources of environmental stress within the region," including the number and concentration of permitted and non-permitted sources of pollution, the presence of toxic pollutants with high exposure potential, and other factors. EPA EJ Guidance at 2.2.2. *Social and Economic Impacts.* Social and economic impacts also are included in the CEQ regulatory definition of effects. 40 C.F.R. § 1508.8. While the regulations state that economic or social effects alone are not intended to require an EIS, when an EIS is prepared and "economic or social and natural or physical environmental effects are interrelated, then the [EIS] will discuss all of these effects on the human environment." 40 C.F.R. § 1508.14. This provision, in conjunction with the requirements to consider **cumulative and indirect impacts**, creates an opportunity for the EIS to consider a broad range of impacts on overburdened communities, provided those impacts are related to a proposed change in the physical environment. *See generally* Mandelker at 8.07[6] (discussion of case law addressing consideration of **cumulative impacts**). As a result of NEPA's broad public participation provisions, this analysis can be fully informed by the comments of the affected communities. The EPA environmental justice guidance discusses the possible need to use cultural or social impact assessments as tools for analyzing specific socio-economic impacts to communities that share a common cultural or spiritual environment. EPA EJ Guidance at 5.3. To assess accurately the potential disproportionately high and adverse effects to communities of color and low-income communities and account for these effects, the guidance notes that EIS analysts may be required to move beyond standard socio-economic modeling and consider such issues as subsistence living, treaty-protected resources, cultural use of natural resources, sacred sites, dependence on public transportation, community cohesion, and a relatively unskilled labor base. Id. [p. 82-83]
Chapter 10: Federal Clean Water Control Act Technology-Based Standards Sections 301, 303, 304	**Section 304** requires EPA to promulgate regulations that contain detailed guidelines for the agency's adoption or revision of effluent limitations under Section 301, and to specify the factors that will be used in determining the BPT, BAT, and BCT standards for different categories of point sources. 33 U.S.C. § 1314(b). The guidelines must be reviewed annually, with public review and comment. 33 U.S.C. § 1314(m). In addition to technical issues and cost, the relevant considerations incorporated into the guidelines may include "such other factors as the Administrator deems appropriate." 33 U.S.C. § 1314(b)(1)(B), (2)(B), & (4)(B). EPA thus could use this broad authority to consider environmental justice issues as a factor when setting appropriate levels of technology-based standards. In particular, where such standards allow or require some consideration of the costs and benefits of a particular technology, this analysis could give weight to the benefits to **heavily impacted communities or sensitive populations**. The Act allows for variances from technology-based standards under certain conditions. In issuing such variances, EPA also could take environmental justice factors into account. For example, **Section 301(g)** allows the agency to modify the BAT requirements for certain

	"nonconventional" pollutants, such as ammonia, chlorine, and iron, as long as the lower BPT standard is still met and
	such modification will not interfere with the attainment or maintenance of that water quality which shall assure protection of public water supplies, and the protection and propagation of a balanced population of shellfish, fish, and wildlife, and . . .such modification will not result in the discharge of pollutants in quantities which may reasonably be anticipated to pose an unacceptable risk to human health or the environment because of bioaccumulation, persistency in the environment, acute toxicity, chronic toxicity (including carcinogenicity, mutagenicity or teratogenicity), or **synergistic** propensities.
	33 U.S.C. § 1311(g)(2)(C). In addition, **Section 301(h)** allows the agency to modify the secondary treatment requirement for municipal waste treatment plants that discharge into marine waters if "the discharge of pollutants in accordance with such modified requirements will not interfere, alone *or in combination with pollutants from other sources,* with the attainment or maintenance of that water quality which assures protection of public water supplies and the protection and propagation of a balanced, indigenous population of shellfish, fish, and wildlife." 33 U.S.C. § 1311(h)(2) (emphasis added).
	The Act thus directs EPA to consider carefully the public health and ecosystem risks prior to granting any such variances, including issues such as **bioaccumulation, synergistic effects, and cumulative impacts**. [p. 89-90]
Chapter 10: Federal Clean Water Control Act	In addition, **Section 303(c)(2)** requires states to include all EPA-listed toxic pollutants in their review of impaired water bodies, and to develop "specific numerical criteria" for these pollutants where their presence "could reasonably be expected to interfere with those designated uses adopted by the State, as necessary to support such designated uses." 33 U.S.C. § 1313(c)(2)(B). Absent such numerical criteria, the states must adopt criteria based on biological monitoring or assessment methods. Id. This section effectively requires toxic pollutants to be included in the TMDL calculations being made under Section 303(d), above. Thus, an EPA decision to expand the toxics listings also would indirectly affect the stringency of water quality standards and TMDLs being developed at the state level. In addition, the option to use biological criteria enables methods like whole effluent testing, which has been called "the only [method] to date that even attempts to measure the **cumulative** effects of what is actually being discharged." Houck article at 10558. This in turn could yield empirical data and standards that are more specifically tailored to heavily burdened communities. [p. 94]
Chapter 10: Federal Clean Water Control Act	**Section 404(a)** of the Act authorizes the Army Corps of Engineers to "issue permits, after notice and opportunity for public hearings for the discharge of dredged or fill material into the navigable waters at specified disposal sites." 33 U.S.C. § 1344(a). In considering a permit application, the Corps first must conduct a "public interest review" that is "based on an evaluation of the probable impacts, *including cumulative impacts,* of the proposed activity and its intended use on the public interest." 33 C.F.R. 320.4(a)(1) (emphasis added). The review consists of a case-by-case balancing of a long list of factors, which includes "conservation, economics, aesthetics, general environmental concerns, wetlands, historic properties, fish and wildlife values, flood hazards, floodplain values, land use, navigation, shore erosion and accretion, recreation, water supply and conservation, water quality, energy needs, safety, food and fiber production, mineral needs, considerations of property ownership and, in general, the needs and welfare of the people." Id. [p. 98]

Chapter 10: Federal Clean Water Control Act	Several of these factors touch on environmental justice concerns. For example, the definition of "historic properties" expressly includes "Indian religious or cultural sites," 33 C.F.R. § 320.4(e), and it has been suggested that the general "needs and welfare of the people" factor allows ample room for considering disproportionate impacts or other environmental justice issues. Hill & Targ at 36. In addition, the express requirement that **cumulative** impacts be considered could be especially important for communities whose watersheds are already severely impacted by dredge-and-fill projects or other kinds of activity. [p. 98-99]
Chapter 10: Federal Clean Water Control Act	Here again, each of these factors could be read to include health and environmental issues relevant to low-income communities and communities of color. For example, the requirement that alternatives be considered could lead to consideration of other possible sites that are not already over-burdened or that already enjoy more environmental benefits. "Significant degradation" is specifically defined in terms of human health concerns, including exposure through the food chain. In addition, the minimization requirement appears to give broad authority to attach permit conditions or to require the permittee to take action to address a wide variety of adverse impacts. **Cumulative** impacts are specifically addressed in 40 C.F.R. § 230.11(g), which requires such impacts to be "documented and considered during the decision-making process concerning the evaluation of individual permit applications, the issuance of a General permit, and monitoring and enforcement of existing permits." [p. 99]
Chapter 11: Clean Air Act	CAA **Section 117(b)** states that EPA shall, "to the maximum extent practicable within the time provided, consult with appropriate advisory committees, independent experts, and Federal departments and agencies" prior to issuing air quality criteria, hazardous air pollutant lists, standards, or regulations. 42 U.S.C. § 7417(b). **Section 117(a)** states that "committee members shall include, but not be limited to, persons who are knowledgeable concerning air quality from the standpoint of health, welfare, economics or technology." 42 U.S.C. § 7416(a). This requirement to include persons who are knowledgeable about public health can be interpreted as authority to appoint committee members from low-income communities and communities of color with first-hand knowledge of health impacts, or others who have public health backgrounds specifically focused on **cumulative** impacts, synergistic effects, and other environmental justice issues. [Advisory Committees, p. 106-107]
Chapter 11: Clean Air Act	**Section 111(j)** allows any person proposing to own or operate a new source to request an EPA waiver from the new source performance standards with respect to any air pollutant, to encourage the use of an innovative technological system or systems of continuous emission reduction. 42 U.S.C. § 7411(j)(1)(A). A waiver will be granted if EPA determines that the owner or operator of the proposed source has demonstrated that "the proposed system will not cause or contribute to an unreasonable risk to public health, welfare, or safety in its operation, function, or malfunction." 42 U.S.C. § 7411(j)(1)(A)(iii). In addition to the reference to public health and welfare, which allows consideration of a broad range of impacts on low-income communities and communities of color, the provision states that the proposed system must not "contribute to" unreasonable risk to public health and welfare. This language could allow EPA to consider **cumulative** impacts when addressing the health risks to a community. *See* Lazarus & Tai at 634. [p. 110]
Chapter 11: Clean Air Act Solid Waste Incineration	**Section 129** requires EPA to establish performance standards under Section 111 for each category of solid waste incineration unit. 42 U.S.C. § 7429(a)(1). **Section 129(a)(3)** states that such standards shall be based on "methods and technologies for removal or destruction of pollutants before, during, or after combustion, and shall incorporate for new units siting requirements that minimize, on a *site specific basis*, to the maximum extent practicable, potential risks to public health and the environment." 42 U.S.C. § 7429(a)(3) (emphasis added). This provision gives EPA authority to establish a range of siting requirements designed to ensure that potential health risks to low-income communities and communities of color from solid waste incinerator air emissions are minimized, including consideration of **cumulative** impacts and meaningful community participation procedures. *See* Lazarus & Tai at 632. [Solid Waste Incineration, p. 111]

Chapter 11: **Clean Air Act**	**Section 110(a)(2)(B)** requires "each implementation plan submitted by a state" to "provide for the establishment and operation of appropriate devices, methods, systems, and procedures necessary to monitor, compile, and analyze data on ambient air quality." 42 U.S.C. § 110(a)(2)(B). Likewise, **Section 110(a)(2)(F)** allows EPA to require SIPs to include "the installation, maintenance, replacement, and implementation of other necessary steps, by owners of operators of stationary sources to monitor emissions from such sources," 42 U.S.C. § 110(a)(2)(F), and **Section 110(a)(2)(K)** requires SIPs to provide for air quality modeling. 42 U.S.C. § 7410(a)(2)(K). Each of these monitoring and modeling requirements could be adjusted to consider **cumulative** exposures, sensitive populations, and other issues of concern to communities of color and low-income communities. [State Implementation Plans, p. 127]
Chapter 11: **Clean Air Act**	Under **Section 105,** EPA may make grants to state air pollution control agencies for the prevention and control of air pollution or implementation of NAAQS. 42 U.S.C. § 7405. The section requires the agency [b]efore approving any planning grant . . .to receive assurances that the [air control agency receiving the grant] has the capability of developing a comprehensive air quality plan for the air quality control region, which plan shall include (when appropriate) a recommended system of alerts to avert and reduce the risk of situations in which there may be imminent and serious danger to the public health or welfare from air pollutants and the various aspects relevant to the establishment of air quality standards for such air quality control region, including the concentration of industries, other commercial establishments, populations and naturally occurring factors which shall affect such standards. 42 U.S.C. § 7405(a)(3). EPA could use this provision to condition grant assistance on consideration of **cumulative** impacts in the planning process for establishing air quality standards, and on considering demographic factors in developing the recommended system of alerts. [p. 129-130]
Chapter 12: **RCRA**	**Section 3001** instructs EPA to identify hazardous wastes subject to Subtitle C by using two different methods: (1) according to its hazardous characteristics, or (2) by listing particular hazardous wastes. A solid waste is classified as a hazardous waste and regulated under Subtitle C if it either exhibits one of the defined hazardous characteristics or it is listed as a hazardous waste, unless it is categorically exempted under the RCRA regulations. 42 U.S.C. § 6921. In promulgating its criteria for hazardous characteristics and listed wastes, EPA is directed to take into account factors such as toxicity, persistence, degradability in nature, potential for accumulation in tissue, flammability, corrosiveness, and other hazardous characteristics. 42 U.S.C. §6921(a). This determination raises environmental justice issues, as it requires EPA to determine the waste's health impact on humans – which inevitably involves a determination of which population or sub-population of humans to base the standard upon. For example, in determining a waste's "toxicity" or "potential for accumulation in tissue," EPA must determine whether its "standard" human subject would be taken from the general population, a sensitive population, or a population that faces disproportionate exposure to the waste or **cumulative** exposures to it and other kinds of wastes. By including these types of factors in its determination, EPA can further environmental justice in its identification of hazardous wastes and their inclusion in the more restrictive Subtitle C regime. [p. 133-134]
Chapter 12: **RCRA**	**Section 3002(b)** requires generators to certify that they have "a program in place to reduce the volume or quantity and toxicity" of their wastes. Generators also must certify that the proposed method of treatment, storage, or disposal "minimizes the present and future threat to human health and the environment." 42 U.S.C. § 6922(b). This health-based language supports consideration of environmental justice concerns; for example, the process of certifying proposed methods of treatment, storage, or disposal could include an examination of the surrounding community to account for possible **cumulative risks and synergistic effects**. [p. 134]

Chapter 12: RCRA	Such information about exposure pathways and **cumulative** risks are precisely the kind of data environmental justice advocates often seek. Under the Section 3019 provisions, EPA has authority to generate this information, at least with respect to land disposal facilities. In addition, **Section 3019(c)** provides that "[a]ny member of the public may submit evidence of releases or of exposure to hazardous constituents from such a facility, or as to the risks or health effects associated with such releases or exposure." 42 U.S.C. § 6939a(c). This section provides an important opportunity for public participation in the health assessment process. [Land Disposal Permits, p. 139-140]
Chapter 13: CERCLA	These general provisions grant EPA considerable authority to respond to releases and threatened releases of hazardous substances. Given the broad statutory language, environmental justice concerns, such as **cumulative** risk and vulnerability of sensitive populations, could presumably be taken into account by EPA in defining "imminent and substantial danger" and determining whether to use its response authority. The statute also provides that EPA actions may be taken to protect "welfare," in addition to public health and the environment. This may provide a basis for EPA to consider non-health impacts, such as social, cultural, and economic impacts, that might be of particular concern to communities of color and low-income communities. [p. 151]
Chapter 13: CERCLA	EPA has rarely used these exceptions to the limitations on its removal and remedial authority. EPA could, however, rely on this section to address hazardous substance releases in low-income communities and communities of color that may otherwise go unaddressed. This may include releases from products, such as asbestos or lead paint, that are part of the structure of buildings. They may also include releases into public or private drinking water supplies due to deterioration of the system through ordinary use, particularly in communities with limited financial resources for maintaining buildings and water systems. In addition, such releases may pose particular public health threats in many low-income communities and communities of color because of factors such as sensitive populations and **cumulative** risks. Furthermore, because many low-income communities and communities of color have limited resources, it may be likely that there are no other authorities with capability to respond to the releases. [p. 151]
Chapter 13: CERCLA	**Section 106(c)** requires EPA to establish guidelines for using the imminent hazard, enforcement, and emergency response authorities granted under Section 106 of CERCLA, which provides the authority for EPA to issue cleanup orders and to request that the Justice Department assist it in securing necessary relief in court. 42 U.S.C. § 9606(c). Among the issues that must be addressed by the guidelines are: the enforcement of standards and permits, the gathering of information, and the imminent hazard and emergency powers authorized in other statutes administered by EPA. Id. This section provides broad, general authority that arguably would allow EPA to take environmental justice considerations into account in developing or amending guidelines for using its emergency response and enforcement authorities. [Abatement Actions, p. 151]
Chapter 13: CERCLA	**Section 102(a)** provides broad authority to EPA to promulgate and revise, as appropriate, the regulations that designate those hazardous substances that, when released into the environment, "may present substantial danger to the public health or welfare or the environment." 42 U.S.C. § 9602 (a). EPA must also promulgate regulations establishing what quantity of release of any hazardous substance must be reported. Id. **Section 103(a)** establishes the actual duty to report releases. This section provides general authority that arguably could allow EPA to take into account environmental justice considerations in designating hazardous substances and their reportable quantities. For example, EPA could consider, as appropriate, **cumulative** exposure scenarios, sensitive populations, and consumption patterns in setting or revising threshold reporting quantities in its regulations. *See* 40 C.F.R. Part 302. [p. 158]

Chapter 13: **CERCLA**	This provision could possibly be used to require EPA to meet its statutory obligation to evaluate facilities in communities of color and low-income communities, if such evaluations have not been completed within the appropriate time frames. This section does not address the factors that EPA should take into account in determining priorities among assessments or determining whether evaluations are warranted on the basis of site inspections or preliminary assessments. Because the statute is silent on these points and Section 105(a) gives EPA broad general authority to determine methods for investigating and evaluating facilities, it is arguable that EPA could consider environmental justice concerns, such as the **cumulative** exposures suffered by a particular community, in determining whether a site should be evaluated. In addition, the statute provides considerable discretion to EPA to develop the criteria used in site evaluations. As discussed above, the criteria for evaluations and for determining priorities among releases for inclusion on the NPL must be based, in part, on "relative risk or danger to the public health or welfare or the environment," taking into account to the extent possible the "population at risk" and several other considerations set out in the statute, as well as "other appropriate factors." 42 U.S.C. § 9605(a)(8)(A). [Assessment and Listing of Facilities, p. 160]
Chapter 13: **CERCLA**	**Section 121(c)** provides that if EPA selects a remedial action that results in any hazardous substance, pollutant, or contaminant remaining at a site, EPA must review the remedial action no less often than every five years after the initiation of the remedial action to assure that human health and the environment are being protected. 42 U.S.C. § 9621(c). In addition, if EPA determines after the five-year review that cleanup action is appropriate, EPA must take or require such action. Id. This is an important statutory provision for purposes of protecting communities of color and low-income communities. EPA's failure to conduct five-year reviews in a timely manner has been well-documented. *See, e.g.,* KATHERINE PROBST, SUPERFUND'S FUTURE: WHAT WILL IT COST, A REPORT TO CONGRESS 63 (2001). EPA has taken steps to meet its five-year review obligations, but it remains to be seen whether it can adequately address the back log and keep up with current demands. Meeting the five-year review requirements is particularly important for communities of color to the extent that EPA is more likely to select containment remedies for sites in those communities than in white communities. *See* Ferris at 673. In addition, remedies that allow contaminants to remain onsite may pose a greater risk to communities of color and low-income communities than other communities because of **cumulative** exposures, consumption patterns, and the presence of sensitive populations. Low-income communities may also have limited resources for taking steps to ensure that EPA meets its review obligations. Thus, this provision could be used to protect these communities from risks posed by contaminants that remain after site cleanups are completed. [Remedy Action, p. 164]
Chapter 13: **CERCLA**	CERCLA contains a variety of enforcement authorities and penalty provisions. The following is a brief outline of the key provisions. Because they are generic provisions, no analysis is provided and the same considerations with respect to environmental justice would apply to these provisions, as apply to most penalty provisions in environmental laws. For example, EPA enforcement authorities should be applied consistently and aggressively in all situations in which private parties or federal facilities fail to comply with administrative orders. This may be particularly important with respect to Superfund sites, given the research that indicates that EPA has tended to enforce more aggressively in white communities. *See* Lavelle & Coyle. In addition, CERCLA and other statutes' enforcement provisions which allow for punitive damages or fines in excess of general caps could be implemented in a manner that takes into account the special harm that noncompliance can cause to members of communities of color and low-income communities because of **cumulative** exposures and consumption patterns. Similarly, statutory provisions that allow for consideration of the "gravity" of the violation or allow for consideration of other "factors as justice may require" may allow EPA to include environmental justice considerations in bringing enforcement actions. For a fuller discussion of statutory enforcement authorities for advancing environmental justice, see Chapter 5. [Enforcement, p. 167-168]

| **Chapter 14:** **FIFRA,** | In establishing tolerances or exemptions pursuant to **Section 408(b)** of the FFDCA, EPA must consider nine specific factors, "among other relevant factors." 21 U.S.C. § 346a(b)(2)(D). As discussed below, some of these factors are of particular importance from an environmental justice perspective.

One important factor that EPA must consider is "available information concerning the dietary consumption patterns of consumers (and major identifiable subgroups of consumers)." 21 U.S.C. § 346a(b)(2)(D)(iv). Thus, the agency can examine the extent to which dietary consumption patterns in communities of color and low-income communities differ from patterns in the general population. For example, some low-income or Native American communities rely on subsistence fishing and hunting, and the animals they consume can contain unsafe levels of pesticide residue as a result of runoff and drift. Low-income communities may also have less adequate diets and lower levels of health generally, which could combine to increase susceptibility to the harmful effects of pesticides. Similarly, agricultural worker communities often consume fresh fruits and vegetables that contain higher levels of pesticide residue than fruits and vegetables that take longer to reach the table.

Another factor that EPA must consider is "available information concerning the **aggregate exposure levels** of consumers (and major identifiable subgroups of consumers) to the pesticide chemical residue and to other related substances, including dietary exposure under the tolerance and all other tolerances in effect for the pesticide chemical residue, and exposure from other non-occupational sources." 21 U.S.C. § 346a(b)(2)(D)(vi). Thus, EPA can consider whether communities of color and low-income communities are exposed to more pesticides from more sources than other communities.

Additionally, EPA is directed to consider "available information concerning the variability of the sensitivities of major identifiable subgroups of consumers." 21 U.S.C. § 346a(b)(2)(D)(vii). This factor gives the agency a means of determining whether members of low-income communities or communities of color may be particularly sensitive to the effects of pesticides. Taken together, these three statutory factors are significant because they refer expressly to the need to consider "major identifiable subgroups of consumers." A fundamental concern about pesticide risk assessment has been that it fails to capture the disproportionate risks borne by population subgroups – particularly communities of color and low-income communities – that suffer higher exposure levels and may have increased susceptibility to health risks. *See* Scott Bauer, *The Food Quality Protection Act of 1996: Replacing Old Impracticalities with New Uncertainties in Pesticide Regulation*, 75 N.C. L. Rev. 1398 note at 1405-06 (1997).

The FQPA has focused attention on major identifiable subgroups, thereby giving EPA a clear means of examining how pesticide residues impact communities of color and low-income communities. In fact, in 1998 the Natural Resources Defense Council and others filed a petition with the agency to designate farm children as a "major identifiable subgroup and population at special risk" to be protected under the FQPA pursuant to these three factors. Petition for a Directive that the Agency Designate Farm Children as a Major Identifiable Subgroup and Population at Special Risk to Be Protected Under the Food Quality Protection Act 4, *In the Matter of Natural Resources Defense Council, et al., Petition to the Administrator* (Oct. 1998), *available at* http://ecologic-ipm.com/farmkids.PDF (last visited Nov. 14, 2001).

Other factors to be weighed in connection with tolerance setting are also important to environmental justice. EPA is required to consider "available information concerning the **cumulative** effects of such residues and other substances that have a common mechanism of toxicity." 21 U.S.C. § 346a(b)(2)(D)(v). This provision is a directive to consider how similar chemicals – which may be present in pesticide residues as well as "other substances" – work together to create harmful effects. Here again, because communities of color and low-income communities are more likely than the general population to face multiple exposures from |
| --- | --- |

	multiple toxic substances, the issue of **cumulative** effects from common mechanisms of toxicity is highly relevant. Finally, it is important to note that the factors listed in the statute represent only a starting point, as EPA may also consider "other relevant factors." 21 U.S.C. § 346a(b)(2)(D). This provides an opportunity for the agency to obtain and review any other demographic and geographical data that might assist in the identification and delineation of specific affected communities. Other factors might also include morbidity in communities of color and low-income communities, as well as susceptibility of such communities to harm from particular toxins. Taken together, all of these factors provide a set of tools not only for obtaining and examining, but also for acting on this information in establishing pesticide residue tolerances and exemptions. [p. 187-188]
Chapter 14: **FIFRA, FFDCA,** **FGPA**	**Section 408(b)** of the FFDCA requires that in the process of establishing a tolerance or exemption for a pesticide residue, EPA must assess the risk of the residue based on certain categories of available information involving infants and children. The agency must consider: • "available information about consumption patterns among infants and children that are likely to result in disproportionately high consumption of foods containing or bearing such residue among infants and children in comparison to the general population;" • "available information concerning the special susceptibility of infants and children to the pesticide chemical residues, including neurological differences between infants and children and adults, and effects of in utero exposure to pesticide chemicals;" and • "available information concerning the **cumulative** effects on infants and children of such residues and other substances that have a common mechanism of toxicity." [p. 188-189]
Chapter 15: **SDWA**	Thus, MCLGs set contaminant levels that protect against all known or anticipated health effects with an adequate margin of safety, while the MCLs included in primary drinking water regulations establish contaminant levels that factor in technological and financial considerations. These SDWA standard setting provisions give EPA authority to act in two important ways. First, the agency can identify any drinking water contaminants that may adversely affect the health of communities of color and low-income communities and ensure that MCLs and MCLGs are adopted to reduce those risks. Second, EPA can ensure that MCLGs reflect health risks that may be of particular concern to communities of color and low-income communities, due to **cumulative** impacts of pollutants, or due to the effects of drinking water pollutants on sensitive populations. [Maximum contaminant load, p. 203]
Chapter 15: **SDWA**	The standard set out in the Act and the regulations provides EPA with broad authority to adopt regulations designed to ensure that state programs do not allow underground injection that may result in adverse effects on human health in communities of color and low-income communities. For example, the regulations could include provisions aimed at addressing situations in which underground injection wells might contribute to **cumulative** health effects from multiple sources of hazardous substances. [Deep Injection Wells, p. 210]
Chapter 16: **TSCA**	EPA can promote environmental justice by considering fully the potential risks to affected communities from the proposed activity involving PCBs before granting any exemptions to the TSCA prohibitions. For example, EPA could consider whether the activity presents unreasonable risks due to unique exposure pathways, such as fish consumption, or due to the **cumulative** and synergistic effects of numerous sources of chemical exposure in the affected communities. [PCBs, p. 228]

Chapter 16: **TSCA**	In determining whether to require testing, TSCA directs EPA to consider whether "manufacture, distribution in commerce, processing, use or disposal of a chemical substance or mixture, or . . .*any combination of* such activities" may present unreasonable health risks. 15 U.S.C. § 2603(a)(1) (emphasis added). In determining whether a chemical may pose an unreasonable risk, EPA can promote environmental justice by considering fully the potential health and environmental risks to communities of color and low-income communities – for example, by considering whether unique exposure pathways exist, whether multiple sources of exposure may produce **cumulative** and synergistic effects, or whether sensitive populations are exposed. **Section 4(b)** establishes the requirements for promulgating test rules once EPA has made the necessary findings under Section 4(a). **Section 4(b)(2)** sets out the types of health and environmental effects for which EPA may prescribe standards on developing test data. The Act specifically includes "**cumulative** or synergistic effects, and any other effect which may present an unreasonable risk of injury to health or the environment." 15 U.S.C. § 2603(b)(2)(A). The law thus gives EPA explicit authority to require testing to obtain information on the types of health effects that are of particular concern to heavily impacted communities. [p. 234]
Chapter 17: **EPCRA**	This statutory authority provides considerable opportunity for EPA to incorporate environmental justice concerns in guidance for state and local entities responsible for emergency planning and response. For example, guidance documents could assist localities in determining whether low-income communities and communities of color may require special medical attention in the event of a chemical release, because of **cumulative** exposures, consumption patterns, or sensitive populations. Guidance documents could also provide suggestions as to how to include and recruit representatives from low-income communities and communities of color on emergency planning teams. [National Response Team Emergency Guidance, p. 239]
Chapter 17: **EPCRA**	**Section 311(b)** provides that EPA may establish threshold quantities for hazardous chemicals, below which no facility is subject to the material safety data sheet reporting requirements of Section 311. The threshold quantities may, in EPA's discretion, be based on classes of chemicals or categories of facilities. 42 U.S.C. § 11021(b). **Section 312(b)** provides that EPA may also establish threshold quantities for hazardous chemicals, below which no facility is subject to the emergency and hazardous chemical inventory form reporting requirements of Section 312. 42 U.S.C. § 11022(b). Under both provisions, the threshold quantities may, in EPA's discretion, be based on classes of chemicals or categories of facilities. 42 U.S.C. § 11021(b), 11022(b). These general provisions provide substantial discretion to EPA and, therefore, presumably could be used by EPA to consider environmental justice concerns, such as **cumulative** exposures, in establishing threshold quantities for hazardous chemicals under two key reporting requirements in the Act. [Hazardous Chemicals Threshold Quantity Regulations, p. 241]
Chapter 17: **EPCRA**	**Section 313(f)** provides that EPA may establish a threshold amount for purposes of reporting toxic chemicals that is different from the amount established in the statute. 42 U.S.C. § 11023(f). The revised threshold must obtain reporting of a substantial majority of total releases of the chemical at all facilities subject to the reporting requirement. The statute provides that the amounts established may be based on classes of chemicals or categories of facilities. Id. These provisions grant EPA substantial authority to shape the toxic chemical release reporting program. Environmental justice considerations could be taken into account by EPA in using this authority. EPA has used this authority in recent years to add chemicals to the list of chemicals that are subject to release reporting and to amend the SIC code list that determines which facilities must report. See, e.g., 62 Fed. Reg. 23834 (May 1, 1997) (addition of industry sectors, including metal mining, coal mining, and electric utilities); 59 Fed. Reg. 61432 (November 30, 1994) (addition of 286 chemicals to reporting list). EPA

	could consider whether any additional changes to the chemical and SIC code lists would be appropriate, in an effort to forward environmental justice goals. Such additions could be based on, for example, epidemiological studies of low-income communities and communities of color. EPA could also apply the toxic chemical release reporting requirements to the owners and operators of particular facilities that use toxic chemicals covered under Section 313, if such facilities pose risks to low-income communities and communities of color. EPA could also use its authority to make additional amendments to threshold reporting amounts. *See, e.g.,* 66 Fed. Reg. 4499 (January 13, 2001) (lowering reporting thresholds for lead and lead compounds because they are persistent, bioaccumulative, and toxic chemicals), codified at 40 C.F.R. Part 372. [p. 241]
Chapter 17: EPCRA	**Section 313(e)** provides that any person may petition EPA to add or delete a chemical from the list of chemicals subject to the toxic chemical release form reporting requirements. 42 U.S.C. § 11023(e). The petition must be based on the same criteria that the statute directs EPA to use in making deletions and additions to the list. 42 U.S.C. § 11023(e),(d)(2). Within 180 days after receipt of a petition, EPA must either initiate a rule-making to add or delete the chemical from the list or publish an explanation of why the petition is denied. 42 U.S.C. § 11023(e). This is a general tool that has been used by industry and environmental groups. It could be used specifically to promote environmental justice, because it authorizes petitions to EPA to list chemicals that may present particular threats to low-income communities and communities of color, due to **cumulative exposures, sensitive populations, or consumption patterns**. [p. 243]

Introduction

The current regulatory approach for siting and operating various types of facilities or activities is predominantly based on a risk-based paradigm from a single source or a single pollutant. In many urban areas, this approach along with zoning areas for mixed-use has resulted in the aggregation of sources (clusters) that are within the risk threshold for individual facilities, but cumulatively produce a higher exposure burden to people living in surrounding areas. This issue is critical in addressing the EJ concerns of a community.

In the current approach, emissions in a given area get weighted against their toxicity potential, but fail to consider the EJ concerns expressed by a community. These concerns include (but not limited to) the number of sources, density of sources, proximity of sources, demographics consideration, or emissions on a per capita basis for comparative purposes.

In light of this concern, USEPA and agencies like CARB and SCAQMD have initiated efforts to develop scientific approaches and tools (models) to evaluate cumulative impacts. The availability of these models for implementation is expected to take many years because of the complex nature of the models and limitations in the data inputs as well as the need to develop consensus among scientific community, industry and community.

Recognizing this inherent delay, the sub-group of the NEJAC concluded that an alternate simpler approach must be adopted in a shorter time frame for identifying communities that bear higher pollution burden and where remedial actions can be initiated. The remedial actions will be site specific and could include a number of options. Examples include proper degree of verifiable emissions controls installation in facilities that are primary/high risk drivers through incentives, strengthening enforcement programs, additional siting, permit and emission requirements for new facilities, etc.

The "Pollution Burden Matrix" proposed for community characterization is a conceptual framework for assessing cumulative impacts using a suite of proxy indicators of neighborhood-scale cumulative emissions, exposure and health effects. The example provided utilizes 20 indices and each is assigned a qualitative value of high, medium, or low to develop a composite "burden level" for a community. Instead, a numerical scale of 1-5 can be applied and the suite of indicators may be increased or decreased depending on the data availability. This matrix approach can be used to identify the communities having the highest burden levels and be given priority for all remedial actions that can be taken.

The PBM serves as a framework for developing a screening tool, which would rely primarily on analyses of existing or readily available sources of data, to identify the most burdened census tracts within a specified region. Optimally, data would be geocoded so that geographic analyses concerning potential problem areas of pollution source over-concentration and/or proximity to sensitive receptors within census tracts can be identified.

Geographical Unit and Demographic Data

Census tracts are chosen as the geographic unit of analysis owing to the availability of demographic data on race and socioeconomic status for the entire country. For each census tract, the following demographic information would be needed:

Total Population and categorical statistics: The severity of the pollution burden is partly a function of population – comparatively speaking, a problem is worse if a large number of people are affected than if only a few people are affected. More detailed information (e.g., % minority, % at or below poverty) is needed to tease out potential differences in environmental burden levels by race and class.

Total area of the census tract (km²): This information is needed to calculate densities of pollution-generating facilities and population. Collectively, a high facility density in a densely populated census tract could be a preliminary indication of the potential for problems due to the over-concentration of pollution sources or proximity of pollution sources to sensitive receptors. As the quality of data on pollution sources could vary significantly among census tracts, the census tracts with the highest facility densities could serve as a starting point for where to target more detailed data gathering or mitigation efforts.

Housing Statistics: Measures of median or average age and cost of housing in a community provide insight on the lead exposure (lead-based paint use in older homes), housing density, and income status. Housing age and density may also be indicators of potential problems with pests (insect and animal), molds, and indoor air quality.

Key Databases

As available, the following pollution source, emissions, exposure, health effects, and/or amenity data should be compiled to calculate the various indices in the PBM:

Inventory of Pollution Sources: For a multi-media assessment, as complete an inventory of air, water, and soil pollution sources is needed. For air, state or local air pollution control agencies may already maintain inventories of major sources (e.g., refineries, cement plants) for SIP-related activities. For water, sources that could potentially affect surface and groundwater quality would need to be identified (e.g., USEPA Toxic Release Inventory, National Water Quality Database). Depending on the principal land-uses in the region (rural vs. urban), sources of soil contamination could include brownfields, chemical applications to agricultural lands, military installations, and toxic storage and disposal facilities (Note: Superfund sites are considered separately -- see below).

Inventory of Major Roadways and Traffic: Major roadways serve as significant line sources for criteria and toxic air pollutants, and potentially significant sources from which contaminated runoff water could be delivered to sensitive aquatic, terrestrial, or human receptors. Where possible, information on traffic density and fleet composition (i.e., passenger cars vs. heavy-duty diesel trucks) would help to refine estimates of line source air emissions, and the source strength of roadways for water/soil contamination due to the build-up of vehicle-associated contaminants (e.g., tire and lubricant residues).

Inventory of Sensitive Receptors: An accounting of all the residences, schools, hospitals, elder-care facilities, etc. is needed to assess potential problems due to source proximity and availability of services. Using a GIS, measurements could then be made to determine an average index of source proximity to homes, schools, and hospitals, inter alia. A measure of hospital density (e.g., number per km², number per 1,000 people) could serve as a measure of the availability of health services in a census tract.

Acreage of Parks and Green Belts: The total "green-space" provides a measure of ecological amenities in urban census tracts. While this is not an indicator of pollution burden, it sheds light on the distribution of benefits within the region. This measure may not have utility for rural census tracts that may have tourism- or agriculture-based economies, where green-space would be a predominant land-use.

Ambient Concentrations of Criteria/Toxic Air Pollutants and Water Contaminants: For air quality related pollution problems, monitoring networks are operated to assess compliance with state and/or federal ambient air quality standards. These data, where available would be used to calculate population-weighted measures of air pollution exposure using peak values or daytime average levels, as appropriate. Drinking water quality data may be obtained from local agencies and/or from national water quality assessments conducted by USEPA.

Presence/Number of Superfund Sites: The existence of a Superfund in a community would, in itself, constitute a major pollution burden. The presence and number of Superfund sites provides an indication of a localized soil pollution problem that could also affect local water supplies and air quality, depending on the contaminant chemistry.

Measures of Health Effects: In addition to the incidence of cancer, a number of other non-cancer health responses should be examined to capture the range of effects that occur in the community (e.g., asthma, nose bleeds). While admissions data from hospitals could be used, consideration should also be given data from community-based organizations that document the extent of pollution-associated health problems where they live.

Other QOL-Reducing Entities: In addition to pollution-generating facilities, there are other activities and entities that reduce the quality of life in communities. These include rendering plants, recycling facilities, landfills, dairies, etc., that are not regulated with respect to emissions to air, water, or soil, but there presence often reduces the overall environmental quality in a community.

Indices of the Pollution Burden Matrix (PBM)

An analysis of the demographic data is first conducted to verify population and area information, to identify which census tracts are populated by low-income communities of color, and to determine if health risks from lead paint are an issue. As selected indices in the PBM are population- or area-weighted, it is important that there is a high level of certainty in these data.

The following of 15-items, for which other census tract-appropriate measures could be substituted, could be used in a PBM to identify the census tracts with the highest pollution burdens in a region. For each item below, the top 25% of values would be considered as having "high" burdens, the middle 50% would be "medium," and the bottom 25% have "low" burdens.

No.	Item	Rationale
1	Total criteria air pollutant emissions (TCE)	Total emissions from stationary, area, and mobile sources, which may be available from state and local agencies or national data compiled by USEPA (tons/day).
2	Total toxic air contaminants emissions (TTE)	As above, except for toxic air contaminants (TAC) (tons/day)
3	Population-weighted air emission burden (PWTE)	For criteria pollutants, TACs, or both. Total emissions are multiplied by census tract population (people-tons/day); the comparative severity of a pollution problem is greater in relation to the number of people affected.
4-6	Facility density -- High, Medium, and Low Emitting Sources. (FD-L, FD-M, FD-S)	After surveying the types of facilities in the region, divide them into three categories based on their emission rates – high, medium, and low. Facility densities (#/km^2) would be calculated for each facility size class.
7	Total Length of Major Roadways (TLR)	A measure of the total length major roadways (e.g., freeways, main thoroughfares with traffic densities above a selected level) as an indicator of community fragmentation and ancillary mobile source impacts (km).
8	Number of Superfund sites (NSS)	The presence of one or more Superfund sites, in itself, constitutes a severe pollution burden, both directly and indirectly.
9	Total release of toxic chemicals from Toxic Release Inventory (TRI) facilities	Although this has overlap with item 2, the TRI database is readily accessible database, and this may also capture releases to media other than air.
10	Presence/number of QOL-reducing entities (QOL)	This is a catch-all category to inventory the presence and number of facilities that may not be subject to air, water, or soil-specific regulations. They would include landfills, dairies, rendering plants, etc.
11	Acreage of Parks/Greenbelts (APG)	Serves as measure of the distribution of a valued amenity. In this case, census tracts with the most park acreage would be ranked low, and those with the least ranked high.
12	Total cancer risk (TCR)	Allows for comparing the cancer risks among census tracts with similar amounts of total TAC emissions; considers the cancer-causing potential of the TACs in ambient air.
13	Incidence of asthma (IOA)	Asthma, or some other respiratory effect, provides a measure of non-cancer health effects most associated with poor air quality.
14	Drinking water quality (DWQ)	County-level data are compiled for maximum contaminant level exceedances in drinking water sources at the point of entering drinking water supplies.
15	Number of leaking underground fuel storage tanks (LUST)	In urban areas, leaking underground fuel storage tanks can be a significant point source for groundwater contamination.

Identification of Census Tracts with High, Medium, and Low Burdens

Depending on data availability at the census tract level, a PBM for the region is question is developed based on the sources of pollution that are most likely to have an impact. There is no right or wrong number of indices to consider in the PBM, and use the maximum number of indices is likely to provide for the most robust analysis to be performed. An example of a PBM could be used in shown in the following table, based on the indices identified in the previous section. To calculate a total score, multiply each "H" by 5, "M" by 3, and "L" by 1, then sum the column (e.g., site 3 = [(6 x 5) + (11 x 3)] = 63).

Index*	Conceptual Comparison of Eight Areas in a Region							
	----------------------------- Areas of Comparison -----------------------------							
	1	2	3	4	5	6	7	8
TCE	H	H	M	M	M	M	L	L
TTE	H	H	M	M	M	M	L	L
PWTE	H	H	M	M	M	M	L	L
FD-L	H	H	M	M	M	M	L	L
FD-M	H	M	H	M	L	M	L	L
FD-S	H	M	M	H	L	M	M	L
TLR	H	M	H	M	M	L	M	L
NSS	H	M	H	M	M	L	M	L
TRI	H	H	M	M	M	M	L	L
QOL	H	M	H	M	M	L	M	L
APG	H	H	M	M	M	M	L	L
TCR	H	H	M	M	M	M	L	L
IOA	H	H	M	M	M	M	L	L
DWG	H	M	H	M	M	L	M	L
LUST	H	M	M	H	L	M	M	L
%P	H	M	M	H	L	M	M	L
%M	H	M	H	M	M	L	M	L
Total	85	67	63	57	43	41	33	17
Rank	1	2	3	4	5	6	7	8
BL	High	High	Med	Med	Med	Med	Low	Low

(*) %P = percent of census tract at or below the poverty level, %M = percent of the census tract that is African-American, Hispanic, or Asian

In this example, sites 1 and 2 have the highest relative burdens in the region, and initial efforts to investigate/mitigate existing EJ problems should begin with those sites. Over time, changes to the list of indices selected for use in the PBM could be made based on verification of or the inability to verify problems on the ground.

STATE CUMULATIVE RISK ACTIVITIES

Texas Commission on Environmental Quality
Staff Report on Cumulative Risk Activities
July 2003

Introduction

In 2001, HB 2912 (77th Texas Legislature) Section 1.12 amended Subchapter D, Chapter 5, Water Code by adding Section 5.130 Consideration of Cumulative Risk which states, *The Commission shall:*
(1) develop and implement policies, by specific environmental media, to protect the public from cumulative risks in areas of concentrated operations; and
(2) give priority to monitoring and enforcement in areas in which regulated facilities are concentrated.

On November 8, 2002, staff presented a status report at a Commissioners' Work Session regarding the implementation of the cumulative risk provisions of House Bill 2912. As a follow up to those discussions, staff was asked by the Commissioners to develop information on the following areas of interest:

- Existing agency regulatory and planning efforts to protect the public from cumulative risks and current agency activities regarding the prioritization of monitoring and enforcement activities in areas where regulated facilities are concentrated.

- Characteristics of the geographic features and programmatic situations that have prompted the agency to consider cumulative risk concerns or to establish monitoring or enforcement activities in areas where regulated facilities are concentrated. Factors may include facility or population densities, quantities of pollutant releases, programmatic criteria (Permitting, TMDLs, etc.), or other elements relating to agency regulatory requirements.

Findings

This report provides the information requested by the Commission at the November 8, 2002 meeting and illustrates ways that agency programs have applied the general concepts of "cumulative risk" and "areas of concentrated operations" in operational activities. Based on this information, the TCEQ can demonstrate that it currently conducts a significant number of activities that provide protection to the public from cumulative risk, especially in areas of concentrated operations, and that its monitoring and enforcement efforts consider concentrations of regulated facilities in areas where problems have been identified. The agency continually evaluates and considers opportunities to enhance its operations and policies to address cumulative risk, within its legislative authority and its technical and fiscal means.

Methodology and Format

Specific definitions of cumulative risk and related terms have not been developed or adopted by the TCEQ. Since this report could facilitate discussions regarding those definitions, a very broad net was cast in preparing a response to this request. To be as inclusive as possible, the Strategic Environmental Analysis (SEA) Group requested agency subject matter experts (SME's) to provide descriptions of all activities that they would interpret as addressing the assessment, control, reduction, or prevention of the combined effects of multiple sources, multiple pollutants, multiple exposure pathways, or similar circumstances; or as influencing the prioritization or implementation of activities based on the concentration of regulated facilities or operations. Staff responses were extensive and, in many cases, included detailed descriptions of program procedures and requirements. Examples ranged from activities that explicitly address cumulative risk in rules or guidance documents to those that, while not specifically designed to address cumulative risk, tangentially affect multiple facilities or pollutants.

The information compiled in this effort, as well as some additional information obtained during earlier work with SME's on this issue, has been summarized in the following tables. Part 1, beginning on page 7, consists of a series of tables, segregated by environmental media, that describe the current activities of the agency that address cumulative risk in some manner. Tables are further divided to distinguish between those activities with a direct objective to address the combined effects of pollutants and/or sources and those activities which more indirectly influence, support, or enhance cumulative risk protection. Part 2, beginning on page 27, consists of tables which describe how agency activities consider the impacts of concentrations of facilities in planning and regulatory efforts and in the prioritization of monitoring and enforcement efforts. The report includes the full gamut of responses, and while the information has been summarized, it does not attempt to screen any of the activities identified by staff.

Observations

<u>Concerning Part 1:</u>
Many air and water quality strategies address cumulative risk by focusing on the improvement and protection of ambient conditions regardless of the number of pollutants or sources that may be contributing to potential environmental degradation. Standards are established to achieve specified health or environmental goals; monitoring, modeling, and other assessments are conducted to evaluate environmental conditions and the extent of source impacts; and control measures are implemented to reduce or prevent overall contributing pollutant releases in affected geographic areas. For example, State Implementation Plans (SIPs) for criteria air pollutants, Total Maximum Daily Loads (TMDLs) for impaired water bodies, and applicable permitting evaluations and control requirements are developed and implemented to ensure that overall air and water quality standards are attained. The Source Water Assessment and Protection (SWAP) Program also considers the potential combined impacts of the type and number of pollutant sources in a contributing zone in determining the susceptibility of a drinking water system to contamination.

Many agency programs utilize monitoring data and/or direct measurements of pollutants in regulatory decisionmaking and risk assessment. Monitoring data (e.g., community air monitoring) can address cumulative exposures by reflecting impacts from all contributing local sources.

Assessment and remediation activities at properties affected by waste contamination also directly address cumulative risk through an assessment of the extent of the contamination, the establishment of human health and environmental levels that are protective of identified cumulative risk, and ensuring that contaminants are remediated to these protective levels. For affected properties remediated under the 1999 Texas Risk Reduction Program (TRRP), exposures from all relevant pathways (air, soil, groundwater and surface water) are considered to determine protective contaminant concentrations. Most of the remediation programs fall within the purview of TRRP. In general, the activities that consider cumulative risk are based on a single property and do not consider the risk from multiple properties that are in close proximity to one another.

The cumulative effects of specific types of pollutants and sources of contaminants on environmental conditions are also addressed indirectly by programs that conduct and coordinate activities to support other assessment, planning, or control functions; provide compliance assistance and enforcement; educate the public regarding relative risks; seek public input in the form of public meetings, hearings, or comment periods; or encourage voluntary actions to reduce contaminant releases. While their primary purpose is not necessarily to assess or reduce cumulative risk, these activities result in the better understanding of overall conditions, information about the effects of multiple pollutants and sources, and/or the reduction or prevention of cumulative impacts of separate sources on environmental quality. Important health-related information and guidance are often used to support or supplement other assessments to characterize or reduce cumulative impacts.

Concerning Part 2:

Following the identification of an actual or potential problem, program areas often implement activities to address the impacts of a concentration of facilities or the impact of adjacent facilities. For example, pollutant source impacts are systematically evaluated in air quality nonattainment areas or in watersheds and affected impaired water bodies subject to a TMDL. In waste permitting activities, the statutory requirements for land use compatibility determine if other related types of facilities or waste management needs will affect permit approvals. While a dense number of waste management facilities and related generators may potentially lead to an increase in total emissions, priority may be given to processing applications for permits in areas where a high volume of waste is generated and/or management/disposal needs exists. Training, technical assistance, and grants are also targeted in areas, businesses, and industrial sectors associated with environmental problems.

Similarly, once areas in which problems exist are clearly identified, the TCEQ targets areas in which regulated facilities are concentrated for monitoring, investigation, or enforcement. Prioritization is given to locating and operating fixed and mobile monitoring stations that can characterize and quantify the impacts of suspected pollutant sources to support planning and compliance efforts. Source investigations, enforcement, and compliance assistance activities are also often focused on specific types and concentrations of facilities, especially close to populated areas. Remediation programs focus on the clean up of identified contaminated properties, rather than on the locations or concentrations of facilities.

Descriptions of Current Cumulative Risk Activities
Air Quality

Assessments of cumulative risk for air quality are addressed within the agency's air permitting, monitoring and planning program functions. Within these programs, subject matter experts (SME's) identified a number of existing program policies, practices, guidance or actions that address cumulative risk to some degree. The technical elements used to evaluate cumulative risk include the use of air dispersion modeling, air monitoring, and tools to characterize risk. These technical elements are also used as an integral part of the planning and development of control strategies to reduce cumulative air emissions and improve air quality.

Direct Approaches
There are several programs that directly assess the cumulative impact of air emissions and conduct planning and regulatory activities to implement controls that improve overall air quality. Air permitting, monitoring, and planning activities directly assess and reduce cumulative risk for criteria pollutants (such as ozone and particulate matter) by addressing the effects of all contributing sources to meet health-based ambient air quality standards. Cumulative risk for specific non-criteria pollutants, including many air toxics, may also be addressed in limited circumstances where ambient monitoring indicates localized health concerns. These activities are often associated with other indirect approaches, such as air dispersion modeling and the use of effect screening levels (ESLs), to offer added protection to the public from cumulative risk.

Activity Description	How It Addresses Cumulative Risk
Air dispersion modeling is used in the technical review of air permit applications for criteria air pollutants	The application of air dispersion modeling for air permit applications of criteria pollutants considers cumulative risk by evaluating single pollutants from one or more sources. • Air emissions used in the air dispersion model are from the facility to be permitted and all other on- and off-property air emissions of the same pollutant from stationary point and areas sources. • A background concentration representing other sources that were not modeled, such as biogenic and mobile sources are added to the modeled concentration.
Representative ambient air monitoring is used to supplement modeling in the effects evaluation of some air permits.	Rather than considering just the concentration predicted to result from site-wide emissions sources, ambient air monitoring reflects existing concentrations of pollutants, regardless of their origin. Modeling may be used in conjunction with existing monitoring to assure that the proposed additional emissions would be acceptable.
The Air Pollutant Watch List is used in the technical review of New Source Review permit applications	Cities and counties are placed on the Air Pollutant Watch List based on elevated concentrations of specific pollutants detected at fixed and mobile monitoring sites. The list serves to alert staff of areas within the state that have - or are predicted to have - concentrations of pollutants that justify the potential scrutiny and restriction of new emissions given existing cumulative air quality.

Activity Description	How It Addresses Cumulative Risk
Fixed monitoring efforts provide information that is used to assist in air quality planning, exposure assessment and enforcement.	Fixed ambient monitoring, which includes continuous and noncontinuous sampling of criteria and non-criteria pollutants, is concentrated in areas suspected to be most severely affected by emissions from clusters of industrial point sources or from the combined emissions from point, mobile, and areas sources. Fixed monitors generally provide the most representative information on community exposure. • Monitoring sites may include several air pollution instruments, allowing a cumulative ambient exposure assessment across different compounds. • Each site operates for a number of years, or even decades, allowing for the assessment cumulative ambient exposure over time. • A network of instruments in most urban areas relay data in near-real time for continuously monitored species. Other species are monitored on a semi-continuous or periodic basis. All of the data allows for cumulative ambient exposure assessment. In addition, the data are used in some cases, such as for ozone, to contour the likely concentrations over a large geographic area.
Mobile monitoring efforts provide ambient air quality data in close proximity to pollution sources of interest.	Mobile monitoring is targeted in areas where there are many sources of a compound or compounds to identify contributing facilities and to use real-time information to focus regulatory activities where needed to reduce cumulative exposures. Mobile monitors provide the most representative information on source-specific pollutant concentrations and characterize short-term community exposure. • Results represent measurements of a compound from a wide variety of potential sources and/or ambient air measurements for multiple compounds. • Results also represent an aggregate concentration of a compound from all upwind sources (mobile, point and non-point) and are used to identify contributions of specific industrial sources to background levels.
Health effects evaluations of results from fixed and mobile air monitoring are conducted.	TCEQ evaluates the results of ambient monitoring data depicting cumulative exposures and identifies concentrations of pollutants which pose air quality concerns and warrant further regulatory efforts. The compounds thus identified may be added to the Air Pollutant Watch List to trigger consideration of whether additions of a pollutant are appropriate given existing cumulative air quality.

Activity Description	How It Addresses Cumulative Risk
Field Operations Division conducts targeted activities to support agency air programs.	Based on decisions and/or data, regional staff conduct targeted compliance investigations of regulated entities, review permit decisions, prioritize monitoring efforts, and initiate appropriate enforcement. This information is used to provide technical assistance, outreach and education. Most investigations are directed to meet TCEQ's obligations to the EPA and/or to respond to complaints, although there are special initiatives that are implemented to address areas of particular concern. These initiatives, which may be statewide or regional, usually address cumulative risk of a particular category of emission source or activity.
Air Quality Planning: Areas of the state that exceed the federal National Ambient Air Quality Standards (NAAQS) are designated as "nonattainment," and the TCEQ is required to develop State Implementation Plans. These regionally specific planning efforts are designed to identify source emissions and implement control strategies to reduce emissions needed to achieve and maintain attainment.	Ambient air quality, emissions, meteorological conditions, atmospheric chemistry, and other factors are used to characterize or predict emissions of all sources (point, area and mobile) that contribute to combined air quality impacts. Extensive research efforts have been conducted in the Houston area (Texas 2000 Study) to help planners better understand the complex interactions of pollutants on ozone formation, transport, and effects. Control strategies are developed based on the results of these assessment activities. These control strategies are designed to address cumulative risk by assessing and implementing controls on the large number and type of sources that emit complex mixtures of compounds that contribute to exceedances of the NAAQS.

Indirect Approaches

The TCEQ uses a number of indirect approaches to characterize air emissions and assess exposure through the air permitting and planning process and to determine the potential adverse effects that may be associated with exposure to specific concentrations of an air pollutant. These activities often support or supplement other air quality assessments used to evaluate or reduce cumulative risk.

Activity Description	How It Addresses Cumulative Risk
Air quality planning is conducted in near nonattainment areas	In areas where air quality is close to exceeding the NAAQS, the EPA, TCEQ, and local communities enter into voluntary agreements to implement strategies to prevent further degradation of air quality in those areas. Voluntary air planning activities include identifying, inventorying, and monitoring current pollution levels and identifying and quantifying potential pollution reduction through voluntary controls. Voluntary planning activities indirectly address cumulative risk by assessing and preventing the combination and interaction of chemicals that may contribute to the degradation of air quality.

Activity Description	How It Addresses Cumulative Risk
Air dispersion modeling of air pollutants not subject to state and federal standards is used in the technical review of air permit applications. The scope of the air dispersion modeling and effects evaluation is determined according to the Modeling and Effects Review Applicability Guidance on a project-by-project basis.	Air dispersion modeling evaluates emissions from relevant sources to predict the resulting maximum ground level concentration (GLC_{max}) of individual constituents. This modeling typically considers worst-case emissions scenarios resulting in conservative estimates of concentrations that would not be expected to occur under normal operations. Generally only emissions from the applicant's property are evaluated except when the applicant has entered into a single property line agreement with another applicant, in which case all emissions from the combined properties are evaluated. If predicted concentrations exceed the effects screening levels (ESLs), additional analysis is conducted that considers frequency and potential exposure, with consideration given to existing concentrations of the same pollutant in the area. The air permitting process indirectly considers cumulative risk by assuming that increased emissions resulting in ground-level concentrations that are less than a specified fraction of the ESL do not significantly contribute to cumulative exposures.
Application of Effects Screening Levels are used in the health effects evaluation of air permit applications	ESLs are used in air permit reviews to address the effects of all compounds for which there are no federal or state standards. Their use indirectly serves to help protect the public from cumulative risk in several ways. • ESLs are set to be protective of public health and welfare, and the environment by incorporating a significant margin of conservatism below the lowest observed effects levels to account for exposures to even the most sensitive members of the population. • ESLs address both short- and long-term exposures, and endpoints in addition to health, such as odor, vegetative damage, and corrosion of materials. • Given the practice in air permitting of evaluating worst-case emission scenarios, and the margin of safety integral to ESLs, application of ESLs serve to limit cumulative concentrations of pollutants in communities. This is supported by the vast majority of community air monitoring which does not indicate air toxics at levels of concern.

Descriptions of Current Cumulative Risk Activities
Surface Water Quality

Municipal, commercial, and industrial facilities commonly discharge treated wastewater and other pollutants into streams, lakes, estuaries, and other water bodies. Runoff into surface waters can also carry other accumulated contaminants from general human activities, such as urban development, agriculture, and mining. Surface water quality strategies address the cumulative effects of the combined releases from all of these point and nonpoint sources as necessary to ensure the normal use of those water bodies. Most pollution control programs of TCEQ address impacts on human health, but perhaps unique among the various environmental media, the water quality standards also address impacts on aquatic life.

Direct Approaches

Cumulative risks are addressed directly through establishing and ensuring the attainment of surface water quality (SWQ) standards to protect human and aquatic life uses, regardless of the type or number of pollutants or sources. Ambient and special purpose monitoring is conducted to support periodic assessments of water quality and to identify water bodies that do not meet these standards or exhibit other concerns. Extensive planning processes, permitting procedures, and control programs are in place to implement efforts to improve water quality and to prevent significant degradation. While many of the standards and related assessment criteria are for single pollutants, the combined effects of some pollutants that may reduce dissolved oxygen, increase total toxicity, or otherwise impair the use of a water body are also considered.

Activity Description	How It Addresses Cumulative Risk
Site-specific SWQ standards are adopted for all classified water bodies and presumed standards for all others.	Standards establish acceptable water quality conditions for designated uses regardless of the type or number of sources. Toxic pollutant standards consider multiple pathway exposure from drinking water and fish consumption, weighted toxicity for certain similar compounds, and total effluent toxicity effects of pollutants on aquatic life. Bacterial standards are surrogates for exposure to a variety of waterborne pathogens.
Five-Part Integrated SWQ Assessment determines water bodies not meeting applicable SWQ standards.	Assessment identifies adverse impacts on ambient water quality from one or more sources of pollutant discharges. Additional loadings of pollutants are restricted in waters listed as impaired.
SWQ Monitoring coordinates monitoring of numerous parameters at sites across Texas.	Monitoring results determine the total pollutant levels in water bodies regardless of the type (point, nonpoint, natural) or number of sources.
Source Water Assessment and Protection (SWAP) Program determines the susceptibility of public drinking water systems to contamination.	Assessment identifies the type, number, and proximity of pollutant sources to ground and surface waters used by public water systems. The assessments includes a ranking of the potential risks from any of 227 contaminants.
Total Maximum Daily Load (TMDL) analyses determine the maximum pollutant loadings that are acceptable for a water body to meet SWQ standards.	Assessments evaluate the amount of a specific pollutant from all applicable point, nonpoint (including aerial deposition) and background sources. Ecological and human health responses to total pollutant levels are predicted and allocations are established to reduce or prevent risks within a margin of safety.
TMDL implementation involves regulatory and voluntary measures to reduce pollutants in impaired water bodies	Implementation protects people and aquatic life from the cumulative effects of multiple sources of contaminants, the combination of certain pollutants (causing low dissolved oxygen or high bacterial levels), and the potential effects of future growth. Prioritized monitoring is conducted to determine the effects of concentrated facilities or evaluate the effectiveness of actions.

Activity Description	How It Addresses Cumulative Risk
Water Quality Permitting establishes effluent limits and other conditions to protect SWQ standards.	For oxygen demanding materials and dissolved salts, ambient levels and existing pollutant loadings are evaluated in determining permit requirements. Background levels of other pollutants are considered negligible. Certain facilities are required to satisfy "total toxicity" or "whole effluent toxicity" requirements to avoid adverse effects of multiple pollutants. Additional nutrient discharge limits may be required where cumulative ecological impacts are of concern. Effluent limits are set to prevent further impacts that would contribute to existing impairments.
Texas Pollution Discharge Elimination System (TPDES) Pretreatment Program establishes local limits on affected Publicly Owned Treatment Works (POTWs) to prevent violations of SWQ standards.	Pretreatment requirements reduce the cumulative effects of multiple industrial wastewater sources that discharge into the same POTWs.
Concentrated Animal Feeding Operations (CAFO) Program conducts annual investigations at facilities in certain areas of the state.	Dairy Outreach Program Areas have been designated to address the potential cumulative effects of the large numbers of CAFOs near Stephenville and Tyler.

Indirect Approaches

The cumulative effects of specific types of pollutants and sources of contaminants on surface water quality are also addressed indirectly by programs that conduct and coordinate activities to support other water quality functions or to provide compliance assistance and enforcement. While their primary purpose is not necessarily to assess or reduce cumulative risk, their activities result in a better understanding of the overall water quality conditions, information about the effects of multiple pollutants and sources, and/or the reduction or prevention of cumulative impacts on water quality.

Activity Description	How It Addresses Cumulative Risk
Field Operations Division conducts routine and special purpose SWQ monitoring.	Monitoring supports the priorities established for assessment and control activities, regardless of the type (point, nonpoint, natural) or number of sources.
Clean Rivers Program coordinates SWQ monitoring, assessment, and public outreach efforts.	Clean Rivers partners provide 60 percent of water quality monitoring data in Texas and supports other efforts to identify and target the immediate risks in associated river basins.
The TCEQ provides Section 401 certification of U.S. Army Corps of Engineers (USACE) dredge and fill permit applications.	Interagency coordination between TCEQ, USACE, and others results in improved mitigation of the adverse SWQ impacts caused by the loss of wetlands and other water body modifications.

Activity Description	How It Addresses Cumulative Risk
On-Site Sewage Facility (OSSF) Program ensures that OSSFs (such as septic systems) satisfy design and operational requirements.	Authorized Agents manage local efforts to ensure that systems to do not individually or cumulatively pollute ground or surface water.
Sludge Beneficial Use Program reduces runoff from participating properties into adjacent waterways.	A proposed project has been submitted for Section 319 funding to monitor and evaluate the effectiveness of this program to reduce overall pollution in specific river basins.
Public Drinking Water Program ensures that certain facilities are inspected annually to reduce public risk to bacterial contamination.	The program targets additional attention on public water systems that use surface water sources or certain groundwater sources that are more susceptible to widespread bacterial contamination.

Description of Current Cumulative Risk Activities
Groundwater/Drinking Water/Water Supply

Programs and staff with regulatory or assessment activities with regard to protecting groundwater and drinking water from contamination include Field Operations programs for the Edwards Aquifer and for evaluation of susceptible public water systems, the Public Drinking Water Section, the Groundwater Planning and Assessment Team, and the Groundwater Protection Team, Water Quality Assessment Section. In general most activities depend on pollutant reduction, regulatory compliance, and educational efforts to reduce contaminant exposure risks, but are not focused on assessing cumulative risk. Since water supply programs do not assess or regulate contaminants, cumulative risk activities are not considered applicable.

Direct Approaches
Many of the groundwater and drinking water programs use drinking water Maximum Contaminant Levels (MCLs) or standards derived from MCLs, such as Protective Contaminant Levels (PCLs), some of which include consideration of cumulative risk. For non-carcinogens, drinking water standards are adjusted to incorporate contributions from other sources of exposure, such as dietary intake. The Source Water Assessment and Protection (SWAP) Program summarizes the contribution of multiple sources of the same contaminant in order to assign high, medium, and low susceptibility ratings.

Activity Description	How It Addresses Cumulative Risk
The SWAP Program determines the susceptibility of public drinking water sources to 227 contaminants. Multiple sources of the same contaminant results in higher susceptibility ratings for the contaminant.	The public is protected from cumulative risks through SWAP susceptibility reports which are provided to public water system operators and summarized in Consumer Confidence Reports.

Public drinking water standards are promulgated by the federal government and adopted by the state to protect consumers.	Where appropriate, drinking water standards are adjusted to consider other, non-drinking water exposures. Also, for certain classes of contaminants (including xylenes, trihalomethanes, radionuclides, and dioxins), additive exposures are addressed by applying an MCL based on class totals.
Promulgated groundwater cleanup standards (e.g. PCLs, MCLs) protect current and future use of the resource.	Groundwater cleanup levels may incorporate adjustments for other non-drinking water contributions to the total exposure and also include consideration for additive exposure from certain contaminants.

Indirect Approaches

Program areas have suggested that activities which reduce overall pollution and contaminant exposure or educate public water systems and consumers have the net result of reducing cumulative risk.

Activity Description	How It Addresses Cumulative Risk
The Texas Pesticide Management Plan developed by the Texas Groundwater Protection Committee (GPC) includes multi-agency policies and responses to protect groundwater from contamination by pesticides. The Interagency Pesticide Database compiles groundwater monitoring results for pesticides.	Groundwater users can determine drinking water threats in their geographical area from information collected by these efforts.
Groundwater monitoring and contamination reports (including the groundwater portion of the Clean Water Act 305(b) report) educates state agencies and the public on groundwater contamination issues. Educational efforts are directed at landowners to plug abandoned wells.	The publications and educational efforts provide groundwater users with information to evaluate public health concerns for groundwater in their geographical area.
Monitoring and compliance activities are conducted by TCEQ to protect public drinking water, specifically including compliance with MCLs, residual disinfectant levels, action levels, and treatment techniques.	Public drinking water program activities are risk assessment and management programs designed to protect the public from the cumulative risk of contaminants by controlling hazard level or duration.
Regulating activities over the Edwards Aquifer includes assessment of sensitive features, application of best management practices, and controls of certain developmental activities.	Reducing pollutants from areas of concentrated development associated with sensitive recharge features protects the public from cumulative risks.

Activity Description	How It Addresses Cumulative Risk
The impact on groundwater is assessed during permitting of certain land-based wastewater storage and irrigation activities (e.g concentrated animal feeding operations). If a potential for groundwater contamination exists, monitoring requirements or a change in facility operations are included in the permit.	Special provisions in a land disposal permit are protective of groundwater resources.
The Field Operations Division inspects susceptible public water systems to ensure compliance with regulations. Technical and managerial assistance is provided to these systems to optimize operations.	Compliance with state regulations protects the public from cumulative risks.

Descriptions of Current Cumulative Risk Activities
Waste Management

Numerous programs within the agency regulate waste management and the assessment, monitoring, and cleanup of properties affected by contamination. These programs protect the public from cumulative risk by considering the cumulative risks of multiple contaminants from a single source, as well as the cumulative risks of multiple releases if the contaminants cannot be separately identified or remediated. Some of these programs consider all releases present at a property (or properties), regardless of source, but generally do not consider the risk from multiple properties with separate and distinct releases that are in close proximity to one another. The hazardous waste combustion strategy is an exception because it qualitatively considers the impacts of other potential sources in establishing control requirements. Most remediation programs fall within the purview of the 1999 Texas Risk Reduction Program (TRRP). Some remediation activities may be grandfathered, and there are certain exclusions to TRRP in various programs. In these cases, program-specific rules or the older 1993 Risk Reduction Rule, which also include certain cumulative risk provisions, may apply. The following information focuses on the current TRRP rules.

Direct Approaches

Numerous activities related to the assessment and remediation of properties affected by waste contamination directly address cumulative risk through an assessment of the extent of the contamination, the establishment of human health and environmental levels that are protective, and ensuring that contaminants are remediated to these protective levels. For affected properties remediated under the TRRP, exposures from all relevant pathways (air, soil, groundwater and surface water) are considered to determine protective contaminant concentrations.

Activity Description	How It Addresses Cumulative Risk
Multi-pathway risk assessments are performed in the review of certain Hazardous Waste Combustion Emissions permits.	Combustion risk assessments of deposition and inhalation exposures may be conducted on a case-by-case basis for certain commercial waste management facilities. Previous multi-pathway assessments of hazardous waste combustion units and other on-property stationary sources in hazardous waste service have demonstrated that, in most cases, emissions have not contributed to significant increases in risk. These assessments sum risk/hazards across relevant pollutants and use health-based criteria, which are set an order of magnitude lower than other regulatory programs, to establish emission control requirements .
Texas Risk Reduction Program (TRRP)-1999 rule which specifies the assessment, monitoring, and cleanup that applies to closures of contaminated properties and waste management units that are regulated by the TCEQ. There are exclusions to TRRP in various programs. Some remediation activities are grandfathered, in which case program-specific rules or an older 1993 Risk Reduction Rule may apply.	Individual impacts are evaluated for the chemicals of concern identified at the contaminated property. The TRRP rules require an evaluation of cumulative risk whenever ten or more specific carcinogenic or non-carcinogenic chemicals of concern are present in an affected area. The cumulative effects of all contaminants present at a property for which closure is sought are considered when certain screening criteria are exceeded. A cumulative risk evaluation which includes off-property contaminants is not required under the TRRP rule. Current procedures require assessing the extent of the contamination, establishing protective human health and environmentally protective levels, and ensuring that contaminants are remediated to levels that are individually and cumulatively protective of human health. Within the affected property, exposure from all relevant pathways (air, soil, surface water and groundwater) is considered to determine protective contaminant concentrations. Measurements of contaminant concentrations in various media are often used to determine the need for remedial action. Certain program requirements may result in the cleanup of contamination migrating onto a property being remediated from an off-property source. In addition, the identification of off-property sources of contamination may prompt separate investigation(s) and remediation action(s).
Superfund Site Discovery and Assessment identifies and ranks properties for remediation under state and federal Superfund programs.	Assessments are conducted and the relative priority for action on Superfund sites is investigated by preparing a Hazard Ranking System (HRS) score. The presence of a single pollutant from multiple sources, or the presence of multiple contaminants and their corresponding concentrations and toxicities are reflected in the hazard ranking score. The cumulative risk of pollutants introduced through multiple exposure pathways are considered by evaluating every complete, or reasonably anticipated to be complete, exposure pathway and assigning weight to those pathways in the HRS.

Activity Description	How It Addresses Cumulative Risk
Superfund Cleanup oversees the remediation and cleanup of federal and state Superfund sites in Texas.	Cumulative risks associated with the introduction of contaminants from multiple exposure pathways are addressed at all federal Superfund sites via a baseline risk assessment required by the National Oil and Hazardous Substance Pollution Contingency Plan. A baseline risk assessment requires an evaluation of multiple exposure pathways operating upon a receptor simultaneously. Most of the state Superfund sites are currently being remediated using TRRP and are subject to the cumulative risk provisions of that rule. Some of the older state Superfund sites were grandfathered from TRRP, and are being remediated under a 1993 Risk Reduction Rule. However, a baseline risk assessment and cumulative risk evaluation are still required.
Industrial Solid Waste and Municipal Hazardous Waste Cleanup Program oversees the cleanup of soil and groundwater contamination from industrial and municipal hazardous and industrial non-hazardous wastes.	The TRRP rules require an evaluation of cumulative risk whenever ten or more specific carcinogenic or non-carcinogenic chemicals of concern are present in an affected area. This criterion is occasionally exceeded at industrial and hazardous waste properties.
Leaking Petroleum Storage Tank (LPST) Remediation oversees the cleanup of LPSTs, including environmental assessments, corrective action plans, remediation, and requests for closure.	Cumulative risk resulting from the release of multiple contaminants from one or more sources, or from pollutant introduction across multiple exposure pathways, is evaluated when LPST contaminant levels exceed Plan A Risk-Based Assessment (RBA) levels. However, the vast majority of properties with LPST's do not exceed this criteria. If a Plan B RBA is performed, cumulative risk is evaluated whenever more than one contaminant is present. The PST cleanup program is scheduled to come under TRRP effective September 1, 2003.
Voluntary Cleanup Program (VCP) provides administrative, technical, and legal incentives to encourage the cleanup of contaminated properties in Texas.	The VCP process requires an investigation of all contaminants in all media present at a property. The cumulative effects of all contaminants present at a property for which a certificate of completion will be issued are considered when certain threshold levels are exceeded. This includes all contaminants of concern released at a property as well as those contaminants which have migrated onto a property from an off-property source. The VCP utilizes the TRRP rules which require an evaluation of cumulative risk whenever ten or more specific carcinogenic or non-carcinogenic chemicals of concern are present in an affected area. This criteria is occasionally exceeded at VCP waste properties.

Activity Description	How It Addresses Cumulative Risk
Spill Prevention and Control Program provides oversight of remediation of contamination resulting from spills and emergencies.	Response actions required as a result of spills can be remediated in accordance with the TRRP rules (see 30 TAC 327.5) and associated cumulative risk provisions. Responsible parties can choose to use TRRP for spill response remediations that are expected to take less than six months, but TRRP is required to be used if a spill response will take longer than six months to remediate.
Licensing of Commercial Low-Level Radioactive Waste (LLRW) Disposal Facilities and Decommissioning and oversight of 18 non-commercial buried LLRW waste sites, and closure of these sites	Assessment of cumulative risk is evaluated using the RESRAD risk assessment model. The model uses groundwater, soil and soil vapor data to conduct a dose assessment from nine exposure pathways (direct exposure, inhalation of particulate and radon, ingestion of plant foods, meat, milk, aquatic foods, water and soil). The model focuses on the assessment of radiological risk from multiple radionuclides, but does not consider additional risk from other nonradiological constituents. However, a separate evaluation may occur under the TRRP for nonradiological contamination. These activities are protective of human health and the environment by providing radiation dose limits to members of the public.

Indirect Approaches

The waste management activities that provide indirect approaches to assess or reduce cumulative risk include programs that conduct and coordinate activities to support municipal and hazardous waste management functions or that provide compliance assistance and enforcement. These indirect activities result in the better understanding of overall conditions, information about the effects of multiple pollutants and sources, and/or the reduction or prevention of cumulative impacts of similar sources.

Activity Description	How It Addresses Cumulative Risk
Groundwater Monitoring of the uppermost aquifer and Corrective Action at landfills is established during permitting.	Enables the TCEQ to focus attention on facilities that appear to be impacting groundwater and ensure that corrective action is performed where needed to prevent the migration of contaminants beyond a facility point of compliance.
Hazardous Waste Permitting and Underground Injection Control Permitting include risk-based considerations.	The techniques intrinsic in permits include risk-based considerations, such as prevention of releases, waste analysis, review of engineering and operational controls at facilities, inspections, and closure in accordance with the TRRP.
Hazardous Waste Permitting reviews consider specific criteria in determining the acceptability of a property.	These regulations preclude properties with certain features from being permitted to store, process and/or dispose of hazardous waste. Demonstrations must show that features of the property have no negative impact on the protectiveness of the facility with respect to human health and the environment.

Activity Description	How It Addresses Cumulative Risk
Municipal Solid Waste Permitting Plan Reviews consider the design, construction, operation, and closure of a municipal solid waste treatment or disposal facility	These activities must be conducted in accordance with standards intended to control and minimize the impact of these facilities on human health and the environment.
Regional Solid Waste Planning provides coordination and funding to address local waste management needs.	Solid Waste Management Plans are developed by regional planning groups every four years. The Regional Solid Waste Grants Program provides funding for the development and implementation of regional plans to ensure adequate landfill capacity and to provide grant funds for citizen recycling, reuse, source reduction actions, as well as illegal dumping enforcement and cleanup programs.
Landfill Gas (Methane) Monitoring is conducted at all Type I and some Type IV municipal landfills	Enables the TCEQ to focus attention on facilities where landfill gas migration beyond the permit boundary is occurring, and ensure that an appropriate remediation plan is implemented.

PART 2:
CHARACTERIZATION OF USE OF GEOGRAPHIC FEATURES
BY AGENCY PROGRAMS
(In Areas Where Regulated Facilities Are Concentrated)

The cumulative risk statute focuses on both monitoring and enforcement in areas where regulated facilities are concentrated as well as activities to protect the public in areas of concentrated operations. Program area responses were keyed to identifying the influence of facilities and geographic features on policies and activities of the TCEQ.

Use in Assessment, Reduction and Prevention Activities
Following the identification of an actual or potential problem, program areas often implement activities to address the impacts of a concentration of facilities or the impact of adjacent facilities. This type of approach is most obvious in air and water quality assessment and control activities. On the other hand, a new waste management facility or expansion may be given greater consideration if its location is in a concentrated industrialized area where existing land use is already compatible and/or where waste management demands are greatest.

Air Quality

Activity Description	How Geographic Features Are Used
Air quality monitoring results are used to define compliance of criteria pollutants under the National Ambient Air Quality Standards (NAAQS).	Geographic areas with air quality monitoring results which exceed the NAAQS are designated as being in nonattainment. Designation can include either a complete county or a part of a county.
Emissions inventories and air quality modeling are emphasized in areas which exceed the NAAQS.	Major stationary sources, primarily in urban nonattainment areas, are required to submit periodic reports of actual emissions. Area and mobile source emissions are estimated based on population or other factors.
Air permits and other control strategies are more stringent in areas which exceed the NAAQS.	Major stationary sources in urban nonattainment areas must control emissions and must offset new permitted emissions. Certain area sources (gasoline stations, dry cleaners, etc.) and mobile source activities (construction equipment) which are concentrated in urban areas must also implement controls.
Air permits are used to control emissions of individual point sources of air toxic pollutants.	Air permits may be adjusted based upon the geographical location and specific pollutants identified in the *Air Pollution Watch List*. The list is based upon monitored data and population exposure potential.

Water Quality

Activity Description	How Geographic Features Are Used
Permits are issued for discharges of treated wastewater to surface waters in the state.	Wastewater permits to a segment may be restricted based upon the permitted load from other discharges and the remaining assimilative capacity of the water body for pollutants of concern.
Control strategies for non-point sources may limit pollutants in certain water bodies in order to meet water quality standards.	Nonpoint source activities in a watershed of a water body that is either impaired or likely to become impaired may be restricted or controlled through best management practices if the pollutant loads exceed the critical load mass of the water body.
The Total Maximum Daily Load (TMDL) Program determines the waste load from all point and nonpoint pollutant sources in an affected watershed.	Point source discharges and nonpoint source activities contributing to an impairment of water quality are evaluated to assess their associated impacts and to determine the appropriate type and level of control measures.
The Source Water Assessment and Protection (SWAP) Program performs a systematic assessment of potential contaminant sources within watersheds and well contributing areas which serve as drinking water sources.	Contaminant risk will include, when appropriate, defining a threat (or susceptibility) based solely on a concentration of facilities near to a water source and in the absence of specific contamination concerns.

Waste Management

Activity Description	How Geographic Features Are Used
Waste facility permits require a legal determination of land use compatibility.	In industrial and hazardous waste permitting, consideration is given of other waste generating facilities in the area. In other programs, land use compatibility refers only to technical considerations at the proposed property.
Underground Injection Control (UIC) operations restrict contaminant disposal to geological formations separated from useable groundwater	Properly designed and operated UIC operations prevent exposure of the environment to contaminants.
Waste management permits and siting in relation to other types of facilities has both positive and negative consequences.	While a dense number of waste management facilities and related client generators may potentially lead to an increase in total emissions, priority may be given to the processing of permits in areas where a high volume of wastes are generated and/or a need exists for management/disposal capacity or a certain technology. In addition to land use compatibility, transportation system burden, regional need, and emergency response capabilities influence siting decisions.

Multimedia

Activity Description	How Geographic Features Are Used
National Environmental Policy Act (NEPA) reviews are conducted on certain proposed construction projects and other major federal actions significantly affecting the quality of the human environment.	Reviews consider existing environmental conditions, such as air quality nonattainment or water quality impairments, in evaluating the potential impacts of a proposed project or action and in determining the appropriate level of controls needed to satisfy NEPA requirements.
Small Business and Environmental Assistance Division provides training and technical assistance to the regulated community and local government.	Training, technical assistance, and grants are targeted to areas, businesses, and industrial sectors associated with environmental problems (nonattainment areas, impaired streams).

Use in Prioritizing Monitoring and Enforcement

Most agency targeting strategies are based upon responding to information which indicates that an actual or potential problem exists (monitoring data, complaints, incidents, investigation results). Once the areas in which problems exist are clearly identified, the TCEQ targets areas in which regulated facilities are concentrated for monitoring, investigation, or enforcement. The choice of where sampling stations are located and the number of monitors may be influenced by a concentration of facilities, among other factors.

Activity Description	How Geographic Features Are Used
The Compliance Planning Process establishes an integrated program of monitoring, investigations, enforcement, and outreach.	Strategies are identified to implement core compliance activities and to address high priority, statewide and regional issues. Efforts are often targeted at specific types of activities in specific locations to address significant or persistent problems.
National Air Monitoring Stations are located to assess attainment of criteria pollutant standards.	A fixed monitoring network is located and maintained in major urban areas to meet specific objectives of photochemical modeling and compliance with NAAQS, including the assessment of air quality downwind of areas of concentrated facilities or other operations (roadways, commercial centers, etc.).
Monitoring station placement in the Community Air Toxic Monitoring Network is designed to evaluate exposure risk to air toxics.	Initial guidance on the placement of air toxic monitoring stations and current planning activities by TCEQ staff considers risks from exposure to air toxics in communities close to industrial point sources.
Mobile air monitoring is prioritized and deployed to areas based upon information that an actual or potential air quality problem exists.	The majority of mobile monitoring assignments are for areas where a concentration of industrial facilities occurs, and usually in close proximity to a large population base.

Activity Description	How Geographic Features Are Used
The Field Operations Division conducts investigations in response to specific incidents, special initiatives, or in support of other agency programs.	Investigations include responding to incidents of visible emissions or flaring, evaluating specific industry-related requirements (e.g. cooling tower inspections in refineries and chemical production facilities), areas of close industry/population interface (e.g. autobody shops) and support to SIP emission reduction activities in nonattainment areas. Results of investigations are used, among other factors, to assess areas for concentrated enforcement.
TCEQ program staff and other partners periodically evaluate the siting and operation of surface water quality monitoring stations.	The coordinated surface water monitoring guidance provides for an increase in the number of sampling stations in a water body to evaluate the impact of a concentration of regulated facilities or other pollutant activities.
The TMDL program responds to surface water impairments by defining additional monitoring and data collection requirements.	In cases where a concentration of facilities is suspected to contribute to the impairment in a segment, subsequent monitoring is established to define the impacts of these facilities and to adjust enforcement schemes.
Groundwater sampling for pesticide contamination is defined by the Joint Groundwater Protection Committee (GPC) as a part of the State Pesticide Management Plan.	Areas of known impact (e.g. detections in public water systems) and high pesticide use are the primary criteria for monitoring site selection. See also the indirect approaches described for the GPC in Part One of this report (page 17).
The Galveston Bay Estuary Program conducts monitoring primarily to assess ecosystem health.	Occasionally monitoring activities are altered to support other TCEQ programs (e.g. TMDL) in which evaluation of impacts from a concentration of facilities is a desired objective.
Groundwater and landfill gas monitoring and assessment is required by the Waste Permits Division at landfills and other waste disposal units.	Groundwater monitoring wells are sited at landfills and other waste disposal units to ensure detection of contamination in the uppermost aquifer, while landfill gas monitoring is required for certain types of landfills. Municipal Solid Waste facilities are sited in accordance with local restrictions, airport safety, floodplains, wetlands, fault areas, and unstable areas.
The Remediation Division oversees clean-up of soil and groundwater contamination from industrial and municipal hazardous and industrial non-hazardous facilities.	Monitoring or enforcement at properties being cleaned up is not based upon where regulated facilities are concentrated. If such prioritization takes place, it is a function of actual or perceived risk at the property.

Remediation Activities

Remediation programs focus on the cleanup of identified contaminated properties, rather than on the locations or concentrations of facilities. Generally all contamination within the property boundaries of the affected property, as well as any contamination which originates on the property and migrates off-property, is required to be cleaned up. Contamination found to be migrating onto the property being remediated from other nearby or adjacent properties, depending upon individual program requirements, may be considered in identifying appropriate responsible parties or may prompt separate investigation(s) and remediation action(s).

APPENDIX N:

LOCAL GOVERNMENT CUMULATIVE RISK PREVENTION/ INTERVENTION EFFORT IN PORTLAND , OREGON

In late 2003, the Protocol for Assessing Community Excellence in Environmental Health (PACE-EH) formed a community health assessment team to identify environmental health concerns by performing pilot assessments in five neighborhoods of inner North and Northeast Portland, in Multnomah County, Oregon. Coalition members had identified a number of sites as ideal candidates for assessment. The five neighborhoods, Humboldt, Vernon, Eliot, King, and Boise, were prioritized as a result of community input from and documentation of significant environmental health issues by concerned members of the Coalition and community residents living in those neighborhoods. The environmental health issues identified by the residents included poor indoor air quality, exposure to lead-based paint, unsafe grounds, and mold and mildew. Upon completion of the assessment, the community coalition will develop and implement a community action plan to address the most significant issues.

Multnomah County PACE-EH is a growing coalition of individuals, community organizations, and local health officials who are committed to improving environmental health and environmental justice in its communities. Under the project, communities can learn more about environmental health and environmental justice, and create action plans based on their needs and values. Through the network, people can become part of the processes of decision making and determining the environmental health of their communities.

The following article discusses the work of the Multnomah County PACE-EH Project. For more information about the Multnomah County PACE-EH Coalition, including copies of its newsletters, visit the organization's website at http://www.pace-eh.org.

Pursuing Environmental Health Through Community Assessment

Latricia Tillman

Local health data indicate that environmental degradation results in adverse health consequences in Multnomah County, Oregon. Breathing contaminated air can exacerbate asthma conditions—the incidence of asthma among children in the Portland public schools exceeds the national average. Exposure to lead-based paints can cause learning disabilities in young children—70% of homes in Portland neighborhoods had composite lead dust levels that exceed federal standards. Consuming drinking water with high levels of volatile organic compounds (VOCs) can cause cancer—several ground water wells in Northeast Portland are contaminated by VOCs. Contact with contaminated surface waters can cause a variety of different illnesses—each year millions of gallons of untreated wastewater are diverted directly into the Willamette River, which runs through Portland and is used by local residents for swimming, fishing, and other recreation.

These kinds of environmental and health concerns disproportionately affect minority and low-income populations. Polluting industries and businesses tend to be located in communities with many low-income residents, who often lack the means to move to a community free from contamination. Low-income residents are often affected by multiple environmental and health concerns that accumulate over years and generations. Additionally, many low-income residents don't have the economic, legal, or political resources to address their health disparities and environmental health issues.

Despite the fact that health consequences of environmental conditions are real, the Multnomah County Health Department (MCHD), in Portland, Oregon, has not developed the internal capacity or the public mandate to deal with environmental justice problems. Environmental health services, which have been sustained historically in the local health department, reflect a traditional public health approach to controlling communicable diseases: fee-based public health services related to inspections of restaurants, swimming pools, and care facilities, vector control, and food safety policies and education. MCHD has tried to develop, with varying degrees of success, new environmental health programs to address childhood lead poisoning and brownfields (industrial or commercial property that is abandoned or under-used and often environmentally contaminated). However, the department has been unable to integrate these programs into the existing environmental health practice model.

MCHD's capacity to address environmental health issues has been hampered by its lack of a systematic way to assess the environmental health of Multnomah County. A climate of mistrust among community members stemming from the perception that the department was unwilling to sustain environmental health programming has also compounded the department's problems.

The Protocol for Assessing Community Excellence

In order to develop a systematic approach to assessing the county's environmental health and respond to community concerns, Lila Wickham, the director of the Environmental Health Division, decided to try the Protocol for Assessing Community Excellence in Environmental Health (PACE-EH).

PACE-EH was developed in 1995 by the National Association of County and City Health Officials (NACCHO) to help local health officials accurately identify environmental health issues at the community level; discover, collect,

---

PACE EH helps local health agencies:

- Be more responsive to community environmental health concerns
- Gain visibility in the community as leaders in environmental health
- Work for environmental justice with disenfranchised communities
- Have community-based coalitions that lobby for local environmental health ordinances
- Have a health department staff that is comfortable being engaged with communities
- Become more effective in engaging community members in environmental health issue identification and problem solving
- Educate communities on the importance of science-based decision making
- Provide state and national policy makers with community-driven findings that could be used to shape environmental health policies and resource allocation
    —Centers for Disease Control and Prevention

and analyze meaningful environmental health data; and identify populations at disproportionate risk of environmental exposure and adverse health outcomes.

PACE-EH offers a way to integrate data-driven assessments of environmental health concerns with the values and perceptions of communities. It promotes leadership among environmental health advocates, involves the community in planning and decision making, and addresses issues of environmental justice. A complete PACE-EH assessment includes 13 interrelated tasks from project planning and assessment team recruitment to environmental health issue identification, indicator development, and action plan development (*see box for complete list*). The tasks walk the participants through planning and assessment and into action in a nonlinear, iterative, and dynamic process.

The initial MCHD planning team included representatives from various divisions in the Health Department: Environmental Health, Planning and Development (the unit responsible for public health data analysis, qualitative and quantitative research, and grant writing), and the director's office, which focuses on community involvement in public health program development. Initial community partners included Portland State University, School of Community Health and the Environmental Justice Action Group, an advocacy group for people of color living in North and Northeast Portland who are affected significantly by environmental health issues (*see sidebar on page 8 for more information on the Environmental Justice Action Group*).

Managing the tensions of community process

The team's first step was to establish a shared philosophical underpinning of environmental justice, with an explicit value placed on developing relationships of trust and understanding the strengths and assets that each individual and organization brought to the team. Meetings and processes were structured to encourage relationship building, leadership development, and sharing and nurturing of the skills, resources, and capacities that contribute to a successful PACE-EH process.

From the beginning of the PACE-EH project, participants have had to learn to work differently. For MCHD staff, this project has required working across organizational work units, which often represent different professional communities. The team approach is different from the hierarchical organizational

structure in work units and requires an appreciation of diversity, in this case professional as well as cultural diversity. Frequent conversations about roles and responsibilities have been necessary as the process unfolded.

The role community members play in the PACE-EH process also differs from past government-led efforts. The strength of the PACE-EH process rests on the degree to which community members become advocates for environmental health with policy makers as well as with their friends and neighbors. "The voices of the community resonate more strongly with elected officials and other sources of funding than would the solitary voice of a government bureaucrat," says Wickham, who believes that organized community engagement is crucial for advancing a sustainable environmental health policy agenda.

Strong community participation will result in community-driven change. Professionals can detach from environmental health threats at the end of the work day and may experience environmental health as subject matter—a luxury community people living in environmentally compromised situations don't have.

Another source of tension is that the PACE-EH process requires working with community partners before the vision, roles, and responsibilities for the PACE-EH project are fully developed. This meant providing sufficient structure so that community partners knew where they could contribute, with enough flexibility that their participation would be meaningful and they could assume shared ownership of the project.

A very interesting tension that has emerged is a result of the multiple roles of government employees—do we participate in a community process only as staff? Are we not also community members? Should the health department have a vote in the process? Is it appropriate for us to take a leadership role or is it more appropriate to encourage leadership among the community members that we are working with? Many involved in the PACE-EH process, county and community members alike, have suggested that the appropriate answer to each of these questions is *yes*. Public health professionals

The 13 Tasks of PACE-EH

1. Determine community capacity
2. Define and characterize the community
3. Assemble a community-based environmental health assessment team
4. Define the goals objectives, and scope of the assessment
5. Generate a list of community-specific environmental health issues
6. Analyze the issues with a systems framework
7. Develop locally appropriate indicators
8. Select standards against which local status can be compared
9. Create issue profiles
10. Rank the issues
11. Set priorities for action
12. Develop an action plan
13. Evaluate progress and plan for the future

Environmental Justice Action Group

"A community that educates and speaks out for itself can best protect itself," is the mission of the Environmental Justice Action Group (EJAG) of Portland, Oregon. EJAG is a community-based, membership-driven organization founded in 1996 by a group of North and Northeast Portland residents to address significant environmental health hazards faced by residents of those communities. EJAG embraces the organizing strategies established during the civil rights movement and is dedicated to developing and using community-based leadership among people of color and low-income communities to address issues of environmental justice, health, and safety. Jeri Sundvall, the executive director, and other EJAG activists have spent the past seven years educating community residents, policy makers, and local power brokers about environmental justice and the effect of policy decisions on low-income communities of color.

EJAG has had several significant victories in its brief history. "Healthy Albina," a report produced by EJAG and the Oregon Environmental Council, mapped many environmental health threats present in the Albina neighborhood in North and Northeast Portland, home to many people of color as well as low-income families. The report showed that 55 percent of all toxic emissions reported in 1995 in Multnomah County originated in the Albina community even though only 13 percent of the county's population lives there. EJAG used a survey on asthma, administered by high-school community organizer trainees, to raise awareness of air pollution as a major factor in disproportionate asthma rates in the community. A follow-up study conducted in partnership with Lewis and Clark University confirmed that asthma rates in North and Northeast Portland are 14 percent, almost three times as great as the city rate of 5 percent and double the national rate of 7 percent.

Sundvall and EJAG recently leveraged their public health data and community organizing strategies to defeat plans to expand the interstate freeway that runs through North Portland. Not only did EJAG's participation in the I-5 expansion project protect vulnerable communities from increased exposure to air pollution, it also educated policy makers about the consequences of their decisions. As a result, policy makers on the I-5 Task Force also voted unanimously to develop a community enhancement fund to provide some redress for past political decisions that have unfairly affected Portland's low-income neighborhoods. That community members and policy makers alike are more aware and proactive about environmental justice is a testimony to the effectiveness of the Environmental Justice Action Group.

have a responsibility to continue to ask questions about our appropriate participation, to listen to a multiplicity of answers, and to balance multiple identities. In doing this, we can help develop community processes in which all participants are encouraged to lead and not dominate, to speak out and to listen, and to fully commit to both the success of the process and the development of the participants.

How the county health department should do its work was only one of the questions. The larger question that the PACE-EH process has moved the broader community toward is "What kind of network needs to be in place, including community organizations, government bodies, and citizen advocacy groups, to ensure that a broad environmental health agenda gets attended to by citizens, elected officials, government bureaucrats, business leaders, and private foundations?" Not only will the county health department have to work differently, community organizations and citizens groups will have to start interacting more effectively with each other and with local government. To the extent that the PACE-EH project can develop a common environmental health agenda and a mutuality of support among its members, there will be a strong multisectoral environmental health agenda and potential for creating a holistic system to manage environmental health threats.

Moving from theory to practice

The Multnomah County PACE-EH Coalition has spent the majority of its first year working on tasks 1, 3, and 5 of the PACE-EH process.

Task 1: Determine community capacity. To build relationships across the multiple sectors of the community, the health department hired two community connectors. The work of the community connectors is to reach out to the various sectors of the environmental health community in the area and engage them in the PACE-EH process. The leadership of the community connectors in the PACE-EH process has been central to the effectiveness of the project.

The community connectors have informed representatives of government, community organizations, environmental health organizations, physicians groups, neighborhood associations, faith communities, social services, and schools about the PACE-EH process. The initial focus of outreach and community capacity assessment was on participants who have a county-wide or community-wide perspective. The community connectors will refocus their outreach and capacity assessment activities when the team has determined a specific community of focus for the assessment.

Hiring the community connectors also sent a clear message from the senior leadership of the health department to the PACE-EH staff and the community that the health department was serious about its commitment to expanding its role in environmental health and to doing so as an active partner with a broad array of community partners. That the commitment happened during a period of budget cutting and tight fiscal controls underscored the value Multnomah County Health Department placed on community mobilization as an effective strategy in promoting the health of the community.

Task 3: Assemble a community-based environmental health assessment team. Over the past year, there have been several community meetings to work out many of the issues raised by community members about the structure and function of the PACE-EH process—and a strong environmental health coalition has evolved. In this evolution, several community members have emerged as leaders and committed advocates for the PACE-EH process.

The coalition operates through several committees. The steering committee is responsible for the functioning of the overall coalition, including fund-raising, developing a shared environmental health agenda, ensuring diversity and leadership development for coalition members, and implementation of the recommendations that emerge from the assessment.

The membership committee is responsible for ensuring diverse representation among the coalition body and on the committees. It will broaden and deepen current community outreach strategies, orient new members to environmental health and the coalition, and ensure that coalition and committee meetings are welcoming to limited English-speaking individuals and participants with children.

The assessment committee is responsible for facilitating the actual work of the PACE-EH assessment. The committee will also work with the coalition to analyze the data, identify themes, and set benchmarks and community standards.

MCHD staff and coalition members are exploring ways to ensure the long-term viability of the PACE-EH coalition and Multnomah County's capacity for attracting more funding to support environmental health, community organizing, and environmental justice. The coalition expects community-based organizations to take more ownership and leadership of the grant-writing and fund-raising process.

Immediate next steps

Task 2: Define the community to be assessed. To define the community for assessment, the members of the assessment team will use criteria of multiple environmental risk factors in low-income communities of color. The research team is analyzing existing data in a geographic information format to identify where these factors overlap. If this method produces clear options for assessment, a second step of investigating the interest and current efforts of the selected community to participate in PACE-EH will follow.

Task 4: Define the goals, objectives, and scope of the assessment. In this task the actual assessment methods will be determined. Given the variety of experience of community members on the assessment team, methods could include community surveys, analysis of existing data, mapping environmental health risk factors, or testing environmental hazards. The environmental justice underpinning of the PACE-EH process suggests that whatever the methodology, the community will be involved in the design, implementation, and analysis phases of the research process.

Task 5: Generate a list of community-specific environmental health issues. This task was initiated early on through a brainstorming process in a community meeting that brought together community-based organizations and environmental agencies. The coalition will revisit the list through a more systematic assessment process once it has selected a community for the formal PACE-EH assessment.

The Multnomah County Health Department elected to use the PACE-EH process in order to build a strong environmental health mandate for the Department and the general community. The focus of the first year has been to develop strong relationships with environmental health advocates in the community. In doing so, an environmental health coalition has developed with a commitment to evolving from a community-focused, health department-driven process into a more community-driven, health department-supported process. The coalition expects to complete the first round of community assessments by the end of 2003, with priorities and strategies for action finalized by the summer of 2004. Many members have expressed their belief that the PACE-EH process will continue beyond the first assessment, and as other communities express interest in environmental health, the coalition will be poised to help them assess their environmental issues and mobilize for action. ❦

Environmental Justice is the fair treatment and meaningful involvement of all people regardless of race, color, national origin, or income with respect to the development, implementation, and enforcement of environmental laws, regulations, and policies.

Resource

PACE-EH EH: A Tool for Community Environmental Health Assessment. National Association of County and City Health Officials. www.naccho.org/project78.cfm

Author

Latricia Tillman, MPH, is special projects manager in the Office of the Director at the Multnomah County Health Department in Portland, Oregon.